BLACK GOLD AND BLACKMAIL

BLACK GOLD AND BLACKMAIL

Oil and Great Power Politics

Rosemary A. Kelanic

CORNELL UNIVERSITY PRESS   ITHACA AND LONDON

The publication of this book is made possible in part by support from the Institute for Scholarship in the Liberal Arts, College of Arts and Letters, University of Notre Dame.

Copyright © 2020 by Cornell University

All rights reserved. Except for brief quotations in a review, this book, or parts thereof, must not be reproduced in any form without permission in writing from the publisher. For information, address Cornell University Press, Sage House, 512 East State Street, Ithaca, New York 14850. Visit our website at cornellpress.cornell.edu.

First published 2020 by Cornell University Press

Library of Congress Cataloging-in-Publication Data

Names: Kelanic, Rosemary A., author.
Title: Black gold and blackmail : oil and great power politics / Rosemary A. Kelanic.
Description: Ithaca : Cornell University Press, 2020. | Includes bibliographical
    references and index.
Identifiers: LCCN 2019031635 (print) | LCCN 2019031636 (ebook) |
    ISBN 9781501748295 (hardcover) | ISBN 9781501749216 (pdf) |
    ISBN 9781501749209 (epub)
Subjects: LCSH: Petroleum industry and trade—Political aspects. |
    Petroleum industry and trade—Military aspects. | Energy security—Political
    aspects. | Great powers.
Classification: LCC HD9560.6 .K415 2020 (print) | LCC HD9560.6 (ebook) |
    DDC 338.2/728—dc23
LC record available at https://lccn.loc.gov/2019031635
LC ebook record available at https://lccn.loc.gov/2019031636

Contents

Acknowledgments	vii
Introduction: The Ubiquity of Oil	1
1. A Theory of Strategic Anticipation	15
2. Oil and Military Effectiveness	48
3. Qualitative Methods for Testing the Theory	67
4. British Vulnerability and the Conquest of Mesopotamia	80
5. The Oil Strategies of Nazi Germany	92
6. American Efforts to Avoid Vulnerability	115
7. Empirical Tests with Fuzzy-Set QCA	159
Conclusion: Oil and the Future of Great Power Politics	173
Notes	183
Index	211

Acknowledgments

Academia is an offense-dominant world. It is almost always easier to attack a scholarly argument than it is to originate and defend one. Thank goodness I did not have to write this book alone. Countless friends and colleagues supported me throughout the arduous process; without their help, this book would not exist.

I owe my greatest intellectual debts to John Mearsheimer, Charlie Glaser, and Bob Pape. John Mearsheimer's wit, mirthful contrarianism, and remarkable clarity of thought provided a constant source of inspiration. Though he relishes playing the "prince of darkness" role in the field, he was unfailingly patient and encouraging. Bob Pape's work on coercion fed my own curiosity about the "oil weapon," and he especially challenged me to develop my ideas into a rigorous theory. Charlie Glaser, more than anyone else, shaped me into the scholar and teacher I am today. I could not have asked for a more brilliant and generous mentor.

I am grateful for the numerous colleagues and friends who "red teamed"—and vastly improved—the ideas in this book, whether in workshops, at conferences, over lunch, or all three (and then some). I especially thank Steve Biddle, Steve Brooks, Ahsan Butt, Dan Byman, Austin Carson, Jon Caverley, Jeff Colgan, Alex Downes, John Duffield, Melissa McAdam Ellison, Keren Fraiman, Gene Gerzhoy, Kelly Greenhill, Eric Hundman, Jenna Jordan, Inwook Kim, Peter Krause, Ned Lebow, Michael Levi, Chad Levinson, Jenny Lind, Julia Macdonald, Rich Maas, Victor McFarland, Emily Meierding, Jonathan Obert, Lindsey O'Rourke, John Owen, Sarah Parkinson, George Quester, Elizabeth Saunders, Sebastian Schmitt, John Schuessler, Josh Shifrinson, Matthias Staisch, Paul Staniland, Caitlin Talmadge, Bill Wohlforth, and workshop participants at Chicago, Harvard, George Washington University, Dartmouth College, and MIT. Early excerpts of the book benefited greatly from feedback provided by discussants and audiences at the annual conferences of the American Political Science Association and the International Studies Association.

While conducting research for this book, I received generous support from the Energy Initiative at the University of Chicago Booth School of Business, the Belfer Center for Science and International Affairs at the Harvard Kennedy School, the Institute for Scholarship in the Liberal Arts at the University of Notre Dame, and my various academic homes over the past several years. I am especially grateful to Charlie Glaser, who gave me space to work on my own research while serving as the associate director of the Institute for Security and Conflict Studies at George

Washington University. I would also like to thank Charlie and the Elliott School of International Affairs at GW for sponsoring a book workshop on an early version of the manuscript. My profuse gratitude goes to Bob Art, Dale Copeland, and Daryl Press, who provided detailed feedback and advice by graciously serving as discussants. My colleagues at Williams College, especially James McAllister and Sam Crane, were incredibly supportive of both my teaching and research. I could not have asked for a more welcoming, good-hearted environment. Finally, I would like to express my thanks to the University of Notre Dame and my colleagues at the Notre Dame International Security Center—Mike Desch, Dan Lindley, Sebastian Rosato, Joe Parent, Anieka Johnson, and Eugene Gholz—for helping me clear the final hump to complete the book. Mike Desch, in particular, offered me indispensable advice at the five-yard line.

I am indebted to my editor at Cornell University Press, Roger Haydon, for his penetrating insights and belief in the project, and to two anonymous reviewers whose thorough and constructive criticisms dramatically improved the book. I also thank Erin Davis, Lisa DeBoer, and the expert production team at Cornell for stellar work. This book contains material from my article, "The Petroleum Paradox: Oil, Coercive Vulnerability, and Great Power Behavior," published in *Security Studies*, 25, no. 2 (April 2016), reproduced here with permission from Taylor & Francis Group, LLC.

I am tremendously grateful to the close friends who guarded my sanity through the trying times of book-writing, especially Mandy Burton, Ahsan Butt, Kristel Clayville, Amir Sean Fairdosi, Katharyn Hanson, Lindsey O'Rourke, Sarah Parkinson, and Jen White. I also thank my family, especially my parents, Mary Flummer and Tom Kelanic, for instilling in me a love of learning while letting me find my own way.

Finally, I thank my husband, Eugene Gholz, for being my rock over the last eight years. His unwavering love and support encouraged me to keep going on days when completing the book felt impossible. I am grateful beyond what words can express. I dedicate this book to him.

Errors of fact or interpretation, which I hope are few, are solely my own.

BLACK GOLD AND BLACKMAIL

Introduction

THE UBIQUITY OF OIL

For over a hundred years, oil has been ubiquitous as both an object of political intrigue and a feature of everyday life, yet its effects on the behavior of major powers remain poorly understood. Researchers recognize that "oil matters," of course, but have focused almost exclusively on formulating specific explanations for distinct events, such as the 1970s oil crises, rather than advancing broad explanations that apply to many cases. We lack generalizable theories that link oil to great power politics in predictable, empirically testable ways.

This book focuses on one particular aspect of oil: its coercive potential. Across time and space, great powers have feared that dependence on imported petroleum might make them vulnerable to coercion by hostile actors. They worry that an enemy could cut off oil to weaken them militarily or punish them economically, and then use this threat as a basis for political blackmail. Oil is so essential to great powers that taking a state's imports hostage could give an enemy significant leverage in a dispute. The vulnerable state might have to acquiesce to an opponent's demands, even when major interests are at stake, because the prospect of losing petroleum access is even worse.

This book presents the first systematic framework to understand how fears of oil coercion shape international affairs. I argue that great powers counter prospective threats with costly and risky policies that lessen vulnerability, ideally, *before* the country can be targeted. These measures, which I call "anticipatory strategies," vary enormously, from self-sufficiency efforts to actions as extreme as launching wars. The core question of the book is, Why do great powers choose different strategies to secure oil?

History is rife with examples of strategic anticipation. Japan attacked Pearl Harbor and seized the petroleum-rich Dutch East Indies to secure oil after a U.S. petroleum embargo cut off 80 percent of its imports. Determined to protect its stockpile and believing war with the United States was inevitable, Japan conquered its own supply and preemptively destroyed the lone naval threat to fuel shipments from the Indies—the U.S. Pacific Fleet.[1] Fear of oil coercion spurred the British and French into the 1956 Suez War. Upon news of President Gamal Abdel Nasser's nationalization of the waterway, Prime Minister Anthony Eden lamented, "The Egyptian has his thumb on our windpipe," and the British cabinet resolved to keep the Suez Canal open by force if necessary.[2] Oil disruption was the foremost concern; two-thirds of British petroleum imports transited through the canal, compared with just one-quarter of the country's total imports. Indicative of this, oil was the only displaced material that received attention by the British cabinet in their emergency meeting following Nasser's nationalization of the canal in July.[3]

Even the petroleum-rich United States has periodically worried about oil coercion. The 1979 invasion of Afghanistan generated alarm that the USSR (Union of Soviet Socialist Republics) might expand into Iran and choke off the flow of oil through the Strait of Hormuz. "The Soviet Union is now attempting to consolidate a strategic position . . . that poses a grave threat to the free movement of Middle East oil," President Jimmy Carter warned in his 1980 State of the Union Address. In this same address he issued a message to Moscow that became known as the Carter Doctrine: "An attempt by any outside force to gain control of the Persian Gulf region will be regarded as an assault on the vital interests of the United States of America, and . . . will be repelled by any means necessary, including military force."[4] To back up this threat, Carter created the Rapid Deployment Joint Task Force, the precursor of CENTCOM, the U.S. regional command responsible for all military operations in the Middle East. Operation Desert Shield, the multilateral effort to defend the sovereignty of Saudi Arabia from Iraq in 1990, and Operation Desert Storm, the campaign to eject Saddam Hussein from Kuwait in 1991, were explicitly motivated by concerns to preserve access to oil.

Scholars acknowledge that oil influenced these developments but have failed to recognize them as belonging to a broad category of behaviors that share a common causal logic. This book is the first to identify the pattern and propose a systematic theory to explain variation in great powers' actions. While fear of oil coercion has spurred some great powers into war, others have instead sought domestic self-sufficiency. No explanation currently exists for their choice.

The Argument in Brief

Anticipatory strategies are policies designed to avert attempts at oil coercion—ideally, though not exclusively, before such attempts ever occur. I argue, based on a careful observation of great power oil policies since World War I, that anticipatory strategies fall into three broad categories: self-sufficiency, indirect control, and direct control. Self-sufficiency utilizes internal policy, such as building up stockpiles and providing government investment for exploration and drilling, to expand domestic supplies of oil. The least costly strategy, it can only relieve minor vulnerability. Indirect control forges security alliances with oil-exporting countries to deter internal and external threats to the ally's resources with the goal of keeping that oil in "friendly hands." These relationships may include arms-for-oil deals, informal alliances, formal security guarantees, and military basing arrangements, among other measures. Indirect control is costlier and riskier than self-sufficiency because it involves the implicit or explicit threat of using military force, but it provides greater oil security benefits. Direct control, the costliest strategy, uses conquest to capture oil-producing territory and transit routes. It offers the greatest potential to expand oil access but entails steep risks. The attempted military invasion may fail outright, devolve into a quagmire, or draw intervention from other great powers, which in turn could escalate to general war.

I argue that two independent variables predict which anticipatory strategy a great power will choose. The first independent variable is the threat to imports, defined as how susceptible oil imports are to deliberate cutoff. The import threat represents the *likelihood* that foreign oil could be successfully denied to the state by an opponent. The second variable is the petroleum deficit, defined as the difference between a state's domestic oil resources and its consumption requirements. The petroleum deficit represents the *magnitude* of harm that would be caused by a deliberate disruption of oil imports. The combination of these two independent variables determines the degree to which a state is vulnerable to oil coercion, and consequently, its willingness to adopt extreme anticipatory strategies. The greater the coercive vulnerability, the greater the costs and risks a state will accept to protect access to oil. This means that as the petroleum deficit and import threat rise, great powers will escalate to more intense anticipatory strategies. If the petroleum deficit and import disruptibility fall, states are less threatened by oil coercion and will select lower-level strategies. Ultimately, states choose whatever strategy meets their oil needs at the lowest possible cost.

Crucially, strategic anticipation can only be understood by accounting for both the economic and the military value of oil. Scholars commonly neglect the latter, but it explains much about why states fear oil coercion so deeply. Simply put, losing oil means losing wars. Ever since World War I demonstrated the superiority of oil-fueled militaries over coal-fueled ones, countries have understood that losing access to petroleum is devastating for military effectiveness. Militaries that are deprived of oil have little chance of prevailing against enemy forces with plenty of it. As a result, disruptions endanger not only economic prosperity but also national survival—the highest goal of states. Although disruption is a low-probability event, its consequences are sufficiently dire to spur strategic anticipation.

Empirically Testing the Theory

The book tests the theory with a mixed-methods approach that combines traditional historical case studies with fuzzy-set qualitative comparative analysis (fsQCA), a method pioneered by Charles Ragin to handle the causal complexity endemic to social phenomena. The bulk of the empirical analysis tests the theory by deploying traditional case studies in two distinct capacities. The first function of the case studies is to test for congruence, which evaluates whether and to what extent the hypothesized causal factors covary with outcomes. The logic behind congruence is correlational and symmetrical. Congruence tests are passed when both the presence of a causal factor (X) coincides with the presence of the predicted outcome (Y) and the absence of the causal factor (X) coincides with the absence of the outcome (Y). The second purpose of the historical cases is to test the theory through causal process tracing. Process tracing is the only way to validate that the observed congruence between causal factors and outcomes is a real causal relationship rather than a correlational apparition.

The fuzzy-set method complements traditional case study analysis because it can parse "the subtleties of causation" by testing specifically for the presence of necessary conditions, sufficient conditions, and causal combinations that may be jointly necessary and/or sufficient.[5] The technique can also be paired with quantitative analysis to assess the generalizability of a theory at standard levels of statistical significance (i.e., 90%, 95% and 99% confidence intervals), as done in this book. The approach, therefore, presents an impartial way for researchers to weigh in on the question of how many (or really, how few) errant cases can occur without disconfirming the theory.[6]

Contributions of the Book

This book contributes to international relations scholarship in several ways. First, it develops a systematic theory about the effects of oil on great power politics, a worthy topic in its own right. International relations scholarship offers surprisingly few generalizable insights about how oil influences great power politics. Yet, oil pervades the modern world, and understanding it better would strengthen our grasp on the politics of everything it touches.

Second, the theory deepens our understanding of past great power behavior by illuminating the systematic ways in which oil influenced the turning points of history. Anticipatory strategies factored into the most consequential developments of the twentieth century, including World War I and World War II; the emergence of the Middle East state system from the ashes of the Ottoman Empire, and particularly, the establishment of its borders; Great Britain's expansion into the Persian Gulf and its retrenchment after the 1956 Suez Crisis; the spectacular rise of U.S. military and economic power; the Persian Gulf War to eject Saddam Hussein from Kuwait in 1991 and U.S. operations to contain him thereafter; and many other events.

Third, the book offers insights relevant to a broad swath of academic research, including literature on trade interdependence and war, trading with the enemy, political coercion, resource conflict, alliance formation, military effectiveness, and grand strategy. For example, seminal research on trade and conflict has been built on case studies involving international petroleum commerce—without drawing distinctions between oil and other traded goods.[7] If foreign oil dependence affects state behavior in a unique way, as my research suggests, general theories derived from or tested against petroleum-related cases could lead to biased conclusions.

The framework also offers valuable insight for understanding contemporary great power politics. China, an emerging superpower, appears to be pursuing an indirect control strategy to reduce its coercive vulnerability to a U.S. naval blockade in the event of a confrontation. Because China relies so heavily on maritime transport for oil, a U.S. blockade could cut off up to 90 percent of the country's petroleum imports. No wonder analysts warn that "China's Achilles' heel may well be imported oil."[8] China has made massive pipeline and infrastructure investments through the Belt and Road Initiative (BRI) for importing Russian, Central Asian, and eventually Middle Eastern petroleum.[9] The major advantage of these investments is that the oil will travel to China overland—beyond the reach of U.S. naval power.[10] Chinese president Xi Jinping has also pursued closer military and economic ties with Indonesia and Malaysia, the two countries that sit astride the Strait of Malacca, a critical choke point for China's oil imports.[11] Analysis suggests that China has good reason to fear the consequences of losing access to the international market. In an air war with Taiwan, China's military fuel requirements would be so massive that if a U.S. blockade forced it to rely on indigenous jet fuel production alone, civilian aviation consumption would have to decrease by as much as 75 percent to maintain a full military effort.[12] Based on the theory developed in this book, despite the substantial dependency, China is unlikely to choose the extreme strategy of fighting a war for oil if the overland projects succeed.

What Do We Know about Oil and International Security?

Present knowledge about oil in international politics is patchy and incomplete. While many experts intuitively believe "oil matters" to geopolitics, consensus on when, why, and how it matters remains elusive. Excellent historical accounts of international petroleum politics exist but do not endeavor to advance causal arguments about general phenomena.[13] Although the 1970s oil price shocks inspired a wave of political science scholarship on oil and international security from the mid-1970s into the 1980s, that research did not yield systematic, generalizable theories.[14] Four decades later, scholarship remains inchoate and largely tangential to the question animating this book. Contemporary research exists on five general subtopics broadly related to oil and conflict, but these clusters of work have yet to cohere into a unified literature or research program.

One cluster of literature examines the apparent connection between natural resource wealth and domestic political ills such as intrastate violence, despotism, gender inequality, and economic backwardness, a phenomenon known as the "resource curse."[15] Michael Ross has shown that, among resources, oil is especially prone to causing strife because the wealth it creates is unusually large, unstable, and easy for states to conceal from their citizens. Moreover, governments with high oil revenue do not have to rely as heavily on taxation to fund themselves, which further separates the state from accountability to society.[16] While excellent, work on the "resource curse" focuses on the internal security ramifications of resource wealth rather than its potential effects on international relations.

A second cluster of research concerns the relationship between oil and interstate war. From the 1990s to the early 2010s, this cluster was dominated by the "resource wars" approach, whereby scholars warned that a combination of rising resource scarcity and outright greed might spur military conflict over dwindling supplies of oil and other resources.[17] Though intuitively plausible, the claim has turned out to be empirically weak, as skeptics found that actual cases of resource conflict—particularly over oil—were rare to nonexistent.[18] Moreover, the early 2010s production boom in the United States, which was driven by new methods for horizontal drilling and hydraulic fracturing (also known as "fracking") and which abruptly reversed decades of production decline, discredited the underlying premise that global oil resources were rapidly depleting. Indeed, some scholars have since turned their attention to investigating what Roger Stern calls "oil scarcity ideology": the persistent yet erroneous fear of imminent oil depletion and the prophesied political consequences it would entail.[19] Others continue to examine whether resources could spark conflict in an era of abundance.[20]

Jeff D. Colgan has advanced the literature on oil and conflict beyond "resource wars" by extending the "resource curse" logic into the foreign policy realm. He finds that revolutionary governments bankrolled by oil profits are significantly more likely to initiate militarized interstate disputes than other states are, largely because oil revenue insulates them from domestic political accountability.[21] Other research supports the broad point that "petro-states" misbehave internationally at above-average rates. Evidence suggests that oil-rich countries are less willing to cooperate in international institutions,[22] and they are especially likely to instigate disputes when oil prices are high.[23] While intriguing, such work is of limited relevance here because net-exporting countries tend not to experience petroleum deficits and thus have no need for anticipatory strategies. The theory advanced in this book generally pertains to net-importing countries, for whom coercive vulnerability is a genuine threat. Elsewhere, Colgan has identified a variety of mechanisms beyond scarcity that could directly or indirectly link oil to war but does not test those hypotheses.[24]

The third research cluster examines the strategic implications of U.S. consumption of foreign oil. Until the mid-2010s, this work focused on the potential hazards of import dependence, which for the United States emerged during World War II and has continued, more or less, into the present.[25] Now some scholars argue that the aforementioned fracking boom will eventually erase American dependence on foreign oil, transform the country into a net oil and natural gas exporter, and create a "windfall" opportunity to boost U.S. political influence through energy exports.[26]

There are two main limitations to the U.S.-centric study of oil. First, while valuable in their own right, arguments about the United States are not generalizable because no other country enjoys such an overwhelming relative power advantage. Extraordinary military preponderance bestows on the United States an advantage that Barry Posen calls "command of the commons": the unfettered capacity to move military forces through sea, air, and space, coupled with the unrivaled ability to deny access to military opponents.[27] Command of the commons renders the United States uniquely invulnerable to oil coercion. It also makes the country the chief military threat to *other* states' access to overseas oil. Second, much of the literature on U.S. oil security is prescriptive rather than explanatory; it aims to provide policy advice for what the United States *should do* instead of explaining what the United States *actually does* to maintain security of supply. Thus, it diverges from this book's primary goal of generalizable, causal explanation.

The fourth category of research analyzes specific scenarios where oil cutoff either was or could be used to coerce. It focuses on individual cases with proper names attached. Some scholars have assessed whether Iran could disrupt global oil supplies by closing the Strait of Hormuz or attacking Saudi production facilities,[28] for example, while others have investigated whether Russia gains political leverage from its consolidation of the European oil and natural gas market.[29] A fascinating piece describes the role of oil-cutoff fears in nearly scuttling Egyptian-Israeli negotiations to return the oil-rich Sinai Peninsula, captured by Israel during the 1973 war, in exchange for peace.[30] Generally speaking, these studies do not address broader questions about coercive vulnerability and the anticipatory behavior it engenders among great powers.

Finally, a handful of studies examine the energy security policies of net-importing countries. These are the closest to this study, in that they try to explain how various countries have responded to the threat of energy supply disruptions. However, they do not tend to answer the headline question about potential military responses and the strategic need for oil supplies. One prominent study, for example, emphasizes public investment in research and development for all types of energy, based on the logic that any energy production can substitute for oil consumption in electricity generation.[31] Unfortunately, most of this investment is irrelevant to the strategic demand for oil, which is based on transportation and for which other energy supplies cannot provide a substitute; electricity generation accounts for roughly 2 percent of oil consumption in developed countries, meaning that no matter how successful the R&D investments, they can free up only a trivial amount of oil supply for strategic uses.[32] In another vein, several authors have written about the political economy processes through which countries affected by past oil disruptions have sought to protect their economies from future disruptions through the use of regulatory and investment policies.[33] These studies are valuable but are limited in the range of outcome strategies that they examine: they are effectively looking just at self-sufficiency efforts without considering the options of indirect control and military action.

In sum, scholarly interest in how oil affects international security is increasing, but we lack systematic theories about its influence on great power politics.

Setting the Record Straight on Oil Coercion

Although strategic anticipation is the object of study, a brief discussion of oil coercion is necessary given the undue influence of the 1973 Organization of Arab Petroleum Exporting Countries (OAPEC) oil crisis in shaping conventional assumptions about the "oil weapon."[34] Oil coercion occurs when a state threatens or disrupts an opponent's petroleum access to obtain political demands. It is an example of what Thomas C. Schelling calls "compellence" because it attempts to *initiate a change* in the target's behavior, as opposed to deterrence, which aims to *prevent a change* in the adversary's behavior.[35] Oil coercion, in my definition, specifically refers to threats intended to change *consuming* states' behavior by denying oil access. It does not refer to threats designed to alter *producer* states' behavior by curtailing their international petroleum sales.[36]

The OAPEC crisis, seared into the minds of those who endured it, fostered at least two myths about oil coercion that persist today. The first myth is that trade embargo is the most salient disruption threat. OAPEC used a trade embargo to disrupt oil, cutting production and suspending trade with the United States. However, coercers can also use military force to interrupt an adversary's supplies—for instance, through a naval blockade. In fact, military force is often the more effective way to deprive oil to an adversary, given the difficulties of enforcing peaceful trade embargos. I discuss this more in chapter 1. Second, the 1973 OAPEC case created the false impression that producer countries are the "typical" perpetrators of oil coercion. On the contrary, because force can be used to disrupt access to oil, would-be coercers need not be oil-producing countries. Rather, coercers can be third-party states with enough military wherewithal to threaten or attack an adversary's imports. Thus, the scenario more apt for triggering strategic anticipation than the unlikely possibility that Iran could sabotage the Straits of Hormuz to coerce the United States is the possibility that the United States could use its naval power to deny oil to China if the two countries entered into a confrontation, most likely over Taiwan.[37] However, even if the coercer is an oil-exporting state, it could still use military interdiction to surgically cut off oil to a particular target without ruining its own economy, as it could still sell oil to the rest of the world.

Dispelling these myths sheds light on why great powers fear oil coercion despite the adaptive mechanisms of the global petroleum market.[38] As long as the international market is functioning, and a state has access to the market, its supply of oil is secure. However, military force can supersede market mechanisms by physically preventing oil imports from reaching the target. In the anarchic international system, where force always lingers as a possibility and the intentions of others are unknowable, states must prepare for worst-case scenarios.[39] Great powers, therefore, must plan their grand strategies mindful of the possibility that an adversary could physically disrupt their oil trade at the crucial moment—when they need to defend themselves in war. Even if the probability of such a calamitous outcome is small, the consequences are sufficiently grave to spur great powers into adopting costly and risky anticipatory strategies. In short, oil disruption is a military problem, not just a trade problem. When force is in the offing, the capability of markets to adjust is beside the point.

Notes on Scope

The theory has two significant scope conditions. First, and most important, the book focuses solely on the anticipatory strategies of great powers. Excluding minor powers' strategies is appropriate, first of all, because the project's central ambition is to develop and test a new theory in a neglected area of the field. Thus, it is an exercise in first-order theorizing—proffering an explanation for behavior that is so understudied that, as yet, it has not even been conceptualized as constituting a single broad phenomenon. In a theoretical void of this nature, it is common practice in international relations scholarship to start at the level of great powers—the first order, in this terminology—before broadening the inquiry to lesser powers. By virtue of their superior capabilities, great powers shape the choices of every state in the international system. Because weak states often find themselves at the mercy of the strong, the actions great powers take to reduce their vulnerability are likely to affect, or even determine, the oil access of minor powers. The decisions of minor powers do not reverberate with such reach.

Focusing on great power anticipatory strategies does not imply that the theory is irrelevant to minor powers. Nor does it mean that minor powers do not follow anticipatory strategies; I am agnostic about whether they do. My point is simply that minor powers' actions depend heavily on what great powers do; ergo, their behavior is a second-order question. From a logical standpoint, we need to understand great powers' strategies before we can predict how minor powers would act. It is less useful, and perhaps impossible, to interrogate a second-order question without at least a preliminary answer to a first-order one.

It also behooves us to stick with great powers because minor powers, if they anticipate, might pursue anticipatory strategies that are very different from those of great powers, reflecting their starkly different material capabilities. Great powers' superlative resources afford them the full menu of options to choose from. Minor powers, by contrast, may be incapable of pursuing intense strategies like indirect or direct control; at the extreme, they may lack the means to engage in strategic anticipation at all. It is also possible that minor powers have adapted strategies that are unique to them because of the vastly different position they occupy in the international ecosystem compared with major powers. All of this is to suggest that the range of anticipatory strategies presented in the book may or may not be directly transferrable to minor powers. I leave this question to future research.

The emphasis on great powers, which are relatively few in number, does not diminish the book's theoretical and empirical value. Six countries qualify as great powers since 1918: Britain (1918–1945), France (1918–1945), Germany (1933–1945), Japan (1918–1945), the Soviet Union (1918–1991), and the United States

(1918 to the present). The emergence of new great powers, most notably China, will increase the number of applicable countries in the future. Nevertheless, even if the theory applies to "only" six or seven countries, this does not mean it explains only six or seven *cases*. Multiple cases exist for each country because coercive vulnerability changes over time, leading to changes in anticipatory strategies. I discuss this in chapter 3.

Notably, the theory does *not* assume that only major powers can be coercers, even though it focuses exclusively on great power anticipation. Minor powers have tried to threaten the oil access of major powers, sometimes tacitly, sometimes explicitly. For example, several oil-exporting Arab states famously targeted Western powers with supply interruptions in 1956, 1967, and 1973. Likewise, Iran has repeatedly threatened to close the Strait of Hormuz, through which some seventeen million barrels of oil flow daily, to retaliate for Western sanctions over its nuclear program.[40] In principle, and occasionally in practice, threats like these from minor powers can spur strategic anticipation by oil-insecure great powers. The theory allows for as much. But for reasons laid out in chapter 1, anticipatory strategies are driven more often by threats from militarily strong countries that can physically interdict oil imports.

The second major scope condition is that the theory obviously applies only to the oil age, which as I explain in chapter 2 dates from roughly World War I to the present (and likely several decades into the future, however regrettable for the planet). Oil politics is necessarily temporally bounded because oil's value is technologically bounded. Though produced in commercial quantities since 1859, oil held little strategic significance until the mass production of internal-combustion vehicles arose in the 1910s. Anticipatory strategies did not emerge until circa World War I; naturally, the theory does not claim to explain great power behavior before that date.

However, the book stands alone in explaining politics for the entirety of the oil age. Even the best political science scholarship on oil politics typically explains only cases that date from the 1970s or later, in part because quantitative data get sparser the further back one goes, but also because some of the phenomena of interest to these studies do not manifest in earlier time periods.[41] An advantage of the deep qualitative analysis found in this book is the ability to travel back further in time than data sets commonly allow. Developing a theory about oil politics that is relevant from World War I to the present—over one hundred years of history and counting—represents an important step forward in our general understanding of oil. Granted, the oil age is historically bounded, but the theory presented here applies to the entirety of it.

Several additional questions about the international politics of oil merit academic study but fall outside the scope of this book. For example, the book does not attempt to explain when and why coercer states wield the "oil weapon," which would require developing a theory about the decision calculus of the coercer. Rather, the book approaches the interaction from the point of view of the potential target, not the potential coercer, and keeps the focus squarely on the target's efforts to anticipate. Certainly, when and why states try to coerce by disrupting oil is a worthwhile question, but it is tangential to the issue of strategic anticipation. Similarly, the book also brackets questions about oil coercion's effectiveness. History generally suggests that oil coercion is ineffective, but not uniformly so. Under what circumstances might oil disruptions achieve political concessions? More research should be devoted to the effectiveness question, but that is not the task at hand.

Another related, but analytically distinct, topic of research is the origins and effectiveness of "reverse" oil coercion, whereby an adversary threatens to block exports of an oil-producing country to deny it revenue. Reverse coercion may have made a difference during President Obama's negotiations with Iran over its nuclear program; multilateral sanctions that hindered Iranian oil sales arguably contributed to Tehran's acceptance of the 2015 deal to restrict its ability to build nuclear weapons. In January 2019, the Trump administration placed sanctions on Venezuelan oil sales to the United States to drain the coffers of Nicolás Maduro's government, which the United States refuses to recognize as legitimate. What are the prospects for the boycott's success in forcing Maduro's resignation? Extant scholarship cannot answer the question. "Reverse" oil coercion clearly deserves scholarly attention, but it is conceptually separate from the question animating this book.

Plan of the Book

Chapter 1 lays out the theory. First, it explains the two independent variables that drive the choice of anticipatory strategies: the petroleum deficit and the threat to imports. When combined, these two independent variables determine the state's overall coercive vulnerability. Next, the chapter explains the causal logic, which holds that the military value of oil is a necessary condition to explain great power behavior. The economic value of oil, while important, is not sufficient to explain why states pursue anticipatory strategies. Then, the chapter fleshes out the dependent variable—the choice of anticipatory strategy—explaining the three categories from which states select: self-sufficiency, indirect control, and direct control. Ultimately, a state will choose the lowest-cost anticipatory strategy capable of fulfilling its oil security needs, given its degree of vulnerability. Finally, the chapter considers whether oil is "different" from other resources. That is to say, it asks whether the theory applies to other strategic resources—coal, iron, and the like—or to oil alone, and why.

Chapter 2 delves more deeply into the military value of oil and traces its origins to the historical transformation from coal to oil as the major military fuel during World War I. In doing so, it firmly explains why the relevant temporal boundary for the theory's applicability is circa 1918. It then explains how oil deprivation influenced Japan's decision to surrender at the end of World War II in the time and manner that it did. The case illuminates in empirical detail the military devastation inflicted by the Allied blockade, which completely severed Japanese oil access.

Chapters 3 through 7 empirically test the theory. Chapter 3 explains the qualitative case study research design, with particular emphasis on why the cases chosen constitute strong tests for the theory. In all, I examined eleven cases using congruence testing and causal process tracing that drew heavily on archival documents and other primary sources, which are invaluable illuminators of the reasoning behind policy decisions. Traditional case studies are the gold standard for demonstrating the validity of a causal inference—that is, for establishing how and why social outcomes occur. They provide the only reliable way to observe the causal mechanism as it operates in real life—"in vivo," so to speak.

I divide the eleven case studies into three chapters, organized by country. Chapter 4 begins with a discussion of British oil policy before World War I. This serves as an observational baseline so that when oil coercion becomes relevant in 1918, we have something to which to compare any changes in behavior. The baseline vignette also confirms the temporal boundary of 1918 as a turning point in policymakers' understanding of oil. Then, the chapter analyzes Britain's choice to pursue a direct control strategy in late 1918 by invading Mesopotamia. Dire vulnerability, underpinned by a yawning petroleum deficit and Britain's severe susceptibility to blockade as an island nation, spurred the government to accept the high costs and risks of securing oil with this most extreme strategy.

Chapter 5 consists of the four cases that span the Nazi era in Germany. Adolf Hitler's anticipatory strategies changed over time, in tandem with his country's coercive vulnerability, intensifying from self-sufficiency before World War II to indirect control at the war's start to, finally, direct control after Operation Barbarossa failed to speedily defeat the USSR. The German cases bear out several "risky predictions" made by the theory—predictions that, if shown to be true, strongly confirm a hypothesis because they contradict our priors (and thus must trigger Bayesian updating). We would expect that the führer, as the most expansionist leader of the twentieth century, would engage in conquest to get oil; yet primarily, he sought oil security through less extreme measures.

Chapter 6 traces U.S. coercive vulnerability, which fluctuated across six distinct cases from 1918 until the volatile 1970s. Like the Britain chapter, it opens with a vignette of U.S. oil policy during the calm pre–World War I years, which likewise establishes a baseline and confirms 1918 as a historical inflection point, before moving on to the cases. Though blessed with generous oil resources, the United States nevertheless encountered periods where its oil security was threatened by a substantial petroleum deficit, a possible disruption of Persian Gulf oil, or both, creating a need for strategic anticipation. The United States never resorted to direct control because, thanks to its singular oil endowment, coercive vulnerability never exceeded moderate levels. This remained true even when the United States assumed the mantle of defender of Europe after World War II, which substantially increased its petroleum demand. Yet, the United States did pursue a sustained policy of indirect control to protect Free World access to Middle East oil from potential Soviet interference. The country also embraced self-sufficiency at two junctures of lesser vulnerability, when flawed geological studies suggested that a mild petroleum deficit would soon emerge.

The qualitative cases strongly corroborate the theory. Process tracing demonstrates the existence of a causal link between coercive vulnerability (qua the petroleum deficit and import disruptibility) and anticipatory strategy. Through the cases, we can see that the causal mechanism works as theorized: leaders' decisions to embark on strategic anticipation were motivated by fears of oil coercion that, in turn, stemmed from the severity of the petroleum deficit and the threat to imports. Moreover, policymakers' fears often had a military rationale above and beyond prosperity concerns. When military threats and prosperity threats coincided, which happened often, anticipatory strategies ameliorated both sets of concerns. In cases where military and economic imperatives collided rather than coincided, military calculations dominated.

Overall, outcomes confirmed the theory's expectations in ten out of eleven cases. How do we evaluate whether that represents a good enough success rate to claim that the theory is broadly generalizable? Chapter 7 uses fuzzy-set qualitative comparative analysis to judge the results against a standard probability benchmark. It finds that we can say, at least at the 90 percent confidence level, that coercive vulnerability is "usually a sufficient cause" of anticipatory strategies, whereby "usually a sufficient cause" means the cause produces the effect at least 65 percent of the time.

The conclusion explores the implications of the theory for great power politics as China continues to rise in the twenty-first century. It predicts that oil will play a major role in Chinese strategy, but not necessarily a violent one.

1
A THEORY OF STRATEGIC ANTICIPATION

Ample historical evidence demonstrates that states are willing to run high costs and risks to reduce the vulnerability of their oil supplies. Such actions underlie a good deal of international behavior and have shaped events as pivotal and diverse as the Pacific War, the Suez Crisis, and the U.S. response to the Soviet invasion of Afghanistan, in addition to many others. These observations prompt the core question of this book: How can we understand the anticipatory strategies countries adopt and predict when and why states will launch wars to protect access, as opposed to creating alliances, relying on peaceful internal measures, or doing nothing at all?

The Independent Variables: Two Determinants of Vulnerability

Two independent variables determine the degree of coercive vulnerability, which in turn affects the cost and risk tolerance for anticipatory strategies. The first and most important causal variable, the petroleum deficit, is defined as the difference between indigenous oil resources and the amount of oil a great power requires for its strategic objectives. It represents the amount of harm that oil denial would cause to a state's security. The second variable, the threat to imports, is defined as the likelihood that an opponent could successfully block the flow of oil to a great power. In other words, it represents the probability that oil denial will occur. The interaction of these two independent variables—the damage from cutoff and the probability of cutoff occurring—is the expected security threat from oil coercion, which I refer to as coercive vulnerability. If either term is zero—if the great power has no petroleum deficit, or if there is no chance its oil imports could be interrupted—then coercive vulnerability is zero, and the great power will not engage in strategic anticipation. Unfortunately for great powers, coercive vulnerability is rarely zero.

These two variables subsume all factors that could potentially impact the size of the petroleum deficit and the threat to imports, respectively. Below I explain and give examples of such subfactors, but the list is not necessarily exhaustive, nor must it be for the theory to work. What goes into the petroleum deficit matters much less for the theory than the simple facts that, first, a deficit exists—that is, there is some demand for oil that could not be met from domestic circumstances in an emergency—and second, policymakers make decisions based on their estimates of the deficit. The theory simply predicts that policymakers will study whatever potential factors influence the petroleum deficit according to their country's circumstances; the precise content of those calculations can vary across cases. Likewise, the exact determinants of import disruptibility need not be uniform across great powers. The theory requires only that some degree of threat to foreign oil access exists, whatever the particulars might be; that policymakers attempt to gauge the likelihood of being targeted; and that they act according to their findings.

Relatedly, the theory assumes that states determine the size of the petroleum deficit and the severity of import disruptibility in a boundedly rational manner. Given their strategic objectives, they perform reasonable assessments of the range and likelihood of threats to their imports as well as how much petroleum they need compared with what they expect to have, considering constraints and the expected responses of others. I do not attempt to validate that official calculations are objectively correct; I merely claim that policymakers will choose the anticipatory strategy that matches their own assessments of the country's overall coercive vulnerability, regardless of whether those assessments are accurate.[1] Ultimately, the theory lets policymakers speak for themselves when it comes to their countries' petroleum deficit and import disruptibility.

Although the petroleum deficit and import threat exist whether or not policymakers perceive them correctly, or even at all, the variables will trigger anticipatory strategies only if policymakers understand that they exist. I argue in chapter 2 that World War I effectively demonstrated to the world that oil coercion was a serious strategic problem, and that ever since, officials should (and do) realize that there is such a thing as coercive vulnerability and that it rests on these two core factors. Before World War I, however, policymakers sometimes failed to grasp these concepts, and thus they neither recognized nor reacted to them. The baseline cases explored in chapters 4 and 6 corroborate this claim.

Whether official assessments of the petroleum deficit and threat to imports are accurate is an interesting question, but it falls beyond the scope of the book. Certainly the argument does not hinge on officials always getting the value of both independent variables right; rather, it requires that policymakers reasonably attempt to do so. The case studies strongly suggest that states do carry out their assessments reasonably, if not always accurately. There were no examples where policymakers obviously or wildly misperceived their state's circumstances, barring the pre-1918 cases, when the concept of the "oil weapon" was not understood. Still, government estimates may err if for no other reason than because certain factors—most notably, estimated oil reserves—are inherently uncertain. At times, states have over- or underestimated their oil reserves or simply misinterpreted their meaning.[2] Official estimates based on the best knowledge available at the time are what matter for assessing coercive vulnerability, regardless of whether these estimates ultimately prove to be correct.

The Petroleum Deficit: How Much Damage Disruption Would Cause

The petroleum deficit measures the magnitude of damage that a great power would experience to its security if it lost access to oil. Conceptually, it is a function of "haves minus needs," which is to say that the damage depends on the severity of the gap between how much oil a great power would have to consume in a cutoff emergency and how much oil it can furnish for itself if it were completely deprived of foreign oil. Obviously, smaller deficits are better for security; as the deficit grows, the potential damage a disruption would wreak increases. At least some level of deficit must exist to create the coercive vulnerability that drives anticipatory strategies.

Importantly, the petroleum deficit can vary based on changes to haves and needs. On the one hand, it is easy to see that changes in the country's petroleum resources will alter the deficit. If a country discovers new oil, as Britain did in the North Sea in 1970, or if it depletes its resources, as Romania did during the twentieth century, its deficit will decrease or increase accordingly. On the other hand, it should also be noted that the "need" side of the equation varies, too, in tandem with strategic threats and objectives. Therefore, even if a country maintains a relatively constant level of petroleum reserves, its petroleum deficit may change to reflect shifts in goals, military doctrine, the strategic environment it faces, and other factors that affect the demand for oil in a potential emergency.

INDIGENOUS OIL RESOURCES: THE "HAVE" PART OF THE EQUATION

Many potential factors can affect "haves," but the two factors that influence this side of the equation most deeply and consistently are current crude oil production, which is determined by the market, and petroleum reserves, which are given by technology and nature.[3] Current production is significant because it represents the quantity of oil available to meet immediate emergencies, while petroleum reserves predict the future oil situation. Both factors show up in official analyses because states do not just worry about their coercive vulnerability today and tomorrow; they are cognizant of long-term needs and threats.

Policymakers understand that, in the short term, crude oil output is sticky. States typically cannot quickly surge production to meet demand spikes caused by crisis or war. This is because developing new oil fields is an unavoidably complex task that takes years to complete, even with massive investment.[4] Under normal peacetime conditions, petroleum industries usually operate at full capacity, leaving little slack for increasing supply without investing in new equipment and infrastructure.[5] This reflects market incentives; it is generally unprofitable to build and maintain costly, nonproductive equipment merely for the option to quickly increase output.[6] Therefore, whatever existing production a state has going into a national emergency is the level it is stuck with for at least several months—or more likely, years.

More nuanced considerations based on the technology of oil production also may affect policymakers' calculations of the have side of the deficit, because at the margins, they can affect the relative ease or difficulty with which a state can boost domestic output. For example, all else equal, the younger a state's industry, the better off the country is in conventional oil production—and the lower the deficit.[7] The productive life of any given oil field tends to follow a bell curve (as does national production, which is the sum of individual fields). At first, extraction is cheap and easy. The porous rocks that make up an oil reservoir are under massive physical pressure. Drilling releases those forces, causing oil to spurt out of the ground on its own.[8] In time, as significant quantities of oil are withdrawn, the subsurface pressure diminishes and less and less oil flows to the surface naturally. Inevitably, production peaks and then moves to the downslope of the curve. Pumps must be installed to remove the remaining oil, raising extraction costs even as the rate of output falls. Once this happens, the oil field is clearly in decline, even though it may continue producing for many years in successively smaller amounts. To keep output steady, a country's industry would have to move on to new fields for extraction, but these tend to be lower quality than their precursors. Oil companies usually exploit the most promising fields containing "easy oil" first because they have the best profit margins. Once these fields are exhausted, production tends to shift toward less promising fields that are more difficult and costlier to develop.

Turning the discussion to oil reserves, it is necessary to clear up popular misperceptions about their nature. Although oil reserves are often erroneously thought of as a "stock problem," in reality, they are better understood as a "flow problem." A country's oil industry continually develops new resources even as old ones are exhausted, assuming oil prices are high enough to stimulate investment. What matters, then, is not a static quantity of oil under the surface, but rather the rate of additions to proven reserves compared to the rate at which oil is removed from the ground. If new reserves are found more quickly than known reserves are drained, overall proven reserves increase. In fact, it is common for proven reserves to increase, or at least hold steady, from year to year.[9] If instead, however, the rate of increase in reserves lags behind the rate of oil extraction, proven reserves will fall.

Another nuance affecting the deficit is that not all additions to proven reserves hold equal promise for future production. The discovery of entirely new, unexploited fields bodes much more positively for future output than revisions to existing fields, which are already on their way towards being depleted. Thus, policymakers may consider the source of year-on-year additions to reserves to gain a full grasp on the petroleum deficit.

SECURITY REQUIREMENTS: THE "NEED" PART OF THE EQUATION

The amount of oil a state needs represents the other side of the deficit equation. Estimated needs typically include emergency military demand as well as civilian requirements. Numerous factors influence the petroleum needs of an individual state. For example, states that have highly motorized economies, as the United States did during the Cold War, need more oil than states where motorization has lagged, such as Germany before World War II. Service-based economies tend to need less oil than manufacturing-based economies. Various characteristics of a state's military forces also impact oil demand. All things equal, more capital-intensive militaries—especially those that use jet airplane technology—likely require more oil than labor-intensive militaries, especially those with underdeveloped air forces. Military strategy and doctrine may affect needs as well. States with attrition-based military strategies, which seek to outlast an opponent's will to fight, will require more oil than those with blitzkrieg-based strategies, which stress quick victories with limited resources. Policymakers' intentions can impact needs, too. Expansionist states typically have greater military demand for oil because their revisionist goals require fighting wars; status quo states can often achieve their goals with deterrence instead of active fighting, and thus their militaries will need less oil.[10]

The speed at which countries can adjust to oil deprivation, as well as the degree, also matters to policymakers and shows up in their analyses. In an emergency, rationing can reduce civilian consumption drastically in favor of military purposes, but just how much petroleum a country can reallocate—and how quickly it can adjust—may vary considerably across cases. By 1944, for instance, Japan had squeezed civilian oil consumption to only 3 percent of pre–World War II levels.[11] The Third Reich's economy was primarily fueled by coal, leaving little extra oil to squeeze from the civilian population. Nevertheless, the Germans managed to free up additional quantities of petroleum from the home front and send it to war, such that by the end of 1943, civilian consumption had been cut to one-tenth of prewar levels.[12] The United States, whose civilian economy relied on petroleum much more heavily than European economies, probably could not have reallocated such high percentages. In any event, crisis demand (military plus essential civilian) often exceeds normal peacetime demand, even with civilian rationing.

Emergency petroleum needs are subject to a great deal of uncertainty, and policymakers' estimates will not always be accurate. History suggests that states tend to underestimate wartime requirements, for example, perhaps due to the Clausewitzian "friction" inherent in war.[13] In practice, precise estimates often are unnecessary because states are too petroleum poor to meet strategic requirements of any size. During most of the twentieth century, for instance, Japan, France, and Britain all faced obvious deficits owing to negligible oil output and virtually nonexistent reserves.

To reiterate, the key premise of the petroleum deficit is that policymakers index oil resources to security needs. Even substantial indigenous oil resources may leave a deficit if a country's strategic requirements are also very large, or very urgent. It is not enough to have a lot of oil; the country must have a lot of oil *relative to its strategic objectives*. Additionally, the specific mix of factors that go into determining petroleum needs and haves can vary across cases without violating the tenets of the theory. What matters is that all states have some level of needs and haves that policymakers can, and do, observe and measure.

The Threat to Imports: The Probability of Foreign Oil Deprivation

The second driver of coercive vulnerability is the threat to imports, which is the likelihood that a cutoff attempt could succeed in blocking the flow of oil to the state. Although several factors influence the threat, three considerations that weigh especially heavily on policymakers are relative power, specifically, a country's military capabilities for defending its oil supply lines from plausible adversaries; the intentions of said adversaries, which captures the probability that opponents would try to cut off oil; and the geography of foreign oil production and transportation. All things equal, the more militarily powerful a state is relative to its adversaries, the less disruptible its imports, because powerful states have better prospects for successfully breaking an enemy blockade than weak powers do. Similarly, countries with better military technology are also safer from disruption than countries with less advanced militaries.

Potential opponents' intentions to cut off oil, or the lack thereof, also shape expectations. For example, if a potential adversary issues an oil disruption threat, and if that threat is credible, policymakers will view disruption as more likely. If no threats have been made, or if those issued are not credible, disruption will appear less likely. As an example, the likelihood of disruption to the United States did not increase in December 2011 when Iran threatened to close the Strait of Hormuz to oil shipping in the dispute over Tehran's nuclear program because the threats were patently outlandish. There is no evidence to suggest that the Obama administration took the threat seriously, and indeed, Iran was bluffing. The United States slapped sanctions on Iran with no retaliation to the strait. In the months preceding the 1973 OAPEC embargo, King Faisal of Saudi Arabia publicly warned that unfettered U.S. support of Israel could provoke use of the "Arab oil weapon," but American leaders reasonably concluded that the threat was not credible because a similar embargo attempt in 1967 utterly failed (see chapter 6). To policymakers, the disruption threat did not increase until the embargo was actually enacted. Even then, they (correctly) understood that although the price of oil would rise, physical access to oil was not in jeopardy. Their reaction in 1973 was an understandable nonchalance.

Policymakers factor geography into their analyses of disruptibility in several ways. All things equal, a country's oil imports are more secure if foreign oil is produced nearby because shorter supply lines are easier to defend militarily than longer supply lines are. Imports are also more secure if they travel overland instead of overseas because land transportation avoids the possibility of naval blockade. Island nations, therefore, face a high level of disruption risk, while great powers that share land borders with exporting states face a much lower risk. Where oil is located relative to enemy territory may affect disruptibility, too. If major producing regions sit in proximity to militarily strong states with motives to attack, imports are more vulnerable to enemy military power and disruptibility is higher. Oil resources that are far away from enemy strongholds are less disruptible. The availability of alternate transit routes for oil can also affect disruptibility. All things equal, states with a diversity of potential transit routes for importing oil are safer from disruption than countries that lack alternative routes.

States may fear disruption through oil embargo, but apropos the 1973 case, there are few, if any, instances where embargo was viewed as the primary threat.

Instead, the threat of physical blockade tends to dominate policymakers' considerations. "Blockade" refers to the use of military force to physically prevent goods from entering or leaving a designated country, whereas "embargo" denotes a nonmilitarized government ban on trade—that is, the peaceful refusal to sell goods.[14] The means of embargo are legal, whereas the means of blockade are martial. The two terms are often used interchangeably, but this is mistaken as they describe fundamentally different concepts. The distinction is critical in the case of oil because embargoes alone are seldom adequate to disrupt petroleum. Blockades, however, can successfully sever oil access, provided the country or countries imposing them have sufficiently strong militaries.[15]

Several obstacles exist to making embargoes effective tools for denying oil to another country. The first obstacle derives from the fungibility of oil and the existence of multiple suppliers and consumers in the international trade system. The presence of multiple suppliers undermines any one state's ability to halt oil to the target through unilateral embargo. With many suppliers to choose from, the country targeted by coercion could easily find alternative sources to make up for lost oil imports. To illustrate this, scholars often envision the oil market as a "giant bathtub" with many spigots and many drains. It matters little whether oil from a specific spigot ultimately reaches a specific drain; what matters is the overall level of oil in the bathtub and the single world market price at which oil is sold. Turning off one spigot cannot stop oil from flowing to a specific drain. Instead, closing a spigot reduces the total level of oil in the bathtub, diluting any price increase across all drains. Despite rhetoric to the contrary, there is evidence that policymakers privately understand this.

Breaking the bathtub requires international cooperation by producers and consumers. Most, if not all, countries must abide by the embargo or else it will fail. Endemic difficulties for cooperation among supplier countries include free riding and other forms of cheating, not to mention the challenges involved in reaching an agreement on what the common embargo policy should be.[16] These issues lessen the chances of organizing an embargo in which enough supply states participate to seriously impact the target's ability to obtain oil.

Yet, even if exporting states cooperated, this would not necessarily be enough for the embargo to gain traction. Oil-importing countries must be brought on board, too. Motivated by profits or politics, third-party net importers may break an embargo by purchasing and secretly reselling oil to targeted countries. During World War II, for instance, Spain illicitly sold some of its petroleum imports to Nazi-occupied France to help Hitler evade the Allied blockade and embargo. Nonstate actors, including organized crime and sometimes even multinational oil companies, also may smuggle petroleum to the target in exchange for premium pricing. Such trickery is very difficult to detect and punish.

Even under the most favorable circumstances, no embargo is airtight. Controlling oil flows without using force is very, very hard to do; evasion nearly always occurs. The case of antiapartheid petroleum sanctions against South Africa aptly illustrates these dynamics. Multilateral attempts in the 1980s and 1990s to institute a strong oil embargo foundered at every stage along the way from policy formulation to implementation. At the time, numerous medium-to-small supplier countries made up most of the international oil market. Imposing an effective embargo therefore required the cooperation of many actors. Although there was widespread international agreement on the repugnance of apartheid, countries could not agree on whether sanctions were warranted, whether they should include oil, or whether they should be compulsory or voluntary. The United States and many European nations blocked efforts to establish a rigid regime. Iran, a major producer, not only bucked the oil embargo but also capitalized on it by becoming South Africa's largest supplier. OAPEC members, and even some African oil exporters including Angola and Nigeria, paid lip service to voluntary export restrictions but in practice did nothing to enforce compliance by their citizens. In all, antiapartheid oil sanctions proved to be "constraints rather than barriers—the oil continue[d] to flow."[17] As leaky and incomplete as it was, the embargo did impose costs on South Africa in the form of higher oil prices that hurt the economy.[18] But this was not enough to coerce.[19] With large quantities of petroleum still reaching South Africa, the government was able to weather the embargo and resist international demands for political change.

Stressing that the main threat comes from military cutoff does not imply that producers cannot attempt coercion or that nonmilitary efforts to restrict supplies fall outside the scope of the theory. To the contrary, the import disruptibility variable subsumes all potential threats to interrupt the flow of oil, including embargoes. Rather, the main point here is that embargo attempts tend to be ineffective, and as such, the threat of them does not loom so large in the eyes of policymakers. Resultantly, when deliberating over whether to pursue anticipatory strategies and which specific ones to choose, the subfactors relating to physical disruption tend to be primary considerations, whereas the subfactors relating to the possibility of embargo tend to be peripheral in policymakers' decision making.

The Causal Mechanism: The Hazards of Coercive Vulnerability

Two independent variables, the petroleum deficit and the threat to imports, determine how vulnerable a great power is to oil coercion. Coercive vulnerability, in turn, spurs great powers into one of three anticipatory strategies: self-sufficiency,

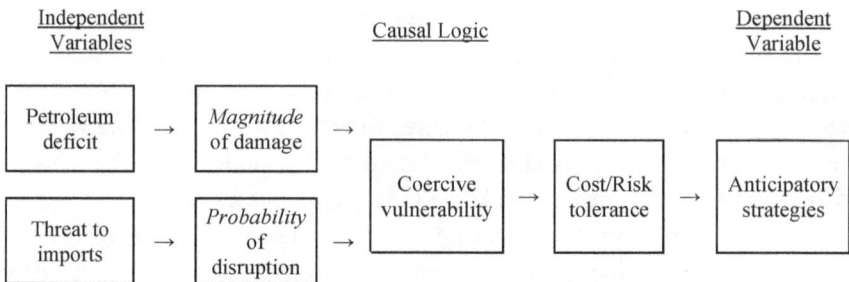

FIGURE 1.1. The theory

indirect control through alliances, or direct control through war. But why would countries adopt measures to preempt a seemingly nonexistent problem—oil coercion—that history shows is rarely used against great powers?

The answer is that coercive vulnerability begets anticipatory strategies because the consequences of failing to reduce vulnerability are potentially catastrophic. Losing access to oil can jeopardize a state's most important goal: maintaining its survival in the international system. This is because oil cutoff can undermine a state's ability to defend itself in war (see figure 1.1).

The economic importance of oil has been the subject of much attention; by comparison, its military importance has been given short shrift. Chapter 2 will say more about how the military importance of oil played out historically with the transition from coal to oil-based transportation circa World War I, and how the great powers reacted. This section articulates in general terms why military considerations, and not simply economic interests, drive anticipatory behavior. I am not arguing that oil is unimportant for economies or that policymakers are indifferent to prosperity concerns. Rather, economic motives simply are not a sufficient cause to prompt anticipatory strategies. Below, I explain why the military component of the coercive threat functions as a necessary cause for undertaking anticipatory strategies.

Economizing on Force: Oil's Special Potential for Coercion

Coercion refers to "efforts to change the behavior of a state by manipulation of costs and benefits" in the target state's decision calculus.[20] Coercion can be thought of as an attempt to achieve a political goal at a lower cost than what it would take to achieve the objective through brute force. Brute force uses overwhelming strength to defeat an opponent and take what one wants—without the opponent's cooperation. Coercion, by contrast, applies selective force to persuade the opponent to cooperate with demands. The aggressor structures the situation such that it is in the target's best interests to comply with the coercer's wishes. From the point of view of the aggressor, the advantage of using coercion instead of brute force to achieve one's goals is that it is less costly.

Scholars often distinguish between two strategies of coercion: denial and punishment. Each of these two strategies aims at altering different parameters in the target's decision calculus. Punishment strategies focus on increasing the costs associated with continued resistance. The logic is to inflict pain on the target until it relents. Punishment can involve threats or attacks against both soft and hard targets; the key distinction is that the attacks are intended to maximize suffering. Denial strategies, by contrast, seek to decrease the probability that continued resistance will achieve the desired benefits. Here the underlying logic is to reduce the material capabilities the target state can bring to bear against the coercer. Typically, coercers accomplish this by destroying the opponent's military forces.[21] In short, punishment reduces will; denial reduces capability.

Existing work suggests that denial is more effective than punishment because it may be better able to persuade target states to concede on high-stakes interests. Punishment strategies can achieve modest coercive goals, but typically only if these entail minor concessions from the target. Short of resorting to bombing cities with nuclear weapons, punishment rarely raises the costs high enough to obtain major concessions on vital interests.[22] Targets may be willing to pay large costs of resistance with major priorities on the line—but only if they face a reasonable chance of success. If denial can drastically reduce the probability that the state will benefit from resisting, the country will be unwilling to continue paying costs and will acquiesce.[23]

Why wouldn't countries always use denial if it is more effective than punishment? One major constraining factor on denial is that it tends to cost more to the coercer than punishment—and in fact, may cost nearly as much as brute force does. Costs hinge on what is required to convince the target that the probability of benefiting from continued resistance is very small. For instance, if an aggressor would have to destroy large portions of the opponent's military in a protracted series of bloody battles to demonstrate that resistance will fail, and thus is not worth further cost, then denial offers little advantage over brute force.

However, if the coercer can find a "shortcut"—a way to convince the target that resistance is futile *without* having to destroy its military completely—then denial emerges as an attractive strategy. After all, an effective coercive device is like a well-functioning lever: it amplifies the effort put in, allowing the coercer to pry seemingly disproportionate concessions from the opponent through the strategic application of targeted costs and risks. The trick is to find a lever that offers the coercer brute force results without having to pay brute force costs. This has been so desirable that military thinkers over the years have tried all kinds of techniques, usually in vain, in hopes of stumbling upon that magic lever that moves the opponent at reasonable cost.

Attacking a target's oil supply is one of very few things that provide a potential shortcut to denial—a way to disable a country's military forces without a knock-down drag-out war of attrition. Oil holds exceptional importance for military power because it determines military mobility, one of the most fundamental ingredients for victory in war. Military transportation in the age of mechanized warfare (i.e., since World War I) depends almost completely on petroleum-based fuels, which offer the best performance. Because oil is the basis of mobility, a country that can deny oil to its adversary in wartime can immobilize its forces and render it unable to win, without necessarily having to destroy the bulk of the opponent's military. This threat amounts to a coercive strategy of denial: it convinces the target state to capitulate without further resistance because all hopes of prevailing in war have been lost.

Oil permeates nearly every part of the military machine and is crucial on both the offensive and defensive sides of the battlefield.[24] For the offense, mobility generates an element of surprise that can be decisive for overwhelming an enemy's defenses. It is generally thought that the offense requires at least a three-to-one majority at the point of attack to break through. Here, mobility can play an integral role by "allow[ing] an attacking force to group itself and regroup itself, to assemble temporary numerical superiorities as it pleases, when it decides to begin battles."[25] With sufficient speed, the offense can mass forces quickly enough so as to give the defender little to no warning about the imminent attack, thus depriving it of response time to redress the numerical imbalance by reinforcing the line at the point of attack. Mobility is perhaps even more crucial for the exploitation phase of battle. Once breakthrough is achieved, the offense must move quickly enough to sever the defender's line of communications before additional reserves arrive. Lack of such mobility presented a huge problem for the Germans in World War I, particularly during the 1918 Ludendorff offensives.[26] On the defending side, mobility means a country can counter incursions along its front by rapidly moving reinforcements to the point of attack. Highly mobile defenders are better equipped to respond to contingencies than slow-moving forces.[27] Petroleum-based fuel is even more critical for military aviation, as it is required to simply get planes into the air, let alone use them operationally.

Petroleum is perhaps even more critical for logistics, given the scale of organization required for modern militaries to supply their combat forces. Highly complex and tightly integrated, logistical systems are composed of interdependent links in the chain that must operate harmoniously to be effective. This means logistics can be especially vulnerable; problems in one link can have rippling negative effects throughout the transportation chain.

Oil also plays an important role in training activities, especially for pilots. Curtailment of training is a common tactic that militaries use to conserve fuel supplies when the petroleum supply is jeopardized or insufficient. The shortages of skilled pilots, navigators, and mariners resulting from a suspension of training activities can drastically diminish military effectiveness.

Finally, oil has unique physical characteristics that make it very difficult to replace for military transportation. Countries are better positioned to disable a military by attacking oil, as opposed to other raw materials, because it is scarce and cannot be renewed or recycled. Otherwise, the targeted country could improvise and stretch supplies with scrap material drives, as is possible for steel and rubber.

In sum, great powers are hardwired to worry about oil coercion because supply disruptions could directly undermine their security. Oil has been *the* critical fuel for military mobility since the rise of mechanized warfare in World War I. Mobility, in turn, can make or break a country in war. No other resource offers the same level of performance for military mobility, and this means a country lacking petroleum is vulnerable to losing wars. An adversary could attack a state's oil supply and render a state's military instrument unworkable, without having to destroy all its military forces. It is much easier to paralyze an adversary's military by denying it oil than it is to destroy the adversary completely. The special potential of oil to disable militaries provides powerful incentives for strategic anticipation.

Why Economic Prosperity Alone Cannot Explain Anticipatory Strategies

My argument differs from the conventional view that oil is most important to great powers as an economic stimulant—that is, because access to abundant oil at steady and reasonable prices is foundational to economic prosperity. No doubt, great powers care about oil as a factor affecting gross domestic product. Prosperity concerns alone, however, are not sufficient to explain the anticipatory strategies we observe. There are two reasons why.

First, debilitating oil cutoffs are likely to occur under circumstances that privilege military goals over national income considerations. Because peaceful trade embargoes are relatively easy to circumvent, as explained above, the most effective way a coercer can deprive oil to an adversary is by targeting its imports with military force—that is, through a military blockade. Generally, blockades tend to happen during war or as an immediate precursor to it.[28] For countries at war, transferring as much oil as possible to the military becomes the overriding goal, and prosperity becomes a second-order concern.

Although the primary threat to oil would occur in wartime, this does not mean that the theory applies only immediately before, during, or immediately after wars. To the contrary, the theory applies nonstop, even during long stretches of peace. Indeed, the case studies of U.S. behavior during the Cold War show that American leaders pursued anticipatory strategies even when they did not believe war with the Soviet Union was imminent or even likely. More to the point, and as realists often emphasize, war is always possible under anarchy, and that fact is enough for states to take precautions against coercive vulnerability even when war is remote—just as most states maintain military forces in times of peace.

Second, if large amounts of oil were physically disrupted through military force, the resulting oil cutoff would hurt militaries disproportionally more than economies. Prosperity would suffer, but despite common beliefs, modern economies without oil would not "grind to a halt." Militaries would. This is because there are substitutes for oil that are adequate for domestic economic uses in a national emergency but inadequate for military purposes.

The importance of oil to modern industrialized economies is often misunderstood. Economies use oil for three main purposes: (1) to fuel transportation, which by far accounts for the majority of consumption; (2) to power industrial production; and (3) to generate utilities such as heat and electricity. Industry and utilities account for a relatively small portion of oil demand in developed countries.

A common myth about petroleum is that is has no substitutes. In fact, several fuels closely substitute for oil for many purposes—transportation representing the one big exception. When it comes to utilities and industry, oil does not offer significantly better performance than substitutes like coal, natural gas, nuclear power, and renewables. Petroleum's one main advantage is that it burns more cleanly than coal does, and thus causes less pollution. But aside from this (albeit serious) environmental concern, coal is just as good at producing heat and electricity as oil is, and it is much more abundant. Natural gas is also more abundant than oil and causes less pollution. Because close substitutes exist, the industrial, commercial, and residential sectors of the economy already rely on nonpetroleum fuel sources, consuming a mixture of coal, natural gas, and renewable energy. Virtually no oil in the United States or other developed countries is used to generate electricity.[29] For this reason, any politician who suggests that investments in clean energy, such as solar and wind, could break a country's dependence on petroleum is either a fool or a knave.

Transportation is the one sector in which oil offers significant advantages over competing energy sources. For this reason, transportation consumes more oil than any other activity, accounting for roughly 70 percent of consumption in developed countries. More importantly, modern transportation relies almost entirely on petroleum as its major fuel source. Roughly 95 percent of U.S. transportation, for example, runs on oil. Transportation in other countries is similarly dependent.

It is possible to run internal combustion engines using alternative fuels, but their performance is far inferior to oil. In other words, they do not substitute for oil for transit purposes as closely as they can for nontransit purposes. These fuels are more expensive and offer lower levels of performance in four key areas: speed, range, reliability, and flexibility.

Petroleum offers superior speed and range compared with other transportation fuels because it naturally occurs as a liquid and is highly energy dense—that is, it contains a large amount of energy per unit of volume. This means that the quantity of oil needed to produce a desired output of energy will be smaller than the quantities of other fuels required for the same energy output. For instance, one ton of coal produces roughly half the energy as a ton of crude oil, and thus it takes about twice as much coal to perform the same amount of work.[30] Because of the energy density of oil, vehicles running on oil can achieve higher top speeds and travel greater distances before stopping to refuel. Its liquid nature also makes it more efficient to carry in compact storage tanks for use "on the go."

Contrast this with fuels with lower energy densities, such as natural gas, charcoal, wood, peat, and coal. All these fuels are capable of powering internal combustion engines. In fact, they were widely used in Europe and Japan during World War II to cope with war-related petroleum shortages (see table 1.1). Converting a vehicle to run on solid fuels is a simple task, consisting of a minor alteration to attach a gasifying generator to the existing engine. A typical automotive mechanic can do the job, and during the war, many people with experience fixing cars did it themselves. Major motor companies began manufacturing large numbers of these "producer gas" vehicles, including Mercedes-Benz, General Motors in Denmark (under Nazi control), Ford in Germany (under Nazi control), Saab, Volvo, Citroen, and Renault. As early as 1939, the Japanese Home Office mandated that

TABLE 1.1 Producer gas vehicles in selected countries, 1942

COUNTRY	NUMBER OF VEHICLES	COUNTRY	NUMBER OF VEHICLES
Germany	350,000	Italy	35,000
France	110,000	Denmark	20,000
Japan	100,000	Switzerland	15,000
USSR	100,000	Belgium	15,000
Sweden	73,650	Britain	10,000
Australia	45,000	United States	6

Source: National Research Council, *Producer Gas: Another Fuel for Motor Transport* (Washington, DC: National Academy Press, 1983), 3.

TABLE 1.2   Energy equivalencies to gasoline (in lb. of solid fuels)

	WOOD	PEAT	BROWN COAL BRIQUETTES	CHARCOAL BRIQUETTES	ANTHRACITE COAL
1 gallon of gasoline	22.4	25	18.3	12.5	10.8
1 pound of gasoline	3.5	4	2.9	2.1	1.7

Source: National Research Council, *Producer Gas*, 75.

all new motor vehicles be equipped to run on producer gas or other alternative fuels. In Europe, the number of producer gas trucks, cars, taxis, buses, tractors, and motorcycles increased from about 9,000 vehicles on the roads in 1938 to 450,000 in 1941 and nearly 1 million in 1942. "To Europe at large, producer gas became the 'civilian fuel'" during World War II. "By March 1944 more than 80 percent of the trucks and other large vehicles and 26% of civilian automobiles (260,000 cars) in Europe had been converted to producer gas."[31] In addition to producer gas vehicles, the Germans also converted thousands of civilian automobiles to run on natural gas. These were "driven through the streets with large canvas gas bags attached, like so many small Zeppelins."[32]

However, the low energy content of alternative fuels meant that producer gas vehicles had significantly lower maximum speeds and seriously reduced range (see table 1.2). At best, these fuels could yield only 80 percent of the energy that petroleum products could. More often, the yield was closer to 50–60 percent. Fuel economy was extremely low. A fifteen-pound sack of wood could power a car for only ten miles. Drivers had to sacrifice cargo space to accommodate bulkier fuels, which, combined with the heavy gasifier attachments, added enough weight to the vehicles to reduce performance further. Huge amounts of fuel were consumed. Sweden's roughly seventy-five thousand producer gas vehicles alone—which accounted for over 90 percent of the cars on Swedish roads in 1943—guzzled ninety million cubic feet of charcoal and seventy million cubic feet of wood per year. Moreover, with producer gas vehicles, "ignition" took on a whole new meaning: the driver had to light an actual fire in the engine to start the vehicle—a clumsy process that could take twenty minutes. And for every two hundred kilometers traveled, the operator had to stop, extinguish the fire, and service the generator by clearing out considerable quantities of ash and replacing the filters; otherwise it could explode. Then, of course, he or she would have to go through the trouble of relighting it. There was no easy way around these issues.[33]

In addition to their low energy content, solid fuels present an additional drawback for internal combustion engines: poor reliability. This problem arises because solid fuels burn neither as smoothly nor as cleanly as liquid fuels do. Internal combustion engines made to run on erratically burning fuels are prone to "knocking," a phenomenon where the fuel causes small, irregular explosions in the engine that manifest as "ping" noises. Knocking seriously degrades engine performance and causes vehicle breakdowns.[34] Furthermore, the dirtiness of solid fuel creates damaging buildup in engines, and with heavy use, this buildup shortens vehicles' operating lives. A telling anecdote demonstrating the reliability problems associated with solid fuels stems from General Douglas MacArthur's first trip to Japan after its surrender in World War II. Upon landing at the Atsugi airfield on August 30, 1945, MacArthur traveled by motorcade to the nearby city of Yokohama. "Though the distance was only twenty miles, the motorcade took two hours to make the trip; the battered vehicles, the best the Japanese could provide, were powered not by gasoline, because there was no gasoline, but by charcoal. They repeatedly broke down."[35]

Finally, any energy source that produces electricity could power vehicles through batteries, rails, and wires—bypassing combustion engines entirely. Electricity can be useful for powering railways and other mass transit systems that draw energy directly from the grid while in operation. However, a reliance on fixed infrastructure entails a significant loss in flexibility. Whereas motor vehicles can move across a plane in any direction, railways and cable cars powered by overhead wires can move only back and forth in one direction (I discuss the military disadvantages of this in chapter 2).

In sum, lack of oil would clearly lower living standards, but it would not paralyze the economy completely. In an emergency, for instance, if oil were disrupted by war, government authorities would almost certainly intervene to funnel as much oil as necessary away from the civilians and to the military. Industrial production and utilities would be the least affected because oil makes a relatively small contribution to these sectors and very good substitutes exist. The effects on transportation would be significant. Motorists would have to face declines in speed, range, reliability, and flexibility, as well as increased transportation costs. Oil prices for civilians might rise, depending on the government's rationing scheme, which may include subsidies or price ceilings. Under normal circumstances, such deprivations would be politically unacceptable. During an emergency, however, nationalistic populations often tolerate oil shortages and other hardships if they believe vital national interests are at stake.

By contrast, armies, navies, and air forces that do not have enough oil simply cannot function effectively if pitted against an adversary with plenty of it. A fleet of "so many small Zeppelins" would spell disaster on a battlefield. All told, oil shortages for the civilian economy are painful; oil shortages for the military are lethal. States therefore worry about the dire consequences of oil cutoff for their ability to defend themselves. This is true even in peacetime because states must prepare for what could happen in the worst-case scenario of war. If a state is cut off from its sources of oil, its military would be immobilized and the chances of winning a war would plummet. The threat of disastrous defeat in war is what makes oil coercion especially potent.

Put together, these two logics suggest that if force is not used, it is very unlikely that an adversary would be able to deprive a target of large enough quantities of oil to cripple its economy. When force is used—for example, during war—petroleum cutoffs are simultaneously more likely to succeed and more likely to cause grave damage to the target's ability to defend itself. In the anarchic international system, states continually prepare for war even as they hope for peace. The fact that war is always possible casts a long shadow over states; it influences state behavior even in peacetime. In sum, embargo scenarios generally pose little threat to states. But for a state that finds itself physically cut off from oil amid a war, the threat is existential.

The Dependent Variable: Anticipatory Strategies

Anticipatory strategies are foreign and domestic policies that secure access to oil. States are motivated to adopt anticipatory strategies by fears that an adversary (or group of adversaries) could use threats to oil access to gain leverage in a crisis or dispute. Oil cutoffs have enormous potential as an instrument of coercion because unimpeded oil access is vital to a state's military and economic power. In ideal cases, anticipatory strategies prevent disruption attempts from ever occurring by making it very unlikely such attempts would succeed.

I conceptualize anticipatory strategies as a continuum of policies that rank from mild to extreme in their relative benefits and costs. The spectrum can be divided into three broad categories. The first, and the mildest, category is self-sufficiency, which consists of all policies that increase domestic oil availability. The second category, moderate in both costs and benefits, is indirect control, which is composed of all policies that keep oil in friendly hands and out of the hands of potential enemies. The third category, direct control, which carries the most extreme costs but offers the greatest benefits, consists of actions to take physical possession of oil territory and supply routes. The three categories encompass all logical possibilities for anticipation. Any given measure a state adopts to protect oil access fits into one—and only one—of the three categories (see figure 1.2).

Two assumptions underlie this conceptualization of anticipatory strategies. First, when it comes to the oil security benefits of each strategy, I assume that great powers "get what they pay for," so to speak. The mildest strategies (those cheapest in costs and risks) buy the least amount of oil security, while extreme strategies

A THEORY OF STRATEGIC ANTICIPATION 33

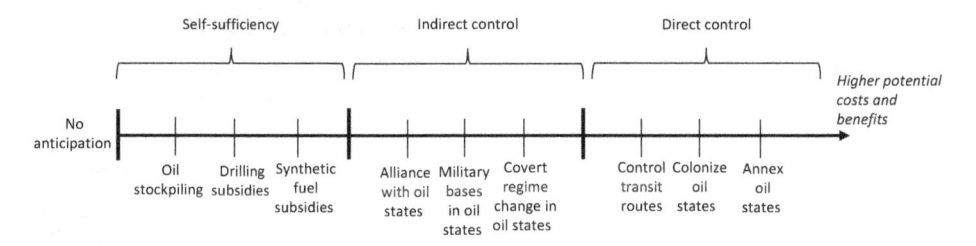

FIGURE 1.2. Spectrum of anticipatory strategies

(those most expensive in costs and risks) buy the best oil security. In other words, the potential benefit of a given anticipatory strategy tracks closely to its costs.

Second, I assume that the hierarchy of anticipatory strategies is generally fixed, such that the costs and benefits of direct control exceed those of indirect control, which in turn exceed the costs and benefits of self-sufficiency *for any given state*. In other words, policymakers consider the trade-offs of each strategy *relative to their own set of options*, not in an absolute sense, and not in comparison with other states' options. For example, direct control of Persian Gulf oil might be less costly for Russia than for Britain, because Britain would have to project power over a much greater distance to conquer oil territory and protect transit routes than Russia would. But the cost of direct control *for Russia* would surpass the cost of indirect control *for Russia*. Likewise, the cost of direct control *for Britain* would exceed the cost of indirect control *for Britain*. The latter cost-benefit comparisons—Russia to Russia, Britain to Britain—are the relevant ones to the theory.

Each anticipatory strategy, by definition, includes a range of policies that share a single logic for securing oil. As a general rule, however, the policies grouped within each strategy differ axiomatically from the policies across the other two strategies, they are discernible as such, and their costs and benefits differ accordingly. Indirect control, for example, could consist solely of military aid, or it could include some combination of military aid, informal security guarantees, formal alliances with basing rights, or even covert intervention to install a friendly leader. On the whole, however, indirect control measures are typically less costly and risky than direct control measures but costlier than self-sufficiency measures.[36]

While anticipatory strategies generally conform to the cost-effectiveness ranking laid out in figure 1.2, it is possible that circumstances could arise in which the costs of a milder strategy overlap with the costs of the next strategy up the hierarchy. I expect any potential overlap across the categories to exist only at the edges—for example, where the costliest indirect control strategy abuts (and perhaps overlaps) the least costly direct control strategy. In a case where costs overlap, the theory would be partially indeterminate; the state could choose either of the two strategies whose costs overlap but should not choose the third.

The example of Britain's experience during the Suez Crisis illustrates how even cheap versions of direct control exceed the costs of expensive versions of indirect control. When Egyptian president Gamal Abdel Nasser nationalized the Suez Canal in 1956, the British pursued direct control by attempting to invade the canal zone. The invasion was relatively low cost as direct control goes—it was a small operation to capture a tiny area from a weak adversary. (Certainly it was less costly and risky than Britain's conquest of Mesopotamia or Japan's attack on the East Indies.) Nevertheless, the action involved direct military costs and significant diplomatic costs. It strained British-American relations so much that Eisenhower refused to extend oil aid to Britain, and it prompted nuclear threats from the USSR. It was less risky than conquering a whole country, but it was risky enough to have failed—British troops did not make it to the canal. The costs of failure were also high: Nasser physically blocked the canal so that no British oil could pass through. Even if the operation had succeeded, Britain would have had to pay occupation costs indefinitely.

Even a very costly indirect control option for Suez would have cost less than direct control did. A counterfactual example of expensive indirect control over the Suez Canal would be covert intervention to topple Nasser and replace him with a sympathetic leader (like the British-sponsored coup in 1953 to oust Mohammad Mossadegh in Iran). Ousting Nasser would trigger some of the same diplomatic costs and risks as the war did (probably not a nuclear threat from the Soviets), but it would avoid the military costs of a conventional engagement. It would also be less risky: if covert action failed, Britain would have plausible deniability, whereas there was no denying the conventional advance of British troops toward the canal zone.[37] Britain would also pay the costs of propping up the friendly regime indefinitely, but these would be smaller than paying direct occupation costs. The Suez counterfactual also demonstrates how direct versus indirect control of sea-lanes can be distinguished. Direct control means that a country uses its own forces to control transit routes, whereas indirect control uses "friendly hands" to control transit routes.

Crucially, the goal of the theory is to predict why great powers choose one strategic tier over another. The theory does not attempt to predict which specific policies a state will choose *within* any given anticipatory strategy—a level of precision that is unrealistic to attain. Even if it were possible to hypothesize at that level of detail, so many additional variables would have to be included that the theory would deteriorate into mere description. Ergo, the present level of abstraction is the appropriate one on grounds of both substantive importance and parsimony. Substantively speaking, the difference between securing oil through alliance and securing oil through conquest is highly consequential: it is the difference between war and peace. Predicting fine gradations in the degree of indirect control—for example, distinguishing the causes of informal security guarantees from the causes of formal security guarantees—is comparatively trivial. In the final analysis, the point of a theory is to distill complex explanations to their most fundamental essence, because doing so allows scholars and policymakers to harvest their insight broadly. When the goal is to generalize, as it is here, theoretical parsimony is virtue, not vice.

Self-Sufficiency

The logic of self-sufficiency is to use domestic policy to make the state as independent of foreign oil supplies as possible. Self-sufficiency decreases reliance on external sources by increasing domestic production, decreasing consumption through conservation or relying on alternative fuels, and/or building a supply cushion. The strategy resembles Kenneth N. Waltz's concept of "internal balancing," insofar as it enhances the state's relative material capabilities in ways useful to its military power and security.[38] Several types of policies fit into this category.

If no oil exists within a state's territory, there is obviously no hope for producing oil domestically. Policy choices would be limited to building up a strategic oil stockpile or conserving oil consumption through some combination of substituting alternative fuels for oil or reducing demand for automotive transportation in general—for instance, by stipulating that workers must live near their place of employment, designating all major roads as high-occupancy vehicle lanes to induce carpooling, or undertaking other creative measures. These measures can only do so much: the country cannot will itself oil resources out of thin air, and the potential for decreasing consumption is limited.

If a state is lucky enough to have petroleum reserves, the government may instead focus on boosting domestic production beyond the level that the market alone would bear. This could be accomplished through a variety of means, including financial incentives for exploratory drilling to discover new fields; subsidies or tax write-offs for building new wells or pipelines, or expanding current ones; direct government funding for new oil infrastructure; opening new public land to exploration or drilling; or subsidizing research and development of new technologies to reach oil that is located deep underwater or in other inaccessible or high-cost areas.

Self-sufficiency is the least costly of the three strategies. That is not to say it is cheap in an absolute sense; rather, it is cheap *relative to the other two strategies that the same state could pursue*. It avoids the military costs and risks of taking territory that are associated with direct control. And, because it employs internal policy, it is the least provocative to other states and thus entails the lowest risk of provoking a broader international conflict and the costs such conflict entails.

Self-sufficiency can mildly decrease vulnerability but is generally inadequate for filling large gaps between oil supply and demand, particularly for military purposes. This is a function of the physical properties of oil noted above. Nothing compares to petroleum for powering internal combustion engines, because oil is uniquely highly energy-dense—that is, it naturally contains more energy per unit of volume than any other fuel.[39] Therefore, it takes much larger quantities of other fuels to produce the same energy output that oil can produce, which makes it cost-inefficient, and usually cost-prohibitive, to substitute other materials when very high volumes of oil are needed. Substitution helps around the margins but cannot sustain an entire war effort for a substantial period of time. There is a reason why large-scale synthetic fuel production only arises when it is subsidized by a government: synthetic fuel is breathtakingly inefficient to produce. The Nazi regime, for example, invested billions in coal-to-oil synthetic fuel production in Germany in the lead-up to World War II (see chapter 5). It required four to five tons of coal, on average, to produce one ton of synthetic oil, and the ratio worsened as fuel quality increased. Because costs were prohibitive, Germany had to settle for producing 87 octane to yield enough synthetic aviation fuel to put the Luftwaffe in the air, contributing to its loss in the Battle of Britain. German aircraft simply could not compete in speed and maneuverability with Allied planes, which burned 100 octane fuel.[40]

The key point here is that the potential for self-sufficiency does not vary meaningfully across industrialized countries; rather, the prospects for self-sufficiency are constant because they derive from these immutable properties of oil. The uniquely high energy density of oil makes it very hard for *any* country to find adequate oil substitutes for transportation (hence the world's continued reliance on the stuff despite its many pitfalls). Widely available but poor-quality fuels (wood, peat, charcoal, etc.) can power civilian vehicles, albeit with dramatically reduced performance, but none of these fuels come close to replacing oil for military power for any state.

Stockpiling is equally expensive for all countries: its cost depends on the global market price for buying oil, to which all countries are subject, plus the costs of storage, which are unlikely to vary much from country to country. Buying and perpetually storing large quantities of oil in strategic reserves is impractical for countries with large petroleum deficits. It is expensive, the reserves take years to fill, and the quantities are epic.

As an illustrative example, the U.S. Strategic Petroleum Reserve (SPR) holds seven hundred million barrels, which the government paid $30 per barrel to purchase (a relative bargain), for a total cost of $21 billion, not counting storage costs. Because the United States produces 65 percent of its own oil, the SPR could replace about four and a half months of imports before running dry.[41] Here the

United States is relatively fortunate compared with other great powers, because it produces so much of its own oil already. If instead it had to use the SPR to replace all oil supplies (if it hypothetically produced no oil), the quantity of oil in the SPR would provide only thirty-six days of total consumption—not much security for $21 billion. At that rate, a whole year's worth of oil would cost over $210 billion in purchase costs alone—a staggering amount. To put that number in perspective, the U.S. defense budget for fiscal year 2016 was roughly $573 billion, which means that the cost of accumulating one year's worth of total oil supplies would equal roughly 37 percent of the U.S. defense budget.[42] Keep in mind, however, that $30 per barrel as an average purchase price is a bargain compared with the price of oil in the 2010s. From 2011 to 2014, the cost of oil, on average, was over $90 per barrel. At that price, purchasing a year's supply of oil would cost $630 billion, eclipsing total annual spending on defense. Clearly, it is impractical to stockpile the massive quantities of oil that great powers need, particularly for countries that produce none of their own oil.

All countries must deal with these physical limitations of oil. Therefore, while self-sufficiency may satisfy the needs of low-vulnerability states, moderate- and high-vulnerability countries must pursue costlier strategies to improve their situation.

Indirect Control Strategies

Indirect control reduces coercive vulnerability through security partnerships that deter rival great powers from intervening in oil-producing countries. The fundamental logic is to keep oil in "friendly hands" and away from adversaries that may interfere with access. It can be thought of as a type of external balancing in response to coercive threats.[43] The strategy may include formal military alliances, securing transit routes, basing, arms sales, military aid, and other measures. Such policies improve the petroleum producer's military capabilities and bolster the credibility of extended deterrence by establishing a public and physical commitment to the producer's defense.

Indirect control also mitigates vulnerability by fostering cooperation. In exchange for protection, the producer state may sit out collective embargo attempts and assist its ally in weathering them instead. For instance, Saudi Arabia, while publicly supporting the 1973 OAPEC embargo against the United States, privately cheated—it secretly provided oil for American forces in Vietnam.[44] Petroleum producers may also supply their protectors at below-market prices or donate oil. For example, countries hosting American forces in the Persian Gulf regularly provide petroleum for military needs at no charge. Saudi Arabia and Kuwait contributed massive amounts of free petroleum as assistance in-kind for the Persian

Gulf War; Operation Southern Watch, which contained Saddam Hussein through the no-fly zone; and the invasion and occupation of Iraq.[45]

Indirect control holds greater potential for boosting oil security than self-sufficiency, but it is also costlier and riskier. Indirect control can expand petroleum access significantly more than self-sufficiency can because it increases the volume of potential oil resources available to the state beyond indigenous output, provided that the producer state remains friendly in a crisis and that the vulnerable state successfully defends the producer's territory and oil transit routes. The costs are higher, however, because there is some risk that the great power will have to use force to defend the producer state against potential aggressors. Other costs include the possibility of being dragged into an ally's conflict, the potential for free riding by allies unwilling to contribute to their own defense, or provoking terrorism or other forms of political backlash by supporting unsavory regimes.[46]

Compared with direct control, however, indirect control is less costly and risky. While the state risks military costs to protect the producer, it pays these costs only if its security guarantee fails to deter aggression. Furthermore, because indirect control defends the status quo, it is less provocative to rival great powers than direct control, which changes the status quo. Therefore, there is less risk that indirect control would provoke retaliation or spark direct conflict with great power rivals. Although it expands potential supplies, indirect control cannot guarantee access. There is always some probability that the alliance could falter at a critical moment. An ally could withdraw cooperation or even switch loyalties, which the West feared Iran's Mohammad Mossadegh might do in the early 1950s, given his perceived Soviet sympathies.[47] Thus, it cannot provide the highest degree of oil security. For that, great powers must turn to direct control.

Direct Control Strategies

Direct control provides the best oil security money can buy. It reduces coercive vulnerability in a straightforward manner: the vulnerable state conquers oil-rich territory and transportation routes that ship oil to its homeland or to military forces deployed abroad. Countries prefer direct control over proxy control of critical resources whenever possible to eliminate reliance on "other help" in a "self-help" system.[48] The best of both worlds, the strategy combines the benefits of indirect control and self-sufficiency while minimizing their drawbacks. Like indirect control, territorial expansion can greatly increase the total amount of oil available, beyond the state's own indigenous output, in a crisis. Yet, unlike indirect control, direct control guarantees access to this oil in an emergency, which is the chief advantage of self-sufficiency because access does not depend on cooperation from a friendly foreign producer.

TABLE 1.3 Summary of great power anticipatory strategies

CHARACTERISTIC	SELF-SUFFICIENCY	INDIRECT CONTROL	DIRECT CONTROL
Logic	Reduce reliance on external oil	Keep oil in "friendly hands," away from adversaries; enhance cooperation	Directly annex foreign oil and transit routes
Means	Domestic policy	Threats, military aid, force if necessary	Military force
Costs and risks	Low	Medium	High
Oil security benefits	Limited	Potentially large, but not guaranteed	Large, guaranteed
Examples	Stockpiles, alternative fuel subsidies, conservation	Security agreements, arms sales, basing	Territorial conquest, controlling sea-lanes

Although the prospects for increasing one's oil security are great, direct control is very costly and risky. Absolute costs can vary greatly, but the relative costs of direct control for a given state always exceed those of indirect control by the same state. With direct control, the state has no choice but to pay the costs of fighting to take and hold oil resources and defend transit routes, whereas indirect control may allow it to avoid those costs if deterrent threats successfully keep oil in "friendly hands." Moreover, direct control could provoke military intervention by rival great powers eager to restore a territorial status quo that favors their interests.

Perhaps the most infamous case of this strategy in action was Japan's anticipatory invasion of the Dutch East Indies in December 1941, which bolstered Japanese oil resources in the short term, but at the cost of provoking a devastating war with the United States. That Japan took such a risk speaks to the desperation its coercive vulnerability engendered. Britain's Mesopotamian campaign during World War I, discussed in chapter 4, is a lesser-known example.

Because of the unavoidable costs of fighting and the risks of wider conflict, countries pursue direct control only when they face dire coercive vulnerability. But success generates high payoffs: the vulnerable state controls the resource directly, rather than indirectly through a friendly regime (see table 1.3).

Choosing among the Strategies: The Theory and Its Predictions

Above I explained the role of each independent variable in determining coercive vulnerability, why coercive vulnerability is sufficiently dangerous to provoke anticipatory strategies, and the spectrum of anticipatory strategies from which states select policies. This section presents the theory's specific predictions—its actionable claims, as it were—for each potential combination of the independent variables.

I argue that states adopt the least costly anticipatory strategy that meets their expected oil security needs. Recall that great powers "get what they pay for"— that is, the *potential* security benefits of an anticipatory strategy track closely to its costs. A hefty reduction in coercive vulnerability comes at a hefty price; there are no free lunches, bargain basements, or semiannual sales. Very vulnerable great powers will pay that hefty price because oil coercion, with its dire consequences for military and economic power, threatens their very survival. Less vulnerable ones will not. The costs and risks of anticipatory strategies are deadly serious— especially those that use military force—so great powers want to avoid "purchasing" more security than they need or overpaying for the security that they get.

Importantly, the *actual* value of a strategy is always pegged to how much it can improve coercive vulnerability *from the state's baseline level*. For example, if a state is invulnerable to oil coercion (rare but not unheard of), the actual security benefit to that state from any anticipatory strategy is zero. The country's oil is already secure, so nothing is gained from anticipation. If an invulnerable state anticipated nonetheless, it would be worse off than if it did nothing because anticipatory strategies always cost *something*, no matter how mild they may be. Incurring costs for no benefit is irrational; the expected value is negative. Ergo, the theory predicts that an invulnerable state will not adopt coercive strategies. To state the claim more generally, countries will not shell out extreme costs for extreme strategies when mild strategies will do. If a state is only mildly vulnerable, the *actual*, incremental security gained from an extreme strategy is too small to be worth paying high costs.[49]

To summarize, if states are boundedly rational security seekers and the costs and potential benefits of each strategy are tightly coupled, as the theory assumes, then the state will select strategies in the following manner.

First, states will adopt anticipatory strategies only if they have some level of coercive vulnerability, which, in turn, happens only when both independent variables are greater than zero. That is because coercive vulnerability echoes the logic of an expected value equation. The petroleum deficit captures the *magnitude* of harm caused by cutoff, and disruptibility represents the *likelihood* of cutoff. As in an expected value equation, if either the magnitude or the probability is zero, then the product—coercive vulnerability—is zero. So, if a country's imports are not disruptible—say, if like the present-day United States, it is the only great power in the system and can militarily defeat any cutoff attempt—then it is invulnerable to coercion regardless of the size of its deficit. Likewise, a state that has no petroleum deficit, that can produce all the oil it needs, is invulnerable to coercion even if its hypothetical imports would be highly disruptible. Put differently, both the petroleum deficit and the threat to imports are necessary causes of anticipation. Both must be present to cause the dependent variable. If either is missing, coercive vulnerability is zero, and the great power will not choose any of the three strategies.

Second, if both the petroleum deficit and import disruptibility are low, coercive vulnerability is also low and the state will adopt self-sufficiency, the mildest of the three strategies. In this scenario, indirect control and direct control would be bad investments; their high costs would overwhelm the *actual* oil security benefits to a low-vulnerability state. For this fortunate great power, there is not much room for improvement over its baseline coercive vulnerability. Thus, most of the *potential* security benefits from an extreme strategy like direct control would be redundant—in effect, wasted—yet the costs and risks would still be massive. Thus, to boost security at minimal cost, the state will adopt self-sufficiency.

Third, a state that combines a high petroleum deficit with high import disruptibility will be highly vulnerable to coercion. The theory predicts that it would choose direct control, the strategy with the greatest potential benefit but also the highest cost. The country has ample room for improving its baseline security, and thus it would reap the full benefits of the most extreme strategy. As a result, it is worth it for the state to invest in the best oil security money can buy—none of it would be redundant. The precariousness of the situation means that the state will be willing to pay high costs to alleviate vulnerability and will seek direct control of oil through conquest.

Direct control is always the logical choice when vulnerability is high—even when the country is an island. Of course, conquest of foreign oil fields does not entirely solve the disruptibility problem for island states because the oil still must travel overseas to reach the homeland. But it remains the best hope. The simple reason is that possessing an adequate supply of oil enhances the state's naval power and strengthens its ability to protect oil shipping lanes. Under high vulnerability, anticipatory conquest pays real dividends; the state is better off grabbing oil territory *before* a blockade rather than after. Preventive action puts the state on its strongest possible footing, given its unfortunate geography.

Fourth, countries that score high on one independent variable but low on the other face moderate coercive vulnerability and will pursue indirect control. A country with a large petroleum deficit but a low import threat, or a country with a small deficit but high import threat, will choose alliances to shore up its situation. Direct control would be overkill: the country is not so threatened by coercive vulnerability as to take the riskiest, costliest path. Self-sufficiency, however, would not be enough to reduce vulnerability.

		Threat to Imports	
		High	*Low*
Petroleum Deficit	*High*	High vulnerability: direct control	Medium vulnerability: indirect control
	Low	Medium vulnerability: indirect control	Low vulnerability: self-sufficiency

FIGURE 1.3. Independent variables and predicted outcomes

A few nuances modify the above predictions. Most important, anticipatory strategies can be additive rather than mutually exclusive. For example, states that experience increases in coercive vulnerability often adopt costlier strategies without abandoning lower-level measures already in place. Rather, the fruits of those measures—for example, higher levels of domestic production thanks to drilling subsidies enacted earlier—get rolled into the state's calculations of its deficit and disruptibility in the present.[50] The anticipatory strategy predicted by the theory is best understood as the *ceiling* of what the state is willing to do to reduce its vulnerability. Similarly, anticipatory policies can get "sticky"; they function more like ratchets than wrenches. States escalate to riskier strategies as coercive vulnerability increases, but, for familiar bureaucratic reasons, they may fail to downshift when vulnerability falls.

Altogether, great powers choose the anticipatory strategy that is commensurate in costs and benefits with their level of vulnerability. Countries do not reduce their coercive vulnerability at any cost; rather, they choose the strategy that adequately supplements their baseline security at minimal cost. Only those states with high petroleum deficits and high disruptibility will fight wars to conquer oil (see figure 1.3).

Is Oil Different?

A final question raised by the analysis is whether the book's theoretical framework applies to other strategic resources beyond oil, such as coal, rubber, or iron ore.

Could these and other raw materials have enough coercive potential to induce similar anticipatory behavior by great powers? In theory, the answer is yes—provided the material in question shares four crucial characteristics with oil. First, like oil, it must be indispensable for military power. Second, no adequate substitutes can exist for military purposes. Third, it must be unusually precious so that a cutoff would restrict a country's access in an especially severe way. Finally, it must be exogenous to the existing balance of power, as oil was at the start of the mechanized age. Few, if any, other resources combine all four of these features.[51] Thus, in practice, oil is exceptional among raw materials in its effect on international politics. The first two criteria—indispensability of oil for military effectiveness and the lack of adequate substitutes for military purposes—were explained above. Therefore, this section focuses on the latter two criteria: the importance of oil's rarity and its relationship to the balance of power at the dawn of mechanized warfare.

Even compared with other critical resources, petroleum is unusually rare. Although many raw materials matter for economic and military power, petroleum is the only strategic resource that is nonrenewable, nonrecyclable, and unusually scarce all at the same time (see table 1.4). Together, these three traits of petroleum reduce the options available for oil-poor states to stretch their supplies in the event of a coercive disruption. First, petroleum is nonrenewable, so unlike water, timber, and food, it cannot regenerate. States could grow their own food to replace imports in the event of a shortage or intentional disruption, but they cannot grow their own petroleum.[52] Second, oil is not recyclable. Whereas durable materials such as timber, metals, and rubber can be collected in scrap drives and reused in the event of wartime shortages, consuming oil means destroying it. Of course, most other energy resources must be burned—and thus destroyed—to produce power. This brings us to the third trait: none of the other major energy

TABLE 1.4 Characteristics of strategic resources

	PROPERTIES		
RESOURCE	NONRENEWABLE	NONRECYCLABLE	SCARCE
Oil	X	X	X
Coal	X	X	
Iron ore	X		X
Rubber			X
Food		X	
Water			
Timber			

sources are anywhere near as scarce as oil. Coal is also destroyed when burned for fuel, but unlike oil, coal is abundant. Petroleum reserves, by contrast, are scarce endowments distributed highly unequally across the world's nations. About half of all countries have no oil at all, whereas the ten countries richest in oil currently possess over 80 percent of proven global reserves.[53]

All told, these three characteristics—scarcity, nonrecyclability, and nonrenewability—exacerbate the difficulty for a country to cope with oil disruption, opposed to the disruption of other key raw materials.

What really sets oil apart from these other resources, however, is the degree to which its location in the world was random, in a geopolitical sense, when it unexpectedly emerged as an important source of motive energy at the turn of the twentieth century. Before this time, oil possessed neither military utility nor much economic value. As a result, very little overlap existed between the balance of power and the geographic location of oil. By contrast, resources such as water, timber, coal, and iron ore were more likely to be found in strong countries because they were important determinants of military and economic power. In other words, these resources were already endogenous to the balance of power at the start of the twentieth century. Oil was not. The following section demonstrates how little oil mattered for relative power before 1900 and discusses its meteoric rise to resource stardom within the span of the first decade of the twentieth century.

Before the invention of the automobile, crude oil's primary commercial value stemmed from its use to make kerosene, a refined petroleum product that could be burned in lamps as a source of light. Kerosene came into use in the United States and Europe in the mid-1800s. As early as 1840, Romanian refineries were producing modest quantities of lamp oil from petroleum, and in 1859, Bucharest became the first city lit entirely by kerosene lamps.[54] Kerosene was highly sought after because it was cheaper than whale oil, which, for the affluent, had been "the standard of excellence in illumination for 500 years."[55] But by the mid-1800s, the whaling industry had decimated the whale population, causing whale oil prices to skyrocket. Kerosene thus became an attractive alternative. However, the primitive oil production techniques of the time, such as skimming oil from the surface of oil seeps or digging pits to bring oil out of the ground by bucket, limited the amount of kerosene that could be produced and traded.[56]

This changed in 1859, when "Colonel" Edwin L. Drake pioneered the use of cable drilling methods to strike oil near Titusville, Pennsylvania. Drake's well was significant because it represented the first successful effort to obtain large quantities of oil for commercial marketing.[57] The Colonel set off a worldwide oil boom. In a veritable reenactment of the California Gold Rush, thousands of would-be oilmen descended on the Oil Creek area of Western Pennsylvania and began frantically erecting derricks.[58] A contemporary observer described the scene vividly:

"Derricks throng the low marshy bottom-land, derricks congregate on the sloping banks, derricks even climb the precipitous face of the cliffs, establishing a foothold wherever a ledge of rock projects or a recess exists."[59]

Similar excitement occurred in the oil-rich regions of Galicia, Romania, and Russia. The Caspian city of Baku, Russia, long known for its surface oil seeps and natural gas flares, was "invaded by investors. The plots were divided again and again until they were so small that people said, 'you couldn't swing a cat by the tail between the derricks.'"[60] Ostentatious displays of wealth accompanied Baku's new prosperity as the upstart oil barons competed to outdo one another, building mansions that "copied Venetian palaces from postcards." One baron even constructed a palace that resembled a dragon, whereby "guests entered through the open jaws."[61] Of course, the kerosene-driven oil craze built fortunes in the United States as well. The most notable tycoon was John D. Rockefeller, whose Standard Oil Company specialized in producing kerosene of consistent quality—a "standard" oil—that was less prone to inadvertently explode when lit. This had been a serious hazard of the new fuel.

Although kerosene made private fortunes for a lucky few, it did not contribute greatly to national wealth or economic development. More importantly, it held no apparent military significance. In its heyday, the market for kerosene remained relatively small. In Europe, kerosene competed with several other substances that could be used to produce lamp oil, including cannel coal, wood tar, lignite, shale, linseed oil, and rapeseed oil.[62] In the American market for illumination, kerosene mostly contended with candles, natural gas, and wood oils such as camphene.[63] Because of the fire hazard involved with all three of these fuels, another popular choice was to avoid artificial lighting altogether.

Furthermore, Thomas Edison's commercialization of the incandescent lightbulb in 1882 cut into the market severely. Within three years, there were over 250,000 lightbulbs in circulation, and by 1902 that number grew to 18 million. As electricity quickly cornered the market for artificial lighting, "the United States market for kerosene, the staple of the oil industry, leveled out and was increasingly restricted to rural America."[64] Because the market for oil was limited and shrinking, and its military value was largely unrecognized, by the end of the nineteenth century, "there was little to suggest that petroleum would in any way become a major factor in international relations."[65]

Several trends conspired to quickly elevate the strategic importance of oil after 1900. First, experiments using oil-burning engines for seagoing vessels led the major powers to conclude early in that decade that oil would soon be essential for naval power. The Italians, uncharacteristically ahead of the pack, had introduced oil-burning vessels into their navy in 1890. The British, Americans, and Japanese followed suit in the early 1900s, embarking on modernization efforts to add oil burners to their fleets. By World War I, "petroleum ceased to be simply another commercial product, and became instead vital to the military welfare of every naval power."[66] On land, the invention of the automobile in 1885–1886 and the subsequent expansion of the automotive industry in the early 1900s made oil even more consequential for national power.[67] The importance of oil grew throughout that decade with the birth of the military aviation industry.[68]

Suddenly, the discovery of oil reserves on a country's territory amounted to hitting a national jackpot. Winning the lottery is an apt analogy here because it reflects the unusual role played by chance in determining which countries had oil resources at the beginning of the twentieth century. It is reasonable to believe that most natural resources are endogenous to the formation of great powers. States located in areas rich in resources like water, arable land, timber, iron ore, and coal were more likely to develop enough economic and military strength to become major powers than those found on barren lands. In fact, it is hard to come up with examples of great powers that sprouted and flourished in resource-poor regions. Raw materials are so important to national power that many international relations theorists assume competition over scarce resources has been a major driver for expansionism.[69] It is not surprising, for instance, that the states that had emerged as major industrialized powers at the end of the nineteenth century were abundant in coal and iron ore. In the words of historian Fiona Venn, "One of the reasons for Great Britain's hegemony in the industrial economy of the nineteenth century was her massive reserves of coal, and the leading industrial and naval powers of the period, Great Britain, Germany and the United States, all had large indigenous coal reserves."[70]

But oil was a different story. Before 1900, oil mattered little for national power, and so strong countries were not any more likely to have oil on their territories than weak countries were. In other words, unlike most other resources, oil was exogenous to great power development before the twentieth century. When it suddenly became important after 1900, possessing oil was largely a product of chance rather than an artifact of being a major power.

As chance would have it, most of the era's great powers found themselves in a pickle. The homelands of Great Britain, France, Germany, Japan, and Italy all lacked substantial petroleum reserves. Contemporary observers speculated that vast oil fields lay under the sands of the Ottoman Empire, but this remained unconfirmed; and Persia, the only part of the Middle East producing commercial quantities of oil, barely churned out 1 percent of world output at the advent of World War I. When it came to oil, all six of these states were out of luck.

Two great powers stood alone as winners of the oil lottery: the United States and Russia. American petroleum dominance was particularly staggering. The United States reigned supreme in the early years of commercial oil production, accounting for 98 percent of the world's petroleum in 1860 and 88 percent in 1880. American output continued to expand in absolute terms from 1880 to 1900, though its share of global oil production declined over these twenty years in tandem with the development of the Russian oil industry.

In 1900, Russia and the United States briefly hit roughly even levels of production, and together accounted for 93 percent of the world's crude. Parity did not last long, however. The 1905 revolution, combined with continued labor unrest in the Russian oil capital of Baku, led to significant decreases in Russian oil output up until World War I. The picture dramatically worsened after the 1917 Bolshevik Revolution; that year, Russia's share of global production plummeted to 5 percent. In fact, the industry was so weakened by the Soviet crackdown on the capitalist oil barons in Baku that the country's share of global production did not exceed 20 percent again until 1980.[71]

Meanwhile, American production continued to grow, buoyed by the major turn-of-the-century discovery near Beaumont, Texas. Spindletop, the first gusher well drilled in the Western Hemisphere, erupted like a geyser on January 10, 1901, producing enough oil to singlehandedly increase world output by 20 percent and bolster American output by a full 50 percent.[72] Oil production in the United States remained steady in accounting for between 65 and 75 percent of annual global production until the 1950s.

It is no coincidence that the two states that emerged as superpowers after World War II were also the two largest petroleum-producing countries. American and Soviet oil was crucial to the Allies' victory. In this regard, World War II helped to partly endogenize oil to the relative power balance, at least for several decades. This could change as China emerges as a superpower.

The critical takeaway is this: by the beginning of the twentieth century, a unique disjuncture had opened between the balance of power and the "balance of oil." This disjuncture did not occur with other strategically important raw materials like coal or iron ore, as these had already gradually become foundational to great power status soon after the Industrial Revolution. Oil's "random" political geography meant that some states would have to depend on trade with others for a resource uniquely crucial to their military strength. Yet, because the international system is a dangerous place, states seek to avoid dependence on unreliable others if doing so is at all possible.[73] Dependence is dangerous because it opens the door for coercion by making a state vulnerable to disruption for the purposes of political blackmail.[74] Unfortunately, several unlucky great powers suddenly found themselves uncomfortably dependent on others for a material crucial to their survival. The inevitable result was an exacerbation of security competition among the great powers. Indeed, the scramble to avoid vulnerability animated a good deal of twentieth-century international relations.

2
OIL AND MILITARY EFFECTIVENESS

As the previous chapter argued, coercive vulnerability drives great powers to adopt anticipatory strategies to protect their access to oil, and the indispensability of oil to military power looms especially large in their calculations. In the age of mechanized warfare, a country capable of denying petroleum to an adversary can threaten the target with certain military defeat. The prosperity costs of losing access to oil are also relevant, as they can worsen the damage to states. However, prosperity threats alone are not sufficient to explain strategic anticipation, given the nature of the global oil market. It is very difficult to disrupt oil without using significant military force, and when force is being used, prosperity concerns tend to recede in importance. Even during a war, petroleum substitutes can offer good enough performance to keep economies humming. But these same petroleum substitutes are inadequate for military ventures because diminished performance makes a country's forces vulnerable to destruction, particularly when pitted against an adversary with plenty of oil.

This chapter puts empirical meat on the bones of theory. First, it examines the origins of oil coercion and the anticipatory strategies used by great powers to reduce vulnerability, explaining how military transformation from coal-fueled to oil-fueled vehicles during World War I imbued petroleum with coercive potential. Oil's superiority over coal was made clear by the conduct of the war, and by its end, all of the major powers understood that oil coercion had emerged as a major international threat. Even countries that lacked oil had no choice but to adopt oil-fueled military technology because coal-related transportation was no longer competitive. This is an example of mimesis—where great powers copy the successful strategies of others to keep pace in the international competition for survival.[1] In fact, the first case of oil coercion happened in World War I, when the Germans attempted to bring Britain and France to terms through the 1917–1918 U-boat campaign, which sank large numbers of Allied oil tankers. This case is analyzed in depth in chapter 4. Even though the technological transition to military motorization was not yet complete, the German attempt almost succeeded. The near miss rattled the great powers because they recognized mechanization was the wave of the future, and like it or not, their militaries were destined to rely increasingly on petroleum-based fuels. Thus, World War I was the turning point that set off an international scramble by vulnerable major powers to secure petroleum access—a struggle that underlay some of the most important events of the twentieth century.

The second part of this chapter presents the historical case study of Japan's surrender in World War II, which demonstrates three things. First, it shows just how debilitating oil shortages are for military effectiveness. Japan's oil access was targeted by the Allies through military means as well as trade restrictions. The result was military paralysis that contributed significantly to Japan's defeat. Second, it reveals a surprising degree of economic resilience to oil denial. Prosperity concerns fell to the background in the face of a national crisis; the population bore the hardships and remained loyal to the regime. Oil shortages devastated Japanese military power, but rationing and substitutes permitted Japan's domestic economy to keep producing despite being starved of petroleum. Third, it illustrates the coercive pressures oil denial puts on military leaders. The Allied military blockade in the latter part of the war did not just contribute to Japan's military defeat. In a way that has not been fully understood or acknowledged, I argue that oil denial played a crucial role in Japan's decision to surrender in the time and manner it did—without an Allied invasion of the home islands. Oil coercion, therefore, was an important, if underappreciated, factor in this successful case of coercion.

From Coal to Petroleum: The Genesis of the Oil Weapon

The transition from coal to oil revolutionized military power and laid the foundation for the coercive potential of the "oil weapon." As important as coal was to military power in the nineteenth century, there was never a "coal weapon" because the two resources are very different animals: coal is abundant and located on the territories of most great powers, whereas oil is scarce and unevenly distributed across the world. Moreover, oil is better suited for military transportation than coal because it offers superior performance, particularly when it comes to speed and flexibility.

From the mid-nineteenth century until the advent of the oil age, militaries ran on coal. In its day, coal-fueled transportation was a major breakthrough. Compared with the human and animal power on which transportation had been based for centuries, railroads fueled by coal were "capable of moving men, weapons, and supplies on an entirely unprecedented scale."[2] Thanks to railways, military forces could travel fifteen times faster than troops were able to march, while "a single train could carry as much as thousands of horse-drawn wagons."[3] This allowed troops in far-flung locations to concentrate quickly against enemy forces, a benefit that proved to be particularly advantageous for internal military mobilization and initial invasions of enemy territory. Railroads altered military strategy and heavily influenced the outcomes of the War of 1859, the 1866 Austro-Prussian War, the 1870–1871 Franco-Prussian War, and the American Civil War. Indeed, most experts agree it was the clever use of railroads that had allowed the Prussians to "twice demonstrat[e] how to win a war against a great power in jig time."[4] Similarly, in the United States, the North's railway superiority played a pivotal role in its defeat of the Confederacy, undergirding such storied campaigns as General William Tecumseh Sherman's capture of Atlanta in 1864.[5]

Nevertheless, the military use of railroads was subject to serious limitations. The most crucial of these, from a strategic point of view, was the loss of flexible mobility. Military forces could move much more quickly, but only at the cost of finding themselves tethered to railway lines of supply. "The fact that railroads could not duplicate the versatility of horse drawn wagons," John Lynn observes, "confined the mode of transportation to a narrower set of operational roles."[6] Location constraints shaped the planning and conduct of warfare as railways "began to assume the role of the 'bones' of strategy," for better or for worse.[7]

The need to use preexisting railroads, which had not necessarily been built with military objectives in mind, for speedy mobilization sometimes had negative consequences for a campaign. One danger was that movements of military matériel might reflect the location of rail networks rather than an ideal military strategy. For example, the 1866 deployment of Prussian troops to the Austrian border, though achieved quickly, entailed a major drawback. "Strategy aside, the dispersed location of existing Prussian railroad lines meant that Prussian forces had to be deployed along an enormous arc of the front, with huge gaps between concentrations." Prussian troops could close these gaps only by marching toward one another, resulting in exhaustion and the quick outpacing of rail supply lines.[8] The redeployment made necessary by the suboptimal placement of the rails effectively defeated the main purpose of railroad mobilization, which was supposed to permit troops to arrive at the front fresh and well supplied.[9]

Additionally, the use of existing railroads for offensives meant sacrificing the attacker's element of surprise, as "defenders were often able to predict likely invasion routes" and react accordingly.[10] Moreover, many European railroad arteries ran straight into fortresses, forcing advancing troops to either abandon the lines and march to their destinations, or pause to construct new lines bypassing the fortress—a mighty and time-consuming task.[11]

Perhaps the biggest weakness associated with railroads was that the construction of new lines and railheads, even under the best of circumstances, could seldom keep pace with the advance. Troops could march about fifteen miles a day, but new tracks could not be laid that quickly. This created a gap between the unloading stations and the front that had to be made up for by using horse-drawn wagons to bring supplies forward. Unfortunately, however, horses had a range of only twenty-five miles per day, whereas each full day of marching increased the round-trip journey from the railheads to the front and back by thirty total miles. The result was that troops constantly faced the danger of outrunning their supply lines.[12] This obstacle underlies the common view that railroads are useful for domestic mobilization and deployment but are not suitable for advancing very far into enemy territory.

Compounding this issue was the fact that railways were prone to congestion and bottlenecks, especially at the termination of the lines where supplies would be loaded and unloaded. Heavy congestion on the lines often blocked supply trains as they competed for space with troops headed to the front. At the same time, the inability to promptly remove cargo at the railhead tied up the lines further. Depending on station capacity, it could take as long as twelve, twenty-four, or even eighty hours to unload supply trains, creating a nightmarish backlog. As trains sat on the tracks, supplies failed to reach the front in time to fulfill military needs, while perishable provisions like food rotted before they could be delivered.[13]

Another major drawback of railways was their susceptibility to sabotage by partisan forces or enemy civilians. Because they were "relatively fragile, vulnerable to even small parties of raiders," rail lines faced the regular threat of destruction and required large military contingents to guard them, and if necessary, repair damage after an attack.[14] "These railroads are the weakest things in war," General Sherman once remarked.[15] His successful use of them in his Atlanta Campaign hinged on his "ability to effectively seize, rebuild, and maintain his rail line in the face of almost daily enemy attacks as he advanced deeper into enemy territory." During the two-hundred-day campaign, Union forces had to rebuild miles of rail lines, including eleven bridges, and lay seventy-five miles of new track.[16] The Prussians encountered similar difficulties. French partisans so effectively demolished lines in 1870–1871 that the Prussians had to devote an entire army corps to railroad defense. Railroad vulnerability to attack especially hampered efforts to pursue retreating armies that routinely demolished the rail lines behind them, effectively slowing down invading forces. Finally, the specifications of enemy rail lines did not necessarily suit invaders' military needs. This could be because the rail lines were not sturdy enough to accommodate heavily laden military trains, as German forces discovered in Belgium during World War I. In other cases, existing lines had to be converted to match the gauge of the invader's trains, a lesson the Nazis learned the hard way during their invasion of the Soviet Union.[17]

At sea, coal was used to power steamships. Compared with wind, the traditional means of propulsion for water transit, coal allowed ships to move at higher velocities, as well as to travel upstream and against the forces of ocean currents. Like railroads, however, steam-powered vessels had serious technological limitations. For one thing, technology put a strong limit on the maximum speed coal-burning vessels could attain. The only way to improve on the top speeds of steamships was to build larger and larger coal engines. However, engine expansion beyond a certain point was impractical, as it required increasingly greater amounts of manpower from coal stokers. In addition to problems of space constraints aboard the ships for both coal and crew, finding men willing to work as stokers was very difficult because the job was low paying and involved laboring under unpleasant and dangerous conditions. Attempts by the British Royal Navy, the most powerful fleet in the world, to increase the speed of its vessels in the first decade of the twentieth century were often held back by "serious shortfalls in the making up of stoker complements."[18]

Coal-powered vessels also lacked flexibility in ways similar to railroads. Refueling could occur only at ports and coaling stations, and in practical terms, this meant that steamships were limited in range and could not operate outside a given radius from their refueling points. Moreover, refueling amounted to quite a headache. It typically took five hundred men toiling for five days to refuel each coal burner, given the large volumes of coal that had to be loaded aboard.[19] Finally, coal storage took up a lot of room aboard steamships, reducing the cargo space available for carrying war matériel. Yet, for all the space that coal occupied in cargo holds, it did not provide ships with a whole lot of energy. Of course, coal does not contain as much energy per unit of volume as oil does. But coal is also a relatively inefficient power source because the two-step process required to convert it into energy creates a greater energy loss. Steam engines do not burn coal directly to do work; rather, the coal heats water to generate steam, and the steam is what does the work.[20] This two-step process inevitably translates into a lower energy capture from the total yield coal would be capable of producing otherwise.

The switch from coal to oil at the beginning of the twentieth century had dramatic ramifications for military power. The contingent nature of war places a high premium on having flexible and portable means of transportation available to militaries so they can adapt to changing battlefield conditions. After all, one of the most defining characteristics of war is its inherent unpredictability. "Every war is rich in unique episodes," Clausewitz memorably wrote. "Each is an uncharted sea full of reefs. The commander may suspect the reefs' existence without ever having seen them; now he has to steer past them in the dark." On the battlefield, mishaps and uncertainties have a way of multiplying to create "friction," the cumulative force arising from those "countless minor incidents—the kind that you never really foresee," which makes military action "like movement in a resistant element."[21] Even small misfortunes tend to cascade and magnify throughout complex military machines until the reality on the battlefield bears little resemblance to initial expectations of progress. Inevitably, according to Clausewitz, war never quite goes according to plan.

Flexibility of movement is the most important advantage oil offered over coal. On land, oil-powered internal combustion engines were a major improvement over railroads because they allowed for free movement of large fleets of vehicles that were not tethered to tracks. "Trucks could take advantage of the road network and off-road possibilities in a way the railroad could not. . . . Far more than the railroad, the truck ushered in a new age of mobility for field armies."[22] Indeed, probably the largest advantage of oil is that, through its use in the internal combustion engines of cars, trucks, and tanks, "it enables land forces to move in any direction over a plane surface, whereas the railway only permits movement in one dimension."[23] Because movement was no longer confined to the predictable path of rail tracks, military strategy did not need to be built around preexisting rail networks and surprise could be restored to the offense.

Better speed was the second major advantage of oil compared with coal. The increased speed that oil-powered vehicles offered ushered in an unprecedented age of mobile warfare and opened up new possibilities for strategic innovation. Whereas previously, the pace of the advancing front was hindered by marching speeds and the inability of railheads to keep up, oil allowed for the creation of the blitzkrieg, or "lightning war" strategy. Speed was also improved by the elimination of railway congestion that had plagued the delivery of troops and supplies. Although military traffic jams did not disappear entirely, they became much less of a problem because convoys could choose any number of different routes along the road network and could even travel cross-country if necessary.

Of course, the uncertainty of war cited by Clausewitz has a flip side. Each unforeseen setback experienced by one of the belligerent parties presents the other with an opportunity to take advantage of a lucky break. When militaries ran on coal, limits on flexibility and speed hindered the capacity of armies to exploit unanticipated successes. Railroads could not directly supply an advance in the event of a major breakthrough, nor could horse-drawn wagons ferrying matériel catch up. Oil eliminated this problem. During the course of World War I, Allied forces began replacing horse-drawn wagons with motor trucks for supplying the front. By 1917, they relied on trucks almost exclusively for this purpose.[24] Motor vehicles could also be used to bring supplies up from the rear directly, provided they did not need to cover long distances.[25] This meant that armies could exploit breakthroughs with less danger of their forces being jeopardized by outrunning supply lines.

Oil also reduced the vulnerability of military transportation to attack. Motorcars were not dependent on a specialized and fixed rail infrastructure that took significant time to rebuild. Although enemy artillery could damage roads more easily than rail tracks, it was harder to render roads impassable to traffic. Usually trucks could still reach their destinations by navigating around torn-up stretches of road. The destruction of a section of rail, however, often took the entire line out of commission until work crews could repair the damage.[26]

At sea, oil provided similar advantages. In fact, naval forces were often the first of the military services to convert to oil-burning engines. Compared with coal, oil was lighter and burned more cleanly. As a liquid, it was easier to transport and handle, and it provided much more energy per unit of volume than coal did.[27] It took up less space aboard ships and lowered manpower requirements by eliminating the need for stokers. Oil also offered major strategic advantages, including superior speed, extra range, and the ability to refuel at sea, thus freeing ships from their tethers to coaling stations.[28] An especially important result of these technical improvements was the ability of oil burners to "gain full power in a short time and maintain that power over a long period."[29] As an added bonus, unlike coal burners, oil-powered ships did not emit thick black smoke, allowing them a better chance at evading enemy detection—at least in the days before radar.[30]

Finally, oil opened up an entirely new dimension of warfare: military aviation. While restricted primarily to reconnaissance in World War I, airpower was used for a variety of purposes during World War II, including strategic bombing, close air support of ground forces, and as a means of delivering supplies to forces in remote regions.[31]

Oil and the Conduct of World War I: A Sign of Things to Come

World War I played a pivotal role in defining the politics of coercive vulnerability because, as the first mechanized war, it demonstrated to the great powers in a concrete way that petroleum would become uniquely indispensable to military victory in the future. Before World War I, most governments had no inkling of the radical changes oil would impose on warfare. By the conflict's end, however, each of the great powers had gotten the message loud and clear. World War I acted as the critical juncture at which a nation's military effectiveness became inextricably linked to its access to oil. From 1918 forward, military power would come to rely on petroleum more than it had ever depended on a single resource before—or since.

Once this fusion between oil and war was established, petroleum took on a new political importance as well. Any country able to control the flow of oil in wartime could confront its adversaries with certain military defeat. This is the basis from which the coercive potential of oil arose. Oil could do much more than make a country rich; a state able to deprive an adversary of oil could potentially inflict its political will on that adversary. Oil-importing countries were now vulnerable to a new instrument of political coercion, and the events of World War I ensured that the threat was universally recognized.

Naval strategists were the first to catch on that oil would become the next big thing in oceangoing transportation. Experiments using oil-burning engines for seagoing vessels led the major powers to conclude that petroleum would soon be essential for naval power. By the early 1900s, Italy, Britain, Russia, the United States, Germany, France, and Japan had all embarked on modernization efforts to add oil burners to their fleets. In 1904, when Russia went to war with Japan, its navy already included significant numbers of oil-burning vessels.[32] That same year, Britain was installing oil-burning engines in all newly constructed destroyers. By 1911, British cruisers were being built exclusively with oil-burning engines, and in 1912, all new battleship designs included oil burners.[33]

Despite successfully anticipating that oil would take on a new role in war, the amount of oil navies expended during World War I far surpassed prewar estimations. This was the case even though only one major naval battle occurred during the conflict—the 1916 Battle of Jutland. Few battles were fought because the Germans sought to avoid open confrontation with the highly superior British Royal Navy. Yet, maintaining the fleets at high readiness during all four years of the war generated enough oil demand to seriously strain fuel supplies, especially because Britain and Germany controlled little to no oil. Even though the British government held a controlling share in the Anglo-Persian Oil Company, the country relied on foreign powers—particularly the United States and Russia—for 85 percent of its oil supplies. Fuel provisioning represented the greatest supply challenge the Royal Navy faced during the war.[34]

Although naval conversion programs were well under way, great power navies still ran predominantly on coal when World War I started. This was true even for the British navy, the largest and most technologically advanced fleet at the time. In 1914, the Royal Fleet's maximum coal-burning capacity stood at nearly three times its oil-burning capacity. By the war's end, however, the fuel mix had reversed. In 1918, oil capacity significantly outstripped coal capacity in the fleet. The war itself played a big role in accelerating the switch from coal to oil. Of course, as technology progressed, and the strategic advantages of petroleum became more apparent, the great powers increased the proportion of new ships built with oil-burning engines. But perhaps more tellingly, the fuel consumption mix also shifted because coal burners were sunk at higher rates than oil burners were. As a result of the shift in primary fuel from coal to oil, oil was being consumed at staggering rates. Over the course of the war, British navy fuel oil consumption increased by almost an order of magnitude—from 400,000 tons annually in 1914 to about 3.6 million tons per year in 1918.[35] Again, this occurred despite the general absence of major sea battles. Given this fact, the skyrocketing of consumption did not bode well for how much oil would be needed in future conflicts. Indeed, it was disquieting to think of the vast quantities of oil the belligerents might consume in the next big war.

Whereas navies had grasped the importance of oil before World War I, armies did not really anticipate how motorized transit would revolutionize the conduct of war on land. World War I thus played a pivotal role in demonstrating to the major powers that oil-powered transportation would have broad military applications on land as well as at sea. It was a rude awakening.

Experimentation with the use of mechanized vehicles on land occurred much later than it did at sea, and major powers envisioned that oil would play only a minor role. For instance, the U.S. Army did not even begin experimenting with motorization until 1906.[36] The British, who had been forward-thinking about the ramifications of petroleum for sea power, did not have official procedures in place for incorporating motor transit on land until 1913.[37] Moreover, by the war's start, the British Expeditionary Force had only 950 trucks and 250 cars at its disposal, amounting to a total engine output of less than fifty thousand horsepower, whereas the ships of the Royal Navy had a combined strength of three million horsepower. "Britain began the First World War, in other words, with an essentially unmechanized army and a highly mechanized navy."[38]

Oil was overlooked by army strategists for several reasons. First, motor technology was simply very new. Although "horseless carriages" had been around for a few decades, early models were so slow, clunky, and expensive that they were regarded as little more than recreational novelties for the rich. It was not until the decade before World War I that mass production of automobiles began in earnest, and so recent was this development that strategists just did not have time to really grasp it before the war began.[39]

Second, the failure of strategic imagination also reflected incorrect expectations held by many that the coming European war would be short and comparable in scale to past wars.[40] Even those who were more pessimistic about the likelihood of a short war failed to anticipate the logistical problems attendant with the need to supply massive forces armed with new firepower technologies for a span of years rather than weeks or months.[41] It had never been done before. It is no exaggeration to say World War I demanded resources on an unprecedented scale. Throughout the period of defensive stalemate from 1914 to 1917, both sides futilely tried to break through the lines by overwhelming the enemy with bigger and bigger forces: more guns, more troops, heavier artillery, and so forth. Ammunition requirements were particularly astounding because technological innovations, such as the machine gun and quick-firing rifles, caused armies to burn through their ammunition stocks very rapidly. For instance, in six months of campaigning during the 1870–1871 war, German troops carried 200 rounds of ammunition per rifle but expended only about 56 rounds. By contrast, German troops came equipped with 280 rounds per rifle at the outset of World War I, and yet they ran out of ammunition within a few weeks.[42] Tragically, throwing greater quantities of resources into the trenches was a waste, yielding no major breakthrough. But in the meantime, the forces at the front, and the elaborate network of supply behind them, ballooned into enormous behemoths. By March 1918, the British Expeditionary Force had grown twelve times larger than it had been in 1914, with total Allied forces numbering five million men stretched across a 450-mile front.[43]

By and large, railways were up to the task of supplying armies during the stationary phase of the war from late 1914 to 1917. Relatively stable lines at the front, which shifted very little owing to the inability of either side to exploit a breakthrough, allowed the armies to build up massive railroad infrastructure to move men and matériel from the rear to the front. Trains were more efficient for transporting large amounts of resources over long distances—provided conditions were stable—and thus motor transit played a niche role in the logistical scheme during the trench stalemate.[44] The artillery barrage, which was capable of hitting targets behind the front lines, made it impossible for standard gauge and even light railways to get too close to the front.[45] Thus, a combination of motortrucks and horse-drawn wagons would pick up most supplies dropped off at the nearest railhead and deliver them an additional several miles to the combat zone.

Yet, even when employed in this limited role, the resources transported were so vast that gasoline requirements skyrocketed beyond all expectations. In 1916, the French army relied on motor transit to deliver about 180,000 metric tons of matériel and 300,000 men monthly.[46] During the 1916 Battle of the Somme, the British Fourth Army alone required over 5,700 motortrucks and cars to move nearly 2,000 tons of supplies per mile of front from the railheads daily. Given the average motortruck got only five miles per gallon, the gasoline requirements for the Fourth Army's motortruck fleet surpassed 12,000 gallons per day, or about 370,000 gallons per month.[47] Less than a year later, during the Allied offensive at Messines in the summer of 1917, British gasoline usage had soared by more than an order of magnitude, to six million gallons per month. But even this figure was not adequate, as the British complained of severe petroleum shortages owing to German submarine attacks on Allied tankers.[48]

Although trains were well suited for stationary warfare, they caused more problems than they solved in periods of open warfare. The use of trains ended up being a major disadvantage for Germany, which had famously relied on an extensive network of strategic railroads for military transit. Along the western front, the Germans had five advanced switch lines that distributed men and matériel at the front, and four additional lines in the rear used by General Headquarters for supply purposes.[49] Although Germany's finely tuned rail system gave it advantages over the Allies during the war of attrition, German reliance on rail proved disastrous in the periods of open warfare.

After the conclusion of the war, Lord Curzon, a member of the British War Cabinet, famously stated that the Allies "'floated to victory upon a wave of oil,' because if it had not been for the great fleets of motor trucks the war could not have been won."[50] Senator Henry Bérenger, the director of France's petroleum committee, agreed that oil was "the blood of victory. . . . Germany had boasted too much of its superiority in iron and coal, but it had not taken sufficient account of our superiority of oil."[51] In the words of the *New York Times*, the war had been "a victory of automobiles over railroads."[52] A U.S. military analyst concluded, "The war, if not actually lost, would have at least been indefinitely prolonged" had the United States not been able to provide sufficient amounts of petroleum to the effort.[53] Fortunately, the United States was more than up to the task. The country produced 90 percent of the total oil used by the Allies in World War I.[54] "As it was, no military undertakings of the Allies on land, or on the sea, underneath the sea or in the air, was ever once interrupted through lack of petroleum supplies."[55]

The other major powers reached similar conclusions. Evidence suggests, for instance, that the lessons of World War I profoundly influenced German and Japanese leaders. These countries imitated the successful practices of Britain in converting their military vehicles and naval vessels into oil burners. German and Japanese leaders in the interwar years also sought to build up domestic synthetic fuel industries and beef up oil stockpiles. "After the Great War demonstrated that other military uses existed for petroleum products, in tanks, submarines, airplanes and motorized transportation, the struggle for control over the world's oil resources intensified," according to Fiona Venn. "The military significance of petroleum had thus been categorically demonstrated."[56]

Once oil proved its superiority over coal for military mobility, countries had no choice but to convert their forces to run on it—even if they possessed no domestic oil reserves. States must emulate the successful military practices of others in order to survive in a competitive international system.[57] Because oil offered unparalleled flexibility and speed for military forces, it quickly became the new standard for military transportation. Simply put, states could not power their armies, air forces, or navies on something other than oil and expect to win a war. All of the improvements that oil offered over coal for mobility translated directly into battlefield advantages that oil-fueled militaries enjoyed over those running on obsolete coal-fueled technologies. Moreover, states could not substitute other energy sources, such as charcoal or synthetics, to harness motor technology and hope to enjoy anywhere near the same level of performance as that offered by oil. No other substance works as effectively as petroleum does in internal combustion engines. The serious decline in performance associated with switching to oil substitutes for motorized forces could be make-or-break when it came to winning a war. As the single most important resource for military mobility, oil became a crucial determinant of success on the battlefield. It was here to stay.

The Case of Japan in World War II: Oil as an Inducement to Surrender

Even more so than in World War I, oil strongly influenced the conduct and outcome of World War II. Whereas the Axis controlled only 3 percent of global petroleum production during the war, the Allies held 90 percent.[58] Much of the oil burned by the Western Allies came from the United States, which provided six out of every seven barrels, or 85 percent, of the oil consumed by Allied forces (excluding Russia) from December 1941 to August 1945.[59] Although it was not nearly as prolific, the Soviet Union was mostly self-sufficient in oil throughout the war, though it did obtain 100 octane aviation fuel from British refineries in Abadan, Persia, and from the United States.[60] American and Soviet oil supplies gave the Allies the military edge they needed to defeat the Axis, providing the basis for their emergence as superpowers.

As for the have-nots, Japan's experience in World War II truly became every oil-importing country's worst nightmare. Japan's coercive vulnerability before World War II was high. The country had no domestic oil resources to speak of, forcing it to import nearly all of its oil, which caused a large petroleum deficit. Additionally, its imports were highly susceptible to military interdiction. As an island, Japan had only one option for attaining oil, and that was through the Pacific Ocean, leaving its imports completely exposed to naval blockade. Making matters worse, Japan was among the weakest of the major powers, which made it difficult to defend its supply lines from stronger rivals such as the United States. As mentioned earlier, Japan's bleak situation of high coercive vulnerability motivated it to pursue a conquest strategy for obtaining oil. It did so at enormous cost and risk: it seized the Dutch East Indies and preemptively destroyed the U.S. fleet at Pearl Harbor—the biggest threat to Japan's oceangoing oil imports. Japan hoped conquest would pay off, particularly if the attack on the United States weakened President Franklin D. Roosevelt's resolve to do anything to stop Japan. However, the high risks caught up with Japan, and the strategy ultimately failed.

It is well known by scholars that Japan's dearth of natural petroleum—exacerbated by a U.S. oil embargo beginning in the summer of 1941—was the primary reason for its aggression in the Dutch East Indies and its attack on the United States. In short, it is agreed that oil played a major role in *starting* the Pacific War. However, even while acknowledging this, academics have not followed up with the case to see whether oil had anything to do with the Pacific War's *ending*. In fact, I argue that Japan's high coercive vulnerability was successfully exploited by Allied attacks on its oil imports, and this contributed not only to Japan's defeat but also the decision taken by its leaders to finally surrender in August 1945.

During the Pacific War, which ensued after the Japanese attack on Pearl Harbor, the United States and its allies gradually fought their way across the ocean toward Japan. By 1943, they began tightening the noose, leading eventually to a full blockade of the home islands. This blockade was devastatingly effective in preventing oil from reaching Japan. In 1943, 75 percent of Japanese tankers were used to transport oil. That year, Japan started with 834,000 gross tons of tankers but lost 388,016 tons of them—roughly 47 percent of the total—to Allied attacks. In 1944, the Allies sank 754,106 tons of Japanese tankers, amounting to 90 percent of the 1943 total. This rate of sinking far outpaced the construction of replacement vessels. A Japanese naval captain interviewed after the war stated, "Toward the end, the situation was reached that we were fairly certain a tanker would be sunk shortly after departing from port. There wasn't much doubt in our minds that a tanker would not get to Japan." And by March 1945, in fact, the Japanese "gave up the ship" so to speak. They abandoned their attempts to sail oil tankers from the Indies to Japan altogether, instead retrofitting their remaining fleet to run on coal.[61]

The hopelessness of Japan's situation was not fully understood until after the war, when American occupation forces discovered all that remained of the Japanese military oil supply: 190,000 barrels the army had ferreted away, and 126,000 kept by the navy. These "were hidden away in remote nooks, caves and countless concealed spots, in order to protect them from bombing and were to be used for suicide flights against the invasion forces," as Jerome Cohen vividly describes. "American military investigators were, however, completely puzzled as to how the

Japanese would have been able to assemble their minutely-scattered hoards in time to service planes, in the event of invasion."[62]

Before surrendering, the Japanese military had attempted to employ substitutes and synthetics to compensate for oil shortages. Included among the materials used to make fuels, or in some cases mixed with petroleum to stretch supplies, were soybean, peanut, coconut, castor, and other vegetable oils; industrial substances such as methanol, ethanol, acetone, butanol, crude rubber, and wood turpentine; and foodstuffs such as potatoes, sugar, and rice wine.[63] The fact that the Japanese government was procuring food items to create alcohol for use as fuel—thus diverting it from civilian consumption—was remarkable because all the while the Japanese population was slowly starving. By July 1945, average caloric intake had fallen 12 percent from what it was in the late 1930s. In the cities, this decline was as much as 20 percent.[64] Even despite severe economic hardship, the Japanese population remained loyal to the regime.

Japan's futile pine root campaign was particularly revealing of its plight. Jerome Cohen offers the following eloquent description:

> In desperation the Navy undertook its fantastic pine root oil project. With the slogan "two hundred pine roots will keep a plane in the air for an hour," people all over Japan were set to work digging up pine roots.... Manpower requirements were amazing. The production of one gallon of crude pine root oil took 2.5 man-days of work. Since the Japanese hoped to obtain about 12,000 barrels of crude per day when the project reached its maximum, this would require 1,250,000 persons per day.

Needless to say, the target was not met. Cohen continues:

> By the time the war ended only about 3,000 barrels of gasoline intended for plane use had been produced and there was no indication that it had ever been tried in a plane. US Army units tried it experimentally in jeeps and found that in a few days it gummed up the engines beyond use. Traces of the pine root oil project were apparent when US forces landed. Monumental piles of roots and stumps lined many of the roadways. Mountainsides were stripped bare of every tree and sapling and the crude stills were to be found in many Japanese villages. Such were the limits to which the Japanese were driven by the sinking of their tankers and the severance of the oil line to the south.[65]

Other outlandish measures to procure fuel were undertaken by the Japanese government. The navy started using submarines to ferry small quantities of petroleum, as these were the only vessels capable of eluding the blockade.[66] Japan instituted a new policy with its German allies whereby the Japanese demanded that any German U-boats seeking to access submarine maintenance facilities at Kobe must carry a full load of oil with them and hand it over to Japan. A German admiral testified in 1945 that "the Japanese were so economical with their oil and gave the Germans such low-grade fuel for the trip from Kobe south that commanders told him they were constantly concerned lest they run out of fuel and become stranded."[67]

Military officials desperate for solutions also considered wild ideas that carried no realistic chance of success. These included plans to construct high-speed tankers that could ferry petroleum from the East Indies around the southern tip of Australia, and then somehow dart through Allied lines in the middle of the Pacific to reach the Japanese homeland. A similarly bizarre proposal suggested using ocean currents to float oil drums to Japan.[68]

The effects of the oil cutoff on Japan's military instrument were stunning. At the outbreak of the Pacific War, Japan had 8 million tons of petroleum products in reserve, including 3,624,000 tons of heavy fuel oil. Estimates indicate that Japan probably needed 6 to 7 million tons of oil annually to wage war, the majority of which was used by the military. By the war's end, only 4,000 tons of heavy oil were left in the country. Moreover, oil losses from tanker sinkings also caused "incredible fuel shortages at the front." In 1944, for instance, Japanese forces in New Guinea, the Bismarck Islands, Burma, and China had received only half the quantity of petroleum they required.[69]

To put these numbers in perspective, Japan's navy alone consumed about 300,000 tons of oil a month under normal conditions, but battles caused consumption to soar. The Japanese fleet burned 200,000 tons of oil during the two-day Battle of the Philippine Sea alone in June 1944 and another 150,000 tons in four days of military engagement in the Battle of Leyte Gulf in October 1944.[70] Even these numbers were not really sufficient, because various navy officers later testified that fuel shortages forced them to make strategically suboptimal choices in each of these battles and at the Marianas. In several cases, Japanese warships "were forced to sail slowly to conserve oil, or to sail by direct routes when good sense called for evasion."[71] Because of fuel depletion, maritime speed and maneuverability declined, combat missions were scaled back or scrapped, and most of the fleet was eventually unable to leave the oil-rich East Indies for want of fuel. Small craft sometimes had to tow each other. Admiral Soemu Toyoda, Chief of the Navy General Staff, later testified, "The fleet fuel situation became very acute early in this year [1945]. Our surface units were restricted even as to their training activities, and any large-scale operation requiring heavy supplies of fuel became almost out of the question."[72] And once inventories fell below one million barrels, which occurred by July 1945, "naval ships had virtually ceased to operate."[73]

Japanese aviation forces—which required forty thousand to fifty thousand tons of oil a month—similarly suffered. Pilot training, reconnaissance, and even combat missions were curtailed in the name of conservation. Kamikaze suicide attacks grew increasingly attractive to military planners because such flights required only enough fuel to travel one way and made navigation training unnecessary, as "pilots were simply expected to follow the leader to the target and few were expected to return."[74] Aviation fuel shortages also hampered the aircraft testing that was supposed to catch mechanical flaws before planes were put in the air. Whereas in 1941 each plane and engine underwent several hours of inspection, "by the war's end, the manufacturers were running only one engine in ten and only for two hours, while aircraft testing consisted of the attempt to fly the plane from the factory to the front."[75]

A strong case can be made that the severance of Japan's oil supply by the Allied embargo explains its leaders' decision to surrender in the time and manner that they did. Several Japanese military and political elites attributed their loss to a lack of materials necessary to prosecute the war; by far the most important of these was oil, "a commodity so vital that any kind of national defense whatever was virtually impossible without it."[76]

Vigorous debate surrounds the question of the timing of Japan's capitulation. It was long known among most Japanese commanders that the war was lost; their objective by August 1945 was to secure the best possible terms for surrender. The only bargaining chip Japan still possessed at that point was its threat to defend the homeland from invasion at any cost. Because this would have caused enormous casualties for invading forces, the Japanese hoped the Allies would shy away from conquering the country and strike a lenient deal with Japan instead.

Conventional wisdom attributes Japan's surrender to the firebombing of civilian centers and the atomic attacks on Hiroshima and Nagasaki. Scholars have cast significant doubt on this claim,[77] but the best alternative explanation for the surrender is also flawed. Robert A. Pape has argued convincingly that Japan's surrender was not because of a desire to avoid civilian casualties but rather because Japan's leaders had finally concluded that the military was too weak to inflict much damage on American invading forces. In Pape's view, the August 9 Soviet invasion of Manchuria is what put the last nail in the coffin, because of what it augured for Japanese military effectiveness. "The rapid collapse of the Japanese armies in Manchuria under Soviet attack indicated by analogy that the home army was unlikely to perform as well against the Americans as had been expected," Pape claims. "Since the Kwantung Army was thought to be Japan's premier fighting force, this had a devastating effect on Japanese calculations of the prospects for home island defense. If their best forces were so easily sliced to pieces, the unavoidable implication was that the less well-equipped and trained forces assembled for Ketsu-Go had no chance of success against American forces."[78]

I agree with Pape that the Soviet entry into the war was the decisive factor in Japan's surrender, but not for the reasons he cites. The Kwantung Army's poor performance in Manchuria was not what convinced Japanese leaders that the military situation was hopeless—the Japanese military already knew that the Kwantung Army was extraordinarily weak. From February to July 1944, the military had redeployed twelve infantry units from the Kwantung Army south in response to the growing threat from Allied forces in the Pacific. In March 1945, four more divisions were removed from Manchuria and sent to the home islands.[79] As a result, "the Japanese officers at GHQ knew ... that the vaunted Kwantung army had been tapped for troops and weapons for the other Japanese campaigns until little was left. It was even said the troops had but one rifle for three men."[80] In short, the Japanese had no illusions about the Kwantung Army for the Soviets to crush. Furthermore, the strength of the army had little relevance for Japanese assessments about their capacity to defend the homeland anyway. Operation Ketsu-Go, the official plan for responding to an Allied invasion, envisioned the creation of a twenty-eight-million-person strong civilian militia; however, Japanese planners knew that the best they could do to arm it, given the shortages in fuel and matériel, was to outfit the volunteers with bows and arrows, muzzle-loading rifles, and bamboo sticks cut into spears.[81] It was not difficult to draw the conclusion that such a force had no chance of success, regardless of how the Kwantung Army fared in Manchuria.

Instead, the Soviet entry into the war against Japan had such a jarring effect on its strategic calculations because it meant the rejection of a potentially game-changing deal that had been put on the table in late June: the Japanese had offered in writing to give up Manchuria in return for Soviet neutrality and Soviet oil.[82] Access to oil would have given the Japanese a new lease on life. An infusion of fuel might have made the Japanese military strong enough to put up a bloody fight in defense of the homeland—one costly enough to persuade the Allies to negotiate a tolerable peace. Certainly, this was the hope of key Japanese decision makers.

The Soviet negotiator was noncommittal in response to Japan's proposal, claiming he "would get back to [the Japanese] when he got an answer from Moscow." But as the summer wore on, the Soviets continually stalled on Japanese requests for serious talks on the matter. At the Potsdam conference in July, Joseph Stalin told Harry S. Truman about his intentions to keep the Japanese on the hook until the planned Soviet attack in August. At around the same time, Japanese ambassador Naotake Sato, stationed in Moscow, had concluded from the Soviets' perpetual stalling that Soviet aid would not be forthcoming. Over the next several weeks, Sato desperately tried to convince Tokyo that the Soviets would not help Japan in the war, but to no avail. He cabled, "I believe that Stalin feels that there is absolutely no necessity for making a voluntary agreement with Japan. On this point I see a serious discrepancy between your view and the actual state of affairs." Yet, the Japanese leadership remained optimistic. According to Toland, they "could not face the truth. They seemed immobilized by a common wishful conviction that the Soviet Union would come to the assistance of Japan." The dropping of the atomic bombs only strengthened Japanese hopes that the Soviets would intervene on their side. The Soviets did not reply to the Japanese until August 8, when Soviet Minister of Foreign Affairs Vyacheslav Molotov summoned Sato to his office and summarily informed him that a Soviet invasion of Manchuria was imminent. Evidently, this was Stalin's way of saying no.[83]

Importantly, Japanese assessments of the situation had been rosy, but they were not unreasonable. Although aware of the Soviet troop buildup in the East and Stalin's promise at Yalta to enter the war against Japan within three months of Germany's defeat, the Japanese were uncertain as to whether these moves signaled genuine intent to invade Manchuria, an attempt to apply pressure on Japan, or simply a desire to maintain East Asia as a Soviet sphere of influence. Even an American intelligence report from May 31, 1945, observed, "From the Japanese point of view the outlook for a negotiated peace probably does not appear hopeless.... The Japanese may also believe that the USSR is interested in maintaining an independent though insular Japan as a barrier to US power and that the Soviets are interested in denying to the United States the political prestige in Asia that a complete victory would bring."[84] Moreover, the Japanese had good reason to doubt that the Soviets would want to open a new front against them in Manchuria, given the heavy casualties sustained by the Red Army on the eastern front.[85]

Faulty intelligence reinforced false hopes. Japanese analysts underestimated the size and strength of Soviet base forces in the Far East, which likely skewed assessments toward unwarranted optimism. Japanese intelligence services estimated that between thirty-five and forty-five Soviet divisions were in the area when, in actuality, Soviet forces in East Asia totaled eighty divisions. This error was highly significant because it put the Soviets well under the threshold of the fifty-five to sixty divisions the Japanese believed the Soviets required to launch operations in Manchuria. The Soviet forces in East Asia also lacked winter gear, leading some Japanese observers to conclude the USSR would not attack until the spring of 1946 at the earliest.[86]

In the end, the Soviet invasion dashed any last hopes that Japan could trade Manchuria for oil and Soviet neutrality. Navy Minister Admiral Mitsumasa Yonai concluded on August 9, "There is no chance whatsoever of victory.... We have reached the end of our resources, both spiritual and material. To continue is out of the question!"[87] In his postmortem analysis of the war, Admiral Toyoda stated his belief that "the Russian participation in the war against Japan rather than the atom bombs did more to hasten the surrender." The official British history of World War II concurs that it was the Soviet invasion that "brought home to all members of the Supreme Council the realization that the last hope for a negotiated peace had gone and there was no alternative but to accept the Allied terms sooner or later."[88] On August 15, Japan capitulated.

This chapter has traced the evolution of the oil weapon, beginning with the transition away from coal to oil at the start of the twentieth century and how this opened the eyes of the great powers to petroleum's importance for military power during World War I. The major powers understood that oil's vital importance to winning wars created an opportunity for countries to use petroleum to blackmail others. A country able to cut off oil to an adversary in wartime could render it incapable of winning a war. This threat became the basis of oil's coercive power. World War I was the juncture at which oil took on its military importance, and therefore, its coercive potential arising from the ability to deny an adversary victory in war.

The second part of the chapter examined what happens when anticipatory strategies fail. In World War II, Japan's experience represented the worst nightmare of great powers forced to rely on others for petroleum. The consequences of oil deprivation to the Japanese military were immense, and these contributed to Japan's decision to surrender in the time and manner that it did—that is, without the United States having to invade the home islands.

3
QUALITATIVE METHODS FOR TESTING THE THEORY

This chapter outlines the historical case study approach, which I subsequently use to test the theory in chapters 4–6, and explains why the cases chosen to test are valuable for causal inference. There is no competing theory to guide the selection of cases, no overarching argument to test against my own. The book deals with that challenge in three ways. First, it examines many cases—eleven full cases in all, plus two additional baseline vignettes—on the principle that the greater the N, the more confident we can be in the results. Second, it uses a combination of longitudinal analysis, which controls for background conditions, and cross-case analysis, to show that the theory travels. Third, the book traces the causal process behind the decision making to see how it conforms to theoretical predictions.

The book uses longitudinal analysis to compare before-and-after observations of the great power over long stretches of its history. The longitudinal method holds constant a wide swath of potential confounding factors, such as a state's regime type, economic system, political culture, wealth, and geographical location, that plausibly influence which anticipatory strategy is chosen. If those factors remain constant but a state's strategy nevertheless changes, we can rule them out as causes of the shift. The United States is the best case for longitudinal analysis because it has been a great power throughout the oil age and its policymakers left a voluminous paper trail, among other reasons. The U.S. case also includes long stretches of peace, which supports the claim that the theory applies throughout the oil era, not just in or around times of war.

Evidence from the United States alone obviously cannot establish a theory's broad generalizability. The book, therefore, includes multiple observations of

Britain, Germany, and Japan to demonstrate that the theory can indeed travel. These particular countries were advantageous for causal inference for various reasons discussed below.

The book also focuses on causal processes, which dovetail nicely with the longitudinal approach for the perhaps obvious reason that causal processes must unfold over time. Each case endeavors to show that policymakers, in effect, evaluated their country's petroleum deficit and threat to imports; that they worried about vulnerability to oil cutoff, and particularly, the havoc it would wreak on the state's military forces; and ultimately, that they chose the anticipatory strategy commensurate with the state's coercive vulnerability. The key objective of process tracing is to determine the extent to which oil security considerations, as opposed to other motives specific to each case, caused policymakers to adopt the policies that they selected.

Though the research design sketched above is straightforward, a good deal of conceptual groundwork must be laid to fully explain the book's approach to theory testing. The chapter does so in the following manner.

First, the chapter defines the unit of analysis—that is, what counts as a "case"—and presents the universe of all case units the theory should be able to explain. A case is defined as a period of time when a state's coercive vulnerability remains constant (that is, there is no major change to the state's petroleum deficit or import disruptibility). If the theory is correct, the state should follow the anticipatory strategy commensurate with its level of coercive vulnerability during that period, and the causal mechanism—that states act to reduce their susceptibility to oil cutoff, particularly because they fear the effect a cutoff would have on their military power—should be clearly observable. Parsing the cases along the independent variables makes for easy viewing of "null" cases, the nonevents when no anticipatory strategy is taken. The inclusion of null cases results in the most conceptually comprehensive case universe possible. The universe consists of every period in which coercive vulnerability is constant for each great power since 1918. Labeling ex ante every case in great power history is impossible because coding the independent variables demands fine-grained knowledge that may only be found through archival documents, not all of which are available to researchers.

Next, the chapter explains the qualitative research design. The book examines in depth eleven distinct cases—a formidable number for close qualitative analysis—across four great powers: the United States, Britain, Germany, and Japan. In combination, the cases span roughly one hundred great power years. The empirical work, therefore, covers a lot of ground. It does not skip and hop from observation to observation, and it certainly does not cherry-pick observations. Rather, it runs a fine-toothed comb over continuous stretches of great power history. The setup of the cases is to compare the theory's predictions of which strategy the state should select, given the values of the independent variables, with the strategy it actually adopted. Historical outcomes that match the theory's predictions count as evidence supporting the theory. If the outcomes contradict the theory's predictions, they count as evidence against the theory.

Not every case perfectly fits the theory's expectations—the world of social science is probabilistic, after all—but the strong majority do. The fact that the theory gets an observation wrong demonstrates the rigor and integrity of the tests: not every case passes. (Too many errors, however, would undermine the theory. Chapter 7, which applies fuzzy-set analysis to the cases, offers an impartial way to judge how many mistakes are too many.) The sheer volume of observations studied should make the empirical evidence more compelling.

The book also features longitudinal and cross-case comparisons to isolate the variables responsible for shifts to more or less extreme strategies. The chapter outlines the logic behind these techniques and explains why the specific cases chosen are appropriate for their application. Finally, the chapter lays out in detail the decision process we should observe policymakers engaging in if the theory is correct.

Defining the Cases and Their Universe

I define cases and the universe of cases according to the values of the independent variables, without reference to the anticipatory strategies a country might be pursuing at a given time. Specifically, in tandem with the book's within-case approach, a case is defined as a time span during which the independent variables—the petroleum deficit and disruptibility—do not significantly change. In other words, each observation captures a period when the coercive vulnerability of a country remains relatively constant.

It might strike readers as surprising to define cases as time units of vulnerability instead of labeling each occurrence of a potential anticipatory strategy as a case.[1] While the object of study here is the anticipatory strategy, it does not make sense to define the case universe as a collection of anticipatory strategies. This is for two reasons. First, it is impractical. Anticipatory strategies are composed of broad categories of state action, spanning both the foreign policy and domestic policy realms. It would be impossible to tally up every drilling subsidy, conservation program, or alternative fuels incentive in a great power's history. Nor would it be useful, because such a catalog would capture a significant amount of noise—that is, oil policies that are unrelated to coercive vulnerability. Government subsidies to boost petroleum exploration, for example, could primarily aim to protect against oil coercion in some cases but be instituted mainly to placate oil-industry interest groups in other cases. I certainly do not claim that coercive vulnerability is the reason behind every conquest, alliance, or domestic energy policy a great power adopts. Many, if not most, social phenomena exhibit equifinality: they originate through more than one causal pathway from combinations of different variables.[2]

The indefinite nature of some anticipatory strategies creates similar noise problems. Whereas many social phenomena—wars, terrorist attacks, elections, and so forth—are relatively discrete, punctuated events, anticipatory measures like oil-based alliances or holding strategic petroleum reserves could continue for decades. Although these policies may have been initially enacted to decrease coercive vulnerability, different factors unrelated to vulnerability could be responsible for their persistence over time—bureaucratic inertia, for instance.

Second, defining the universe of cases according to the dependent variable would exclude cases where the dependent variable was absent—the negative cases or "nonbarking dogs"—which are crucial for establishing causality. Logically, for the study to include cases where the dependent variable is absent, the overarching universe must also include cases where the dependent variable is absent.

Methodologists of all stripes agree that it is advantageous, if not strictly and in all cases necessary, to include negative cases in a qualitative research design. Doing so strengthens causal inference by demonstrating that both sides of a hypothesized relationship function as specified: that A causes B, and that the absence of A causes the absence of B. If we defined the universe as all cases of anticipatory strategies, we could demonstrate only the first part of the relationship: that coercive vulnerability causes strategic anticipation (or more specifically, that as coercive vulnerability increases, states choose more extreme strategies). We could not, however, test whether a lack of vulnerability causes a lack of anticipation, because cases of nonanticipation would not appear in the universe. Moreover, it would also be impossible to find at least one type of discrepancy that should cast doubt on the theory: instances where coercive vulnerability is high, yet the country takes no anticipatory measures. It is far better to have a universe that could capture this potentially disproving data point.

The next logical step is to establish how one can recognize the beginning and the end of an observation. Conceptually speaking, an observation ends and the next begins when one or both independent variables change significantly enough to register with policymakers and prompt official reassessment of oil vulnerability. Once anticipatory measures are successfully put in place, leaders generally leave them there and move on to other concerns, rather than reassess continually. Gradual change—increased home production, for example—tends not to get their attention. Significant changes to the petroleum deficit and the threat to imports typically result from exogenous shocks. For example, Germany first used self-sufficiency to boost its home production from 1936 to 1939. Although output increased as a result, the Germans did not update their approach to reflect higher production. Instead, reassessment occurred only after the Anglo-French blockade in September 1939. At that point, the results of self-sufficiency—increased natural and synthetic production—are counted in the "haves" part of the deficit. But the reassessment was prompted by something other than the self-sufficiency measures themselves—in this case, the blockade.

General Characteristics of the Case Universe

The universe of cases consists of every period of relatively constant vulnerability for each great power since 1918, the first full year when the strategic value of oil was widely understood. Since 1918, six countries have qualified as great powers in the eyes of most scholars: Britain (1918–1945), France (1918–1945), Germany (1933–1945), Japan (1918–1945), the Soviet Union (1918–1991), and the United States (1918 to the present).

Limiting the scope to great powers allows me to control (at least somewhat) for perhaps the most important variable in international politics: relative power. Certainly great powers vary in their capabilities, so the control is imperfect, but their capabilities far outclass those of lesser powers. The scope limitation creates a broader and more meaningful range of strategic anticipation to observe, because great powers, by virtue of their superior capabilities, can choose from the broadest range of possible options. In methodological terms, such cases produce better empirical tests because they exhibit the greatest variation on the dependent variable.

As a concrete illustration, consider that empirical cases of self-sufficiency among minor powers would likely provide less compelling evidence than cases of great powers pursuing self-sufficiency. It would not be surprising if minor powers adopted self-sufficiency, because costlier measures like indirect or direct control may simply exceed their capabilities. Ergo, power is an alternative explanation for the same evidence, which weakens the test. The United States, however, has been a great power since the late 1800s, so its pursuit of self-sufficiency at various times, instead of indirect or direct control, conveys more information about the validity of the hypothesis than a minor power's use of self-sufficiency would.

The largest downside of defining observations on the independent variables is that presenting a full universe of cases requires coding every change in the petroleum deficit and import disruptibility of a great power for its entire life span as a great power. If the observation was simply a dyad-year, for example, the exact number of potential cases would be easy to calculate. Unfortunately, changes in coercive vulnerability are so difficult to detect without intimate knowledge of the cases that it is impossible to code the vulnerability over time of all six great powers that have existed since World War I. Therefore, it is impossible to be exhaustive in identifying the entire case universe.

The reason why capturing the bookends of observations—where one ends and another starts—is difficult is because it requires access to primary documents that contain the private deliberations of policymakers. Secondary accounts, even excellent detailed histories, are likely to miss changes in coercive vulnerability unless they are specifically looking for them (and to my knowledge, no existing studies have). This is because many of the key factors relating to coercive vulnerability are sensitive, and as such, are tightly held by governments. For obvious reasons, governments do not publicize what their military and essential civilian oil requirements would be in a war, nor do they openly report on the military vulnerability of their imports. Even the United States does not disclose its military oil requirements, though it fosters the illusion that it does. The U.S. military publishes data on how much oil it *purchases*, but evidence suggests it *consumes* more oil—perhaps much more—than it actually pays for.[3] Strategic aims, doctrine, and other factors that influence how much oil a country would need in war may be similarly concealed. And of course, policy documents that reflect leaders' thinking about sensitive oil data are also withheld from the public.

In the final analysis, I did an immense amount of research to code the vulnerability of four of the six great powers—the United States, Britain, Germany, and Japan—during their time as great powers. I have identified twelve potential observations. Of these, the book examines eleven in depth.

Without digging into the cases, it is impossible to know how many potential observations exist for the other two great powers, Russia and France. Fully coding the coercive vulnerability of Russia is effectively impossible because its archives are closed, thwarting the fine-grained research required to identify cases. For this reason, Russia is omitted. I left out France simply because I could not include everything. I have no reason to believe it behaved differently than the other great powers. As explained below, the United States, Britain, Germany, and Japan cases provide strong evidence in support of the theory, because they combine within-case and cross-case congruence testing with process tracing of the causal mechanism.

Research Design and Case Selection

Although the originality of the theory is a major strength of the book, it does pose methodological challenges when it comes to testing the theory. Crucially, because there is no single, overarching theory that competes with my argument, I could not select observations according to what would best test my theory against a rival hypothesis. In other words, I am in a "two-cornered fight" between my theory and the null hypothesis, which assumes that no causal relationship exists, rather than a Lakatosian "three-cornered fight" among my theory, a rival theory, and the null hypothesis.[4] As a result, some of the techniques lauded within the qualitative methods literature as particularly "strong tests" simply cannot apply to this project. For example, the lack of a competing argument removes the joint most-likely/least-likely case design as an option.[5] However, although there is no overarching rival theory, case-specific alternative explanations exist, and I rebut these within the cases.

Within-Case Comparison Controls for Omitted Variables

The research format adopted here compensates for the lack of a three-cornered test by controlling for numerous confounding factors (i.e., the kernels of would-be competing arguments) through the technique of longitudinal or within-case comparison. Within-case analysis examines several observations of the independent and dependent variables within one country over time. A key benefit of such tests is that they "gain strong controls from the uniform character of the background conditions of the case," effectively "creat[ing] a semi-controlled environment that limits the effects of third variables by holding them constant."[6]

To see how uniform background conditions help to limit potentially confounding omitted variables, such as regime type, culture, and the personality of leaders, consider the within-case analysis of Nazi Germany (chapter 5). It deftly eliminates regime type as a potential competing explanation because anticipatory strategies changed in 1939 and again in 1941 even though regime type remained constant (under the same leader, no less). And, of course, constants cannot explain variables. Ergo, we can eliminate regime type as a potential cause of the change in Germany's strategy.

Some scholars may worry that longitudinal analysis introduces endogeneity problems, insofar as leaders' decisions in one period may depend on the strategy chosen in previous periods. Of course, it is true that the choice of policy at one time affects the size of the petroleum deficit later. For instance, if a country adopts self-sufficiency at some point in time (t_1), it will decrease its petroleum deficit in the future (t_2), all else equal. But as long as the policy decision in t_2 depends only on the values of the independent variables at t_2, there is no endogeneity problem. The estimate of the causal effect of the petroleum deficit on policy choice will be correct. In other words, if countries react the same way to the same size petroleum deficit regardless of whether past efforts contributed to that deficit, then the observations are independent, and the past events do not affect the causal theory. Only when countries react differently to the same size petroleum deficit depending on what anticipatory strategy they chose at a previous time would there be an endogeneity problem. Empirically, this would show up in the case studies as leaders in t_2 referring to decisions in t_1 as part of their rationale for choosing a particular strategy. I looked for this in the case studies and found no evidence of leaders basing their decisions on previously chosen strategies.

Cross-Case Analysis Demonstrates Generalizability

While the study's use of within-case analysis helps control for omitted variables, the cross-case analysis tests the theory's generalizability and the preconditions under which it operates. Note that the German case as a stand-alone would not eliminate regime type as an antecedent condition—it could be argued, for instance, that authoritarian government was a necessary precondition for anticipatory strategies to shift over time. However, the book's research design counters this argument by making cross-case comparisons with the United States and Britain (chapters 4 and 6), two democracies that exhibit similar behavior to Germany when faced with comparable circumstances.

Why These Cases

The eleven cases chosen for examination in the book, particularly in combination, provide rigorous testing of the theory for several reasons. First, the sheer number of cases should boost confidence in the findings. The more data included, the more robust the results. Second, the cases collectively exhibit significant variation on the independent and dependent variables, which makes it possible to test the full range of predictions the theory offers. All three levels of coercive vulnerability (as determined by the petroleum deficit and disruptibility of imports) are represented among the cases, and each of the three types of anticipatory strategies—self-sufficiency, indirect control, and direct control—is observable as well. Third, individual characteristics of the eleven cases, discussed below, make them strong tests.

The United States is the best possible country for within-case analysis because it offers the most observations over time. The country is a great power throughout the period of interest, and it can be closely observed thanks to its political openness. Indeed, the book surveys American oil vulnerability from circa 1900 to the 1970s, the most recent decade for which a large body of declassified material is available. Six distinct observations are discernible (though only five are codable; the 1945–1950 era was indeterminate because the United States had not fully committed to protecting Europe from the Soviets indefinitely). Because the background is similar across observations, we have greater confidence that changes in anticipatory strategies can be attributed to the independent variables rather than confounding factors.

Observations of the United States should weigh heavily because they are difficult, or least-likely, cases from a common knowledge point of view. Initial assumptions suggest that the United States, as a major oil-producing country (indeed, the largest global producer from the 1860s until well into the 1970s), would not need to adopt anticipatory strategies. Yet, the theory predicts self-sufficiency and indirect control at various historical junctures. These constitute "risky predictions" that, if confirmed, strongly corroborate the hypothesis.[7]

The U.S. cases are also valuable because they include numerous wartime and peacetime observations. This means that they can assess whether the theory applies only in times of great power war. If only the wartime cases passed the empirical tests, this would suggest that ongoing military conflict is a crucial antecedent condition for strategic anticipation. In that case, because war is a relatively rare occurrence, the results would narrow the scope of the theory and, consequently, limit its substantive importance. If instead the peacetime cases match the theory's predictions, the broad scope and substantive importance of the theory is confirmed. The Cold War U.S. cases, specifically, perform this role. They demonstrate that policymakers worried about vulnerability to coercion from the Soviet Union into at least the mid-1970s, three decades after the most recent great power war.

The Nazi Germany case, while more temporally compact given its scant twelve years as a great power after the devastation of World War I, also contains a surprising amount of variation on the independent variables across four observations. Again, because the context is relatively steady across the four periods that make up the case, changes in strategy are more likely to reflect the hypothesized causal factors rather than lurking variables. Fine-grained research is also possible, thanks to the large cache of German documents retrieved by the Allies after World War II.

As in the American cases, the theory's predictions are least likely or risky based on prior knowledge of the case. Default expectations suggest that Hitler, an expansionist bent on aggression, would employ direct control to seize oil-rich territory. Risky predictions on the case are those that foresee measures short of conquest, namely, indirect control and self-sufficiency. If the predictions are fulfilled, the results are especially significant because they clash with a priori beliefs.[8] The U.S. and German cases, because they are difficult cases, thereby present an opportunity for what Jack Levy calls "Sinatra Inference," as in, "if I can make it here, I can make it anywhere."[9]

The cases from Britain and Japan, parallel in certain respects, serve three primary purposes. First, beyond the simple demonstration that the theory applies across two additional countries, the independent and dependent variables take on extreme values in both cases, which means that other factors are less likely to overwhelm the predicted outcome. Consequently, there are fewer "third factors with the strength to produce the result that the test theory predicts, which lowers the possibility that omitted variables account for passed tests."[10] In both Britain and Japan, the petroleum deficit is very large, as neither country has oil resources. The import threat is also high because both countries are islands. As predicted, Japan and Britain pursue the most extreme strategy: direct control through conquest. The chances are relatively small that some other factor would cause such a result.

Second, the two cases present even more evidence that the theory can travel. It is significant that the Britain-Japan pair, as two countries that bear little resemblance to each other on a superficial basis, nevertheless pursue the same anticipatory strategy. That the independent variables predict the actions of both countries, despite contrasting background conditions (such as dissimilar regime types, economic systems, and strategic goals), testifies to the theory's broad applicability.[11]

Finally, the cases play unique historical roles. The British case clarified the importance of oil to other great powers, which watched as the country nearly succumbed because of German attacks on its oil. The contribution of the Japan case is that it exemplifies the worst-case scenario of the damage wrought by oil cutoffs on military effectiveness.

Analytical Techniques within the Cases

Two main qualitative techniques are applied to the cases: the congruence procedure and causal process analysis.

Congruence Testing

Congruence testing, at its most basic level, lays out specific predictions of what combinations of independent and dependent variables we should observe if the theory is correct, and then compares those predictions with the historical record. If the predictions are borne out in a particular case, the case provides support for the theory. If the predictions are not consistent with observations, the case counts against the theory.[12] For example, in cases where the independent variables combine to create a moderate level of coercive vulnerability for a great power, that country should embark on an indirect control strategy, provided that the theory is correct. If the country does so, the case strengthens the empirical validity of the theory. If the strategy taken does not comport with the level of vulnerability—for example, if the country pursues direct control instead—the case counts against the theory.[13]

While a passed congruence test is suggestive of a causal relationship, one test alone cannot establish causality. Thus, congruence procedures should be overlaid and combined to strengthen claims that the relationship between variables is causal rather than spurious. The book incorporates several best practices to this end. One technique is to test as many observations as possible, especially cross-case observations.[14] The book achieves this by examining observations across four countries: the United States, Britain, Japan, and Germany. Another recommended technique is to test the negative side of the relationship by evaluating whether the absence of the independent variables leads to the absence of the dependent variable. If absence begets absence, the theory is strengthened.[15] The book accomplishes this by examining three observations where the petroleum deficit is functionally absent—the baseline cases of Britain from 1900 to 1918 and the United States from 1900 to 1918, and the full case of the United States from 1920 to 1941—and finds that no anticipatory strategies are taken.[16]

Causal Process Tracing

Process tracing of the causal mechanism bolsters the findings of congruence tests.[17] Process tracing "explores the chain of events or the decision making process by which initial case conditions are translated into case outcomes."[18] The technique also looks for consistency between theoretical expectations and historical realities, but it focuses on confirming that the causal mechanism operates as postulated instead of gauging the degree to which the independent and dependent variables agree. The researcher may use minutes from meetings, memos, reports, diplomatic cables, memoirs, and other written records that indicate the reasoning behind a given action to ascertain whether the proposed causal logic is driving the decision, an unidentified logic is at work, or the decision reflects idiosyncratic causes.[19]

If the theory is correct, the following steps in the causal process should be observable.

First, there *must* be some kind of evaluation (or reevaluation) of the country's oil security. Often, an exogenous shock is what illuminates the need for an assessment of the oil situation, but this need not necessarily be the case. In an unfolding crisis, the evaluation process may simply consist of an emergency meeting where leaders diagnose the situation and plot a course of action. In that case, evidence might consist of personal memoirs, diaries, official meeting notes, recordings, and other such sources. Alternatively, where circumstances permit for extended study and deliberation, leaders may order a formal inquiry into the country's oil security situation that culminates in an official report with policy recommendations and a robust paper trail.

Second, the official assessment of the oil situation *must* try to determine what are essentially the petroleum deficit and disruptibility of imports (though likely expressed in different terms), and it should draw policy conclusions based on their values. Recognizable components of each variable should appear in the conversation or report. For the petroleum deficit, factors such as the country's oil output, expected future output, size of its reserves, age of its oil industry, new discovery rates, and expected demand for civilians and military should frame the analysis. Potential threats to oil access should also be considered, including whether overland imports are available, the distance imports must travel, the capabilities of potential interdictors, and the likelihood that a cutoff occurs.

Third, there *must* be evidence that principals—actual heads of state or cabinet-level advisers—are directly involved in deliberations that arise from the report. For instance, an evaluative report of the country's oil position could be presented at a meeting attended by the leader; the report's recommendations could be adopted and bear his or her signature; or, witnesses or the principal himself or herself could indicate in private papers that coercive vulnerability was a driving force in the decision. The most convincing evidence consists of behind-the-scenes private or classified material, which is more likely to represent the "true" intentions of policymakers than statements made for public consumption. Public statements still constitute evidence, of course, but it may be more difficult to parse whether they accurately reflect policymakers' sentiments or amount to mere rhetoric. In any case, a report by a low-level aide that never crosses the desk of a policymaker, and the contents of which are never communicated up the chain of command, does not qualify as strong evidence.

Fourth, if coercive vulnerability is threatened, there *should* be evidence that policymakers are concerned not only about prosperity but also about the consequences of an oil disruption for national security, especially the consequences for military effectiveness in war. Closely related, policymakers *should* worry about losing physical access to oil as much as or more than they should worry about the consequences of higher oil prices, which are linked to prosperity rather than security in a traditional sense. However, because the theory allows that oil coercion threatens both prosperity and survival, if military threats are not considered, it does not undermine the theory—it merely suggests that the military motive may not be as strong as postulated.

Fifth, if coercive vulnerability is threatened, the leader *must* respond by choosing the anticipatory strategy commensurate with the country's degree of coercive vulnerability, according to the theory. If the country is not vulnerable, the leader *must not* pursue any of the three anticipatory strategies.

Sixth, the leader *must* explicitly cite oil security as a decisive rationale for anticipatory strategies, as opposed to motivations such as greed or domestic politics. An example of a greed-based action would be conquering oil-rich territory primarily for profit, not security. Domestic factors might include lobbying by oil companies that are eager to maintain or expand their activities at home or abroad; pressure from environmental groups interested in conservation and alternative fuels; or pressure from legislators or other officials keen on subsidies for oil-producing constituents, among other possibilities.

The eleven cases examined across the next four chapters are strong tests of the theory, both individually and collectively. Although there is no single competing theory that acts as a foil to guide case selection, the cases, particularly in combination, are nonetheless rigorous tests.

4
BRITISH VULNERABILITY AND THE CONQUEST OF MESOPOTAMIA

Until 1917, the threat of oil coercion was poorly understood. Mechanized warfare was new, and resultantly, petroleum had not been targeted in previous conflicts. That year, however, Germany's unrestricted submarine warfare destroyed large numbers of oil tankers destined for Britain, demonstrating that the evolution from coal-based fleets to ships running on petroleum—which Britain lacked—made the country exceedingly vulnerable to coercion in future wars. Behind this vulnerability lay two factors: Great Britain's large petroleum deficit, and the susceptibility of its oil imports to naval blockade. As my theory predicts, Britain took a direct control approach by annexing Mesopotamian oil resources and establishing a regional mandate after the war. Mesopotamia produced no oil at the time and could not affect the outcome of World War I, but it was believed to possess massive resources that could determine the winner of future wars.[1] Direct control was costly and risky to the British; the invasion risked fracturing the Western alliance and provoking conflict with the United States over the division of Ottoman spoils.[2]

This chapter presents the British case in the years before, during, and after World War I—the turning point for oil-fueled warfare, marking the onset of coercive vulnerability logic. In the first period, before 1917, there was some concern in the Admiralty that the ongoing switch to oil-burning propulsion could be strategically problematic; but policymakers as yet did not understand the coercive potential of the "oil weapon," and they did little to protect access.

The second period of study considers Germany's attempt in 1917 to coerce Britain into surrendering by attacking its imports of American petroleum with unrestricted submarine warfare. This inaugural use of the oil weapon was a near miss: it failed to force British capitulation, but just barely. German U-boats successfully destroyed large amounts of petroleum destined for Britain, causing severe oil shortages that nearly immobilized the Royal Navy. Only at the eleventh hour was Britain saved by emergency petroleum shipments provided by the United States. The British feared what would happen if the Americans did not bail them out should they be faced with the oil weapon again in the future. This leads to the third era, strategic anticipation, when the logic of coercive vulnerability theory sets in. This shift set British policy on a course it would follow until the start of World War II.

Evolving Views on Oil's Importance before World War I

In the decade before World War I, the British government was becoming increasingly aware of the importance of oil for military power. But few officials anticipated that oil would become so indispensable to war that a country would be unable to prevail in a conflict without it. Nor did British policymakers seem to grasp that oil's unique military value meant that supply cutoffs could potentially be used for political coercion. Calculations involving oil were not yet driving British grand strategy. "It cannot be argued," according to Marian Jack, "that oil was recognized by the British government before the war as a peculiarly vital commodity over which it should have general control."[3]

Only a small number of individuals in the Admiralty had sensed oil's new importance for warfare. Admiral John Fisher was perhaps the most influential among them. During Fisher's tenure as First Sea Lord from 1904 to 1910, the Royal Navy embarked on a massive transition from coal-fueled ships to oil-burning vessels. The many performance advantages petroleum fuel had to offer, such as higher top speeds, faster acceleration, and increased range, had convinced Fisher that conversion was crucial for maintaining British naval superiority in the face of German competition. Winston Churchill, a disciple of Fisher's who was appointed First Lord of the Admiralty in October 1911, expanded the program, and by 1912 all destroyers, cruisers, and battleships ran on oil.[4]

The problem associated with conversion, of course, was that it required Britain to switch from a fuel found in abundance domestically (coal) to one that it did not possess (oil). Nineteenth-century British naval power owed a lot to the country's massive coal resources, which were "far superior to those of any other nation," and which included large amounts of premium Welsh steam coal for high-speed propulsion. In fact, British soil was so rich in coal that the country became one of the world's premier coal exporters, with coal accounting for 85 percent of the country's total export tonnage in 1913.[5]

Early Efforts to Secure Fuel for the Royal Navy

The absence of domestic petroleum reserves raised concerns in the Admiralty as well as in Parliament about ensuring a steady supply for the Royal Navy, particularly given the expected twenty-year life span of the newly built oil-burning vessels. Urged on by the Admiralty, the British government took modest steps toward this goal as opportunities presented themselves. However, these efforts were ad hoc—not a comprehensive plan for safeguarding oil access.

The most important step taken was the government's involvement in creating and maintaining an exclusively British oil concession in Persia. Under his own gumption, William Knox D'Arcy, an Australian with financial backing from British banks, had negotiated an exclusive deal with the shah of Iran in 1901 for a sixty-year unlimited petroleum concession. The investment quickly bore fruit with the speedy discovery and exploitation of Persian crude. In 1905, D'Arcy decided to bring in more capital by partnering with the French Rothschilds to develop the concession further—that is, until the British government dispatched its spymaster Sidney Reilly to break up the deal. In a stunt reminiscent of a 1980s Eddie Murphy movie, Reilly disguised himself as a priest and persuaded D'Arcy, a religious man, to instead sell his rights to a good "Christian" firm—the Anglo-Persian Oil Company (APOC).[6] The concession thus passed into the hands of a company entirely controlled by British nationals. Over the next several years, the British government extended diplomatic support to APOC in its efforts to obtain a concession in Ottoman Mesopotamia, while the Admiralty pressured APOC to retain strictly British ownership over Persian oil.[7]

Matters were more complicated in 1912 when APOC asked the British government for financial assistance in light of tough competition from Royal Dutch-Shell—a company Anglo-Persian successfully painted as "foreign" despite its 40 percent British ownership.[8] The Admiralty rejected the plan for funding Anglo-Persian at first. Churchill and his officers thought it unwise for the government to assume the financial risks associated with the business of oil exploration. Moreover, the Admiralty wanted to maintain its freedom to purchase oil from diverse sources, particularly if those sources could offer it more cheaply. For its part, Anglo-Persian made the strategic argument to the country's political leaders, contending that national security would be better served by the preservation of an all-British petroleum conglomerate. But this was not enough to sway the Admiralty. Only when it became clear that Anglo-Persian was willing to offer very favorable long-term contracts to the Royal Navy did Churchill come around. "The argument that really caused the Admiralty to change its mind," as Marian Jack tells it, "was the chance of a good bargain." As a result, the British government bought a 51 percent controlling share in Anglo-Persian in May 1914. It was an unprecedented move; never before had such an arrangement been negotiated with any major company.[9] But the impetus behind it was more a matter of cost cutting than one of national security. The British did not yet appreciate the danger posed by petroleum cutoff, nor did they understand the extent to which the country's lack of oil made it vulnerable.

Strategic Priorities in the Middle East: India Overshadows Oil

Of course, the growth of German political and economic influence in the Ottoman Empire that was occurring at the time alarmed the British. The possibility that German firms could beat British interests in obtaining Ottoman oil concessions prompted serious economic and strategic concerns. But oil was just one aspect of the Anglo-German rivalry in the Middle East—and not necessarily the most important one. Above all else, the British wanted to preserve their supremacy in the Persian Gulf for the inevitable day when the Ottoman Empire, the "sick man of Europe," would finally collapse. The British position in the region mattered chiefly because of its implications for the defense of the empire's "Jewel in the Crown": colonial India. If Germany succeeded in obtaining a political toehold in Ottoman Turkey, it could seriously compromise Indian security. The primary maritime and overland routes to India ran smack through the Middle East. German penetration in the region, therefore, threatened to cut the empire in half in the event of a European war.

These priorities are reflected in the actions taken by the British in the first few years of the war, before the vital strategic nature of oil was illuminated. Although the British could not ignore the Middle East given its instrumental value in protecting India, Europe remained the clear priority. Thwarting German expansion on the continent was vital to the security of the British Isles, and preserving the sovereignty of the home islands naturally trumped threats to the empire. This compelled the British to concentrate the great majority of their resources along the western front. Moreover, to sustain strong alliances with France and Russia, which were necessary for Britain to have any hope of defeating Germany, the British had vowed to refrain from annexing any Ottoman territory until the war's conclusion.[10] The promise was in keeping with Britain's historical policy of preserving the integrity of the Ottoman Empire for as long as possible, out of the belief that a Turkish collapse would set off a dangerous scramble for territory among the major powers. Such a scramble pitting the Entente powers against each other could undermine the primary war aim: vanquishing Germany. Finally, the Middle East was not yet producing oil on a large scale. The only productive area in the region was the Persian concession, which contributed a mere 1 percent of global oil output in 1914.[11] During the war itself, Persia provided just 15 percent of the Royal Navy's fuel requirements; the rest of Britain's oil came from the Western Hemisphere—predominantly from the United States.[12]

In summary, the actions Britain took in the Middle East from 1914 to 1917 were commensurate with the primary British objective in the region—the protection of communications with India—and revealed only modest concern over oil. Shortly after declaring war on Turkey in November 1914, the British sent a small contingent of troops to guard the Abadan naval fuel refinery in Persia and dispatched a modest Mesopotamian Expeditionary Force to defend the port city of Basra on the Persian Gulf. Both moves served to shore up Indian security; the two contingents were composed of Indian troops and fell under the command of Lord Hardinge, the viceroy of India. The administration of the occupied areas fell under the preserve of the Foreign Office, not the cabinet.[13] Once deployed, these troops largely remained in a holding pattern, deterring attacks against communications with India until early 1917. There was no significant attempt to overrun Ottoman territory or take control of promising petroleum areas. Britain lacked the resources to penetrate far into Mesopotamia given the action on the western front and could not do so in any case without risking its European alliances. The other main military operation undertaken by the British against the Turks was the ill-fated Gallipoli Campaign of 1915, which had nothing to do with petroleum. Rather, British and French forces opened a new front against Turkey in the Dardanelles at the request of Russia, which was facing severe pressure from Ottoman forces in the Caucasus.[14] Only the seizure of Abadan could reasonably be described as defending an oil interest.

Prelude to a Shift in British Foreign Oil Policy

Behind the scenes, however, circumstances were aligning to set the stage for a shift in British objectives in the Middle East. Two factors held particular importance. First, in the context of the Gallipoli Campaign, Czar Nicholas II made clear his expectation that control of Constantinople would pass to Russia upon conclusion of the war—a concession to which the British and French reluctantly agreed. This prompted the British to consider, in turn, what they should demand by way of Ottoman territories after hostilities ceased. To that end, Herbert Henry Asquith's government formed a committee under the leadership of Sir Maurice De Bunsen of the Foreign Office to determine Britain's strategic interests in the Middle East and make recommendations as to British war aims in the region.

In its report of June 1915, the De Bunsen Committee reaffirmed the importance of maintaining the Persian Gulf as a British sphere of influence for the land defense of India and called for the annexation of Basra. But the committee also recommended an additional objective: control of Mesopotamia all the way north through Baghdad to Mosul. By 1915 it was widely suspected that these lands held massive petroleum reserves,[15] which the committee, in conjunction with the Admiralty, argued would prove vital to British naval power in the future. Given the Royal Navy's unexpected and skyrocketing demand for petroleum as the war waged on, "the hypothetical oil of Iraq was rapidly becoming an asset that none of the British officials concerned could ignore." Although no immediate action was taken to occupy these regions, the De Bunsen recommendations did factor into the secret Sykes-Picot negotiations with France that began in December 1915 and resulted in an agreement on the partition of the Ottoman Empire in May 1916. Concurrently, a group of geologists from APOC prospecting in southern Iraq confirmed that sizable petroleum deposits existed in the area.[16] In the final draft of the Sykes-Picot Agreement, Britain ultimately laid claim to Mesopotamia up through Baghdad; Mosul, however, was ceded to France. This oversight would come back to haunt the British in postwar negotiations.

The second factor that laid the foundation for a change in Britain's Middle East war aims was the fall of Asquith's government in December 1916, and the rise of a coalition government under David Lloyd George. The new prime minister was much more hawkish than his predecessor and escalated the war by ordering a new offensive against the Ottomans in early 1917. He also brought in advisers sympathetic to the Admiralty's evolving views on the significance of oil to naval power. The most important was Maurice Hankey, whom Lloyd George appointed as secretary of the newly formed War Cabinet. A former captain in the Royal Fleet, Hankey had served on the De Bunsen Committee and strongly favored expansion into oil-rich Ottoman territories.[17] Arthur Balfour, Lloyd George's choice for the position of secretary of state for foreign affairs, also had navy ties, having served as first lord of the Admiralty under Asquith's government from May 1915 to December 1916. Yet another strong advocate of conquering Mesopotamia, Lord George Nathaniel Curzon, was appointed chairman of the Middle East Committee and thus given authority over all matters within the region. Therefore, by the start of 1917, the highest levels of the British government were stacked with men predisposed toward making control of oil a major war aim.

In sum, while oil was viewed as important by the British government during this period, it represented one of many competing considerations associated with Middle East policy. It did not trump other concerns, nor does it appear that the British government understood oil to be unique among raw materials useful for war. Although certain members of the Admiralty foresaw that a lack of petroleum could pose difficulty for the Royal Navy, especially if supply at a reasonable cost could not be guaranteed over the life span of newly built vessels, even they failed to fully appreciate the political vulnerability Britain faced.

The Blockade

Everything changed in February 1917, when Germany strengthened its blockade of Great Britain by resuming unrestricted submarine warfare against merchant shipping in the North Atlantic. The Germans had tried this tactic on a much smaller scale in 1915, but the backlash it provoked from the United States and other neutral countries forced them to abandon the campaign. By the start of 1917, however, Germany was so desperate to end the war that its leaders were willing to run grave risks. Targeting raw material shipments crucial to Britain's war effort, they believed, offered Germany the best chance of forcing Great Britain to the negotiating table. The Germans fully recognized that the resumption of unrestricted U-boat warfare would bring the United States into the war against Germany, but they gambled that if they could interdict enough tonnage, they could knock Britain out of the war before the Americans could mobilize. The bet almost paid off.

Fuel Shortages Cripple the Fleet

The tightened blockade threw the British armed forces into a crisis almost immediately. Of all the materials Great Britain lost to U-boat torpedoes, petroleum did the greatest damage to its war machine, and the Germans soon went out of their way to target fuel tankers and oilers. By 1917, Britain was relying on the United States for nearly 90 percent of its total petroleum needs.[18] American oil, of course, had no other way to reach Britain than by sea, and therefore it was entirely vulnerable to German submarine attacks.

Petroleum shortages emerged in early spring and grew increasingly severe each month. Civilian rationing was imposed; yet the real danger the blockade posed was to Britain's military power. Nearly all of the oil imported by Great Britain went directly to the armed forces. As J. C. Clarke, an Admiralty official, reported to the War Cabinet at the height of the crisis in July 1917, the Royal Navy "was practically the sole user of oil fuel in this country."[19] Tanker losses caused stockpiles of fuel oil to plummet from five months' consumption in February to two months' in May.[20] By summer, the situation was precarious. Admiralty reports described Britain's position as "very grave" and recommended "strictly limiting the speed of all oil-burning vessels of the Fleet, except in the gravest emergency," as well as the "limitation of Fleet movements to the utmost possible extent."[21] The

Admiralty similarly told British officials in Washington, "The Navy Fuel situation is giving us the greatest anxiety and we are within measurable distance of seeing the Fleet immobilized."[22]

Uncomfortable Dependence on the "Goodwill of the USA"

The British had little choice but to make desperate entreaties to the United States for emergency shipments of petroleum. Fuel shortages were so acute that British and French leaders warned that they might be forced to negotiate an end to the war with Germany if something was not done immediately to ensure the delivery of American oil. "The Germans are succeeding," reported the U.S. ambassador in London in July. "They have lately sunk so many fuel oil ships, that this country may very soon be in a perilous condition—even the Grand Fleet may not have enough fuel. . . . It is a very grave danger."[23] That same month, Arthur Balfour, the foreign secretary, sent a cable to Alfred Harmsworth, Lord Northcliffe, the British commissioner in the United States, informing him that the British fleet would be immobilized by September unless three hundred thousand additional tons of oil could be obtained from the United States. Balfour cited two reasons for the crisis: the Royal Navy's soaring demand for petroleum combined with the loss of oil tankers to German U-boats.[24]

Although Britain's coercive vulnerability was severe, pursuing a direct control strategy to remedy the situation was impossible at the height of the crisis for three main reasons. First, British forces could barely keep the Germans at bay on the western front, precluding any realistic chance of opening a new campaign to capture oil resources. Second, there was no readily attainable oil to be found. Global production was already dominated by distant great powers—namely, the United States and Russia—or countries within their spheres of influence.[25] Third, and most important, the mistake had already been made. Britain's weakness at the time reflected a failure to anticipate before the war just how quickly oil would supplant coal during the course of the conflict. Had Britain acted more strenuously to secure supplies before the war, perhaps it could have avoided such a situation through anticipatory measures; but by the summer of 1917 that opportunity had passed. In fairness to the British, anticipating the threat was probably impossible. No one foresaw just how much oil would be needed to fight, both because World War I was the first major mechanized conflict and because its conduct turned out to be unprecedented in scale. Perhaps more to the point, oil coercion had never been attempted before, and therefore states had not fully grasped the consequences. The British experience let the proverbial cat out of the bag, revealing to all the great powers the significance of the new threat.

Ultimately, Britain squeaked through the crisis thanks to three factors. The most important was the emergency delivery of additional oil from the United States, which more than doubled oil exports to the United Kingdom from 1.33 million tons in 1916 to 2.75 million tons in 1917. Harsh conservation measures adopted by the Royal Navy, including speed restrictions and a virtual grounding of the fleet, also played a role. Finally, the development of the convoy system curtailed losses to German submarines.[26] By early 1918, the worst had passed.

Britain narrowly escaped coming to terms with Imperial Germany, but the near miss shook up those in the highest echelons of government and convinced leaders that Britain could not be caught unprepared again. It was not lost on officials that the primary reason Britain survived the U-boat campaign was "the goodwill of the USA" in providing emergency oil supplies.[27] This near-total dependence on the United States raised alarming questions. What if in the next war the Americans did not rush to the rescue? After all, the country had deep isolationist tendencies. Could Britain really count on another nation, even an ally, to come through in a crisis? The British now understood that petroleum was too vital a resource to depend on others for access. The growing voices in the Admiralty finally had an opportunity for advocating strong anticipatory policies to prevent Britain from falling victim to oil coercion in the future. They were pushing on an open door.

The Slade Memo: A New Course for British Grand Strategy

In the months following the petroleum crisis, the Admiralty went to work determining what steps needed to be taken to reduce the country's vulnerability. In July 1918, they released a lengthy memorandum explaining the threat of oil coercion and sketching the foundation of a grand strategic plan for protecting Great Britain from it. This memo, written by Admiral Sir Edmond Slade, would guide decades of British strategy.

Slade's memo demonstrated a clear understanding of Britain's high vulnerability, which would worsen in future wars, and explained the need for strategic anticipation. British naval security, Slade argued, relied on the control of oil. Because the superior performance of oil-burning vessels was quickly rendering coal obsolete, Britain had no choice but to fuel its navy with petroleum—despite lacking domestic oil resources. "The gradual substitution of Oil for Coal will in the future," Slade warned, "wrest from our grasp one of the principal factors on which the maintenance of our Naval position depends. . . . It is no exaggeration to say that our life as an Empire is largely dependent upon our ability to maintain the control of bunker fuel." As a result, Slade argued, "it is consequently of paramount importance to us to obtain the undisputed control of the greatest amount of Petroleum that we can. This control must be absolute and there must be no foreign interests involved."[28]

Heightening the urgency, Slade noted that Britain's traditional sources of supply were facing steep decline. Before World War I, Britain received 62 percent of its petroleum from the United States, 12 percent from Romania, 8 percent from Russia, 8 percent from the Dutch colonies, and 4 percent from Mexico. Yet for a variety of reasons, Britain would not be able to count on these sources in the future. Slade cited official reports from the U.S. Department of the Interior indicating that American oil fields were in serious decline, with perhaps as little as twenty years of U.S. domestic consumption remaining. According to Slade, the situation was creating "a great deal of anxiety in the States." He predicted that within the next decade, "the amount of Petroleum that we shall be able to draw from the United States will be greatly diminished if not entirely stopped," not least because American officials would attempt to conserve oil resources for as long as possible and earmark them for domestic consumption. In Russia, political turmoil made it very unlikely that Russian oil fields would produce enough oil for an exportable surplus. Romania, having surrendered to the Central Powers in May 1918, had effectively fallen under enemy control. Even if it regained its commercial independence after the war, British experts believed that the Romanian oil industry would soon decline, leaving little to no surplus for export. Mexican oil would likely be consumed by the United States given its geographical proximity and the deep American involvement in Mexico's petroleum industry. Finally, total production in the Dutch East Indies would be far too small to supply British needs.[29]

To make matters worse, Slade contended, the tight supply situation likely to emerge in the future would prompt aggression from Britain's oil-importing rivals, which would similarly struggle to maintain access. "It is therefore clear that competition will be most severe," especially from Germany, which "will hesitate at nothing that will prevent the control of liquid fuel from passing into our hands and will endeavor by every means in her power to secure it for herself.... Germany recognizes the great strategic importance of securing a dominating position in the control of oil supplies.... We must take prompt action if our oil position is to be safeguarded."[30]

Only the Middle East, believed to hold vast petroleum resources, could provide enough oil for future British needs in an age of oil-powered navies. "It is evident that the Power that controls the oil lands of Persia and Mesopotamia," Slade argued, "will control the source of supply of the majority of the liquid fuel of the future... and will be in a position to dictate its own terms to all shipping in case of war." Strengthening British naval power was the only solution for defeating future blockade attempts and defending the far-flung empire. Although Middle East oil was far away and could reach the British Isles only by sea, direct control would boost the capabilities of the Royal Fleet, already the world's preponderant navy, to defend its supply lines from weaker foes such as Germany. Furthermore, Britain could use its exclusive control to ban sales of Mideast oil to rivals—extending its relative advantage even more. Therefore, Slade concluded that Britain must establish exclusive control over Middle East oil "at all costs" to secure its military position and "enjoy all the advantages that this will give us if we find ourselves forced into another war."[31]

Evidence suggests that Slade's memo had a direct impact on British policy. Maurice Hankey, the secretary of the War Cabinet who had sat on the De Bunsen Committee, found Slade's memo compelling and made certain it crossed the desks of the most powerful principals in Lloyd George's government. He personally forwarded the memo to Prime Minister Lloyd George; to Arthur Balfour, the secretary of state for foreign affairs; and to Eric Geddes, who was then serving as the first lord of the Admiralty.[32] Now that defeat of Germany appeared inevitable—the "black day of the German army" famously lamented by Erich Ludendorff had occurred on August 8—time was of the essence for Britain to make its move in the Middle East before the severe competition foreseen by Slade could come to pass.

On the eve of the pivotal Imperial War Cabinet meeting to revisit British war aims in the Middle East, Hankey lobbied hard in favor of conquering oil-rich Mesopotamian territory beyond the current British lines. Balfour was a critical target because he was slated to give a speech at the meeting. Hankey wrote to Balfour: "As I understand the matter, oil in the next war will occupy the place of coal in the present war.... The only big potential supply that we can get under British control is the Persian and Mesopotamian supply. The point where you come in is that the control over these oil supplies becomes a first-class British war aim. I write to urge that in your statement to the Imperial War Cabinet you should rub this in." Balfour scribbled "I entirely agree" on his copy of Hankey's cover letter.[33]

At the meeting, Balfour echoed Hankey's concerns and advocated for reopening the Mesopotamian campaign in order to seize petroleum resources. "I do not care under what system we keep the oil, whether it is by a perpetual lease or whatever it may be," Balfour argued, "but I am quite clear it is all-important for us that this oil should be available." This represented a major change in Balfour's thinking compared with the start of the war, when he believed annexing Mesopotamia would be a mistake. Lloyd George agreed with Balfour's new conclusions. Thus, the Imperial War Cabinet decided to occupy all oil-rich land in Mesopotamia before the war ended—with particular emphasis on capturing Mosul.[34] Because the Sykes-Picot agreement had shortsightedly ceded Mosul to France, it was imperative that Britain move quickly to create "facts on the ground" to gain leverage in postwar negotiations over the city's final status. Thus began a race against time for British forces to advance as far up the Tigris as possible before peace could be concluded with Turkey. By the time an armistice was signed with the Ottomans on October 30, British forces were still several miles outside Mosul. Aware that time had run out, they nevertheless pushed on, capturing the city days after formal hostilities ceased.[35]

Britain's direct control strategy in the Middle East paid off handsomely. Once they officially won their claim to Mosul in exchange for ceding Syria to France at the 1920 San Remo conference, the British had acquired control over vast quantities of petroleum. That year, the oil fields of Mesopotamia were estimated to contain reserves equal to those the United States was estimated to possess—about nine billion barrels.[36] Before the war, only 5 percent of the world's oil production came from territories under British control. But as a direct result of the British Middle Eastern mandate, 50 percent of known global oil reserves were now controlled by British companies.[37] As will be discussed in chapter 6, Britain's new oil prominence provoked serious security concerns in the United States, setting off a major rivalry over petroleum concessions. Nevertheless, through conquest, the British dramatically improved their oil security situation.

5

THE OIL STRATEGIES OF NAZI GERMANY

"Shortage of petrol! It's enough to make one weep."[1] So lamented Erwin Rommel, the German field marshal nicknamed the "Desert Fox," after his defeat in North Africa by British forces at El Alamein in 1942. Dearth of oil famously hampered Germany's military power in the latter half of World War II. When the Soviets broke through at Stalingrad in January 1943, Wehrmacht forces had practically exhausted their fuel supplies.[2] By the final two years of war, large portions of the army and air force could no longer be deployed. "Reports from every German frontline complained of the lack of oil.... Tanks were dug in as artillery. Oil use was rationed to only the most essential operations."[3] Albert Speer, the minister of armaments and a close ally of Hitler, encountered the Tenth Army stationed near the Po River and witnessed a remarkable reminder of the damages the oil shortages had wrought: "a column of a hundred and fifty trucks, each of which had four oxen hitched to it."[4] On the western front, entire army groups dissolved in the face of Allied attacks because the lack of oil rendered them immobile.[5] "There was little petrol and everything moved on foot and in wagons," recounted a German commander who forbade his forces from using gasoline "except in battle."[6] Captured German vehicles were found to have empty oil tanks.[7] The absence of fuel was blamed for the failure of the Ardennes counteroffensive, as well as the Wehrmacht's inability to prevent Russian forces from capturing Silesia.[8] In the east, twelve hundred tanks were immobilized because of the lack of fuel and overrun by Soviet forces at the Baranov bridgehead.[9] "Lack of gasoline in countless local situations was the direct factor behind the destruction or surrender of vast quantities of tanks, guns, trucks, and thousands upon thousands of enemy troops," General Omar Bradley of the U.S. Army reported.[10]

Given this nightmarish ending, it is easy to forget that Germany's oil position was not always so desperate. In fact, as late as December 1941, the Reich possessed adequate supplies to meet its demand—a point that is often obscured by the dramatic tales of shortages during the latter stages of war. While not awash in oil, Germany faced a far more favorable situation than commonly recognized, for several reasons. To begin with, Germany's economic backwardness offered a counterintuitive blessing: slow to motorize, the country still ran predominantly on coal and consumed very little oil compared with other great powers. Second, Germany possessed a small oil industry that had not yet modernized, providing hope that investment in new technologies could rapidly boost output. Third, breakthroughs in coal-to-oil hydrogenation technology in the 1920s opened the possibility for producing synthetic liquid fuels in commercial quantities. Meanwhile, Hitler cobbled together additional productive resources through the absorption of several minor oil-producing regions, including Austria (1938), Western Galicia (1939), and Alsace (1940). Finally, the Reich enjoyed favorable geography that mitigated vulnerability to blockade. Romania and Russia, both major producers at the time, could transport oil to Germany overland.

Consequently, all of Hitler's planning in the run-up to war and through the early phases of conflict sought to meet Germany's demand through self-sufficiency and indirect control, and did this more or less successfully. Hitler switched to a direct control strategy only when his war plans went awry during the winter of 1941–1942 on Russia's frozen steppe. In fact, what makes Nazi Germany such an interesting case is that Hitler did not pursue oil primarily through force. He was arguably the most conquest-obsessed leader of the twentieth century, yet he never conquered Romania, the Reich's most crucial source of oil. In truth, it was unnecessary. Germany was secure enough in oil that Hitler could rely on self-sufficiency and indirect control strategies. Although Hitler probably could have squeezed more oil from Romania through direct control, trade agreements with the country sufficed. Cheaper and less risky anticipatory strategies could meet projected demand, so the führer did not need to undertake costly conquest.

Hitler never annexed Romania, but in June 1941 he famously invaded the Soviet Union, one of the world's foremost oil producers. This has prompted some to suggest that Operation Barbarossa was fought for oil, but this interpretation is unsatisfying.[11] While Operation Blau, the summer 1942 campaign, certainly had the capture of Caspian oil as a central objective, it occurred only because Hitler's plan to quickly knock out the Soviets in 1941 had failed. And, the initial decision to invade the USSR reflected motives that ran much deeper than oil. These included, most importantly, a desire to eliminate the Soviet security threat; Hitler's hatred of Bolshevism; the confiscation of more lebensraum, or "living space," for the Reich; and the addition of Soviet industrial might to the Nazi war machine.[12] The fact that Hitler did not attempt to occupy Soviet oil fields in his initial invasion suggests oil was not his driving goal.

The German experience is especially valuable for theory testing because both explanatory variables change across the Nazi period. The Reich's petroleum deficit fluctuated in terms of needs and haves. Oil needs grew considerably owing to Hitler's massive military and economic buildup, yet domestic conventional oil production also climbed substantially, expanding the Reich's petroleum resources. Meanwhile, the susceptibility of German oil imports to cutoff increased dramatically with the imposition of an Anglo-French blockade in September 1939.

I divide the Nazi Germany case into observations based on the values of the independent variables: the petroleum deficit and the susceptibility of oil imports to interdiction, which together determine the country's degree of coercive vulnerability. When one or both independent variables shift substantially, I consider this the beginning of a new observation, and I expect Hitler's anticipatory strategy to shift in response to Germany's new level of coercive vulnerability. If coercive vulnerability increases, German behavior should shift up to a costlier strategy (for example, from indirect control to direct control). If vulnerability decreases, we should observe Germany shifting down to less costly measures (for example, from indirect control to self-sufficiency). Evidence of shifts that correspond to changes in coercive vulnerability would provide support for the theory. However, if coercive vulnerability changes but German anticipatory measures either do not change or move in the opposite direction than predicted, this would provide evidence against the theory. If vulnerability stays constant but we observe a change in Germany's anticipatory strategy, this also would cast doubt on the theory.

From the beginning of the Nazi regime in March 1933 until its defeat in April 1945, I identify three major turning points: (1) Hitler's announcement of the Four-Year Plan in September 1936; (2) the imposition of an Anglo-French naval blockade against Germany on September 3, 1939; and (3) the shift from blitzkrieg to attrition warfare against the Soviet Union in December 1941. This divides the case into four distinct periods: March 1933–August 1936; September 1936 until September 3, 1939; September 4, 1939, until the end of December 1941; and January 1942 through the end of the war in April 1945.

As a special note, there is an immense literature on Nazi Germany, and nearly every decision Hitler made has been debated extensively. My goal is not to resolve these well-worn debates but to highlight and clarify one particular, misunderstood aspect of his regime: oil policy and its relation to German grand strategy.

Thus, for places where there is dissent, I use the "conventional" view of today but note disagreeing interpretations throughout.

Period I: March 1933–August 1936

When Hitler assumed power in March 1933, Germany's economy was in shambles. Economic growth had remained stagnant during the 1920s, even as other industrialized countries had bounced back from the devastation of World War I. GDP per capita in Germany lagged behind that of the United States, France, and Britain throughout the 1920s.[13] So did German wages, which did not rebound to pre–World War I wage levels until the end of the decade.[14] Worse, the Great Depression hit Germany disproportionately hard. From 1929 to 1933, roughly 40 percent of full-time German workers lost their jobs, compared with 25 percent in the United States.[15] It was in this context that the Nazi party came to power on its campaign promise of "Bread and Work."[16]

Although Hitler privately intended to rearm Germany and favored strategic self-sufficiency in raw materials, having lived through the devastating effects of the Anglo-French blockade during World War I, his policies from 1933 to 1936 necessarily focused foremost on reversing the country's grim economic fortunes. He accomplished this through a variety of economic stimulus programs designed to both stabilize the economy and build general industrial capacity that he could later use for war. These efforts focused on building employment in the civilian economy, rather than in the military sector, with the majority of work-creation funds devoted to civilian public works projects such as home construction, road building, and bridge repair.[17] From December 1932 through the end of 1935, the regime spent over 4 billion reichsmarks on work-creation programs alone, which at their peak in March 1934 directly employed over 630,000 full-time workers.[18] The goal, of course, was to put people to work on projects with spillover effects that would stimulate private investment long after the work-creation programs had finished. In addition, the government worked to increase private investment by lowering interest rates, increasing liquidity in the credit market, and extending tax relief and subsidies for new investment in the agricultural and industrial sectors.[19] Finally, the regime instituted price controls to prevent inflation.[20]

What Hitler did not do in this period was make a concerted, coherent effort to reduce Germany's coercive vulnerability in oil. This is not to say that Hitler did nothing in the oil realm during his first few years in office, but simply that his behavior is difficult to distinguish from domestic economic stimulus. Nazi policies affected the German oil position in three ways. First, some stimulus funds were used to expand conventional German oil production. Second, moderate assistance was given to the finically distressed chemical giant IG Farben as it developed synthetic fuel technology. Third, Hitler invested heavily in the motorization of Germany as a bootstrap to lift the economy out of depression. Notably, motorization actually *increased* German vulnerability by expanding domestic consumption of oil.

Low Vulnerability: Germany's Surprising Oil Security

Germany experienced a relatively low petroleum deficit in this period for several reasons. First, civilian needs were minor. The economy relied overwhelmingly on coal, which made up 97 percent of total energy consumption, and in which Germany was a net exporter.[21] This made Germany the least oil dependent of the great powers. Liquid fuels consumption per capita was remarkably low—only 12 gallons a year, compared with 33 gallons per person in the USSR, 36 in France, 52 in Britain, and 267 in the United States. Largely this reflects the slowness of the country to motorize compared with its rivals. In 1933, there were only nine motor vehicles for every one thousand Germans, whereas Britain had forty-three vehicles per thousand of population, France had forty-seven and the United States had two hundred.[22]

Military needs also were small. Owing to the military limitations imposed on Germany by the Treaty of Versailles, the German military was virtually nonexistent. The peace agreement ending World War I circumscribed German military power by limiting the size of the military forces, forbidding the acquisition of certain types of weapons such as heavy artillery, tanks, and submarines, and imposing a demilitarized zone in the Rhineland.[23] Consequently, the German army consisted of just one hundred thousand men, roughly equal to Czechoslovakia's military forces and half the size of Poland's.[24]

On the "haves" side of the equation, Germany possessed a small oil industry in the northwest part of the country that had tantalizing possibilities for new discoveries. Production was tiny (just 240,000 tons in 1933), though this met almost 10 percent of demand, given how little petroleum Germany consumed. But the future appeared bright. While we know today that Germany never possessed large reserves, in the 1930s the future was wide open. The country had never conducted a systematic geological survey, so the full extent of its resources was unknown. It is important to remember that the global oil situation of the time differed profoundly from that of today. Many of the world's largest reservoirs, including the great oil fields of Saudi Arabia, lay undiscovered. Countries with no history of petroleum production were striking oil for the first time. Neighboring Austria was among them, in 1930.[25] That same year, the largest reserve then discovered—the East Texas Oilfield—gushed to life, containing more oil than the twenty largest U.S. oil fields combined.[26] Germany itself enjoyed the thrill of a new discovery at Thuringia in 1931. The first new oil field found in over a decade, Thuringia "opened up vast new prospects along the south margin of the North German Plain . . . [prompting] German authorities to realize that there was probably more oil in the Reich than was generally supposed."[27] Although no one expected to find reserves on par with Russia or the United States, optimism pervaded that Germany could boost its production significantly.

Vulnerability to interdiction was moderate. Germany lacked the military wherewithal to resist any attempts to interrupt imports, but there was no realistic threat of disruption on the horizon because outside powers had no burning reason to intervene. Hitler cooperated with his neighbors during the first few years of his regime. Rearming in secret and avoiding open provocation, the führer did not publicly breach the Versailles agreement until introducing conscription in March 1935. More aggressive steps, such as remilitarizing the Rhineland, would not occur until 1936. Additionally, geography played to the Reich's advantage. Although some 70 percent of German oil imports came from the Western Hemisphere, making them vulnerable to blockade, sources from continental Europe could replace them. Romania, for instance, produced six million tons of exports annually—more than enough to meet the Reich's tiny demand.[28]

Stimulus Meets Self-Sufficiency

In its first three years, the Nazi regime pursued only two types of self-sufficiency measures: subsidies to increase domestic conventional oil production, and government investment in synthetic fuels research and development. The extent to which these measures reflect strategic anticipation, however, as opposed to domestic motives to combat unemployment and build general productive capacity is not clear. Germany did not begin stockpiling oil in large quantities until 1936. Conservation was not pursued—in fact, quite the opposite occurred. Hitler launched a motorization program that actually *increased* consumption, potentially worsening coercive vulnerability.

Under Hitler, the government began modest investments in conventional oil production and scaling up emerging technologies for converting coal into synthetic gasoline. To encourage the discovery of new oil fields, the government offered 50 million reichsmarks in cheap loans to defray exploratory drilling costs, causing annual drilling to more than double from 1933 to 1936.[29] It also created a national geological service and undertook the first modern survey of German petroleum resources. From 1933 to 1945, the Central Geological Survey and its predecessor organizations identified some two hundred promising areas for exploration, and through subsequent drilling, discovered twenty-five new oil fields.[30]

Second, Hitler also helped save the domestic chemical conglomerate IG Farben, whose risky gamble on coal-to-oil hydrogenation technology had put it on the financial precipice. It is unclear, however, whether Hitler helped Farben because he viewed hydrogenation as a strategic godsend or because he was simply trying to prevent the failure of a major German company at a time of economic crisis. Pioneered by the German chemist Friedrich Bergius in 1909, hydrogenation was capable of producing synthetic oil from coal, a substance Germany possessed in large quantities. In the 1920s, IG Farben began experimenting with the technology in hopes of finding a way to produce commercial quantities of synthetic fuel at a competitive price. From 1926 to 1932, the company invested 100 million reichsmarks to build its first major hydrogenation plant at Leuna, but it encountered major problems scaling up the technology, doubling production costs over the original projections. A more devastating surprise was the emergence of a global oil glut that caused prices to plummet by 70 percent over the five years it took to get large-scale production going, leaving Farben with a break-even cost ten times higher than the market price.[31]

By this point Farben was teetering on the edge of ruin. The company's sole lifeline was a high tariff on imported oil, which was extremely unpopular and strongly condemned by the Nazi party. When Heinrich Bruning's government collapsed in late 1932, paving the way for a Nazi takeover, the directors of IG Farben feared their lifeline would be withdrawn and initiated a meeting with Hitler in November 1932 to persuade him to leave the tariff in place.[32] He obliged, but took no further action to assist the company. Some scholars suggest that Hitler attended the meeting because he already believed that synthetic fuel was necessary to protect Germany from blockade and wanted to build a strong relationship with IG Farben, but others doubt that Hitler saw much potential in hydrogenation in 1932 and argue instead that he continued the tariff to prevent a major chemical company employing thousands of Germans from going under.[33] The following year, the Nazi government went one step further with the Feder-Bosch contract, which offered price controls and a guaranteed market for synthetic fuel in exchange for a commitment by Farben to expand production to 350,000 tons annually by the end of 1935. This agreement is generally interpreted as evidence that Hitler was already pursuing fuel self-sufficiency through synthetics but could also be explained as further measures to reduce unemployment and conserve foreign exchange by lowering petroleum imports.[34]

Motorization: The Opposite of Conservation

A third program adopted by Hitler involving oil is difficult to account for with the theory: Hitler's quest to motorize the civilian economy, which boosted oil consumption and actually *decreased* self-sufficiency. Why did Hitler do this? At least three reasons seemed to be at work. First, the main motive behind the effort was to use motorization to bootstrap the civilian economy into recovery.[35] The auto industry, Hitler recognized, was uniquely positioned to stimulate growth across the whole economy because of its many linkages across sectors. Stimulus occurred on three levels. On the first level, policies to encourage motorization obviously provided a direct stimulus to the automobile industry by increasing demand for cars, spare parts, drivers, mechanics, roads, and bridges. Estimates suggest that by 1935, one million new jobs were created in these industries alone.[36] As a secondary effect, motorization raised demand for a broader range of manufactures used in auto production, such as steel, glass, rubber, lubricants, conventional and synthetic fuels, and even textiles. A tertiary economic boost came from the qualitative improvement in transportation, which allowed goods and passengers to move more quickly and efficiently. Altogether, motorization was arguably the single most important catalyst for Germany's economic recovery from 1933 to 1936, even more important than rearmament.[37]

The second reason Hitler sought to motorize the civilian economy was his personal love for automobiles, which he viewed as symbols of prosperity and modernization. Expanding car use would improve the German quality of life, which had long trailed living standards of the country's Western competitors. Finally, manufacturing automobiles would help build the general industrial capacity that could someday be used for war. Plants used to build cars for civilian consumers could later be adapted to build military vehicles, for example. Even something as simple as increasing the number of German civilians who knew how to drive cars would be useful for military purposes once rearmament was under way.

All told, the first few years of Nazi rule focused foremost on regime consolidation and economic recovery. Oil played a role in this as a means of supporting the automobile industry, which Hitler hoped would stimulate the economy, and as a means of direct employment in the conventional and synthetic fuels industries. Strategic anticipation did not begin in earnest until 1936, however, when economic stabilization allowed Hitler to turn his attention to war preparations and the problem of Germany's oil supplies.

Period II: 1936–1939

The year 1936 was a major turning point for the Nazi regime, marking a transition in policy focus from immediate economic stimulus to Hitler's broader strategic goals. Several things had changed since Hitler assumed power. Most notably, the German economy had recovered enough to reach full employment.[38] In a few short years, the Nazi regime had dramatically turned the country's economic fortunes around. Second, in March, Hitler remilitarized the Rhineland over the protests of Britain and France and in direct contravention to the Versailles agreement—providing cause for an intervention, though a military response seemed unlikely. Third, economic preparations for war began in earnest under the Four-Year Plan announced in September. The plan itself was spurred by a fourth development: the major foreign exchange crisis that rocked the economy in early 1936, causing severe shortages of raw materials such as food and petroleum. The crisis prompted the first comprehensive survey of Germany's raw materials position in light of plans for rapid growth in the size of the armed forces. While oil was not the only subject of the study, Nazi officials placed special emphasis on measuring oil needs and haves—in other words, on estimating the petroleum deficit. The projections set in motion efforts that would lead to the development of a new agency for economic planning under the leadership of Hermann Göring, head of the Luftwaffe. In doing so, they formed the basis for Hitler's calculations of German coercive vulnerability and his decision to pursue the anticipatory strategy of self-sufficiency.

Foreign currency shortages had plagued the Nazi regime from its beginnings. The fundamental problem arose from the disjuncture between growing demand for agricultural and industrial imports, which was spurred partly by economic recovery but also by government price controls that distorted domestic markets, and German export weakness perpetuated by trade protectionism abroad. However, several factors conspired to turn the chronic problem into an acute crisis from late 1935 to early 1936. One was the poor harvest of the fall of 1935, which necessitated an increase in food imports. Another cause was Hitler's rearmament program, which boosted demand for foreign raw materials, from wool and leather for military uniforms to oil, iron ore, and alloys for munitions and equipment—all of which had to be purchased in foreign currency.[39] On top of this, the amount of foreign exchange necessary to buy oil was about to increase, with both the Soviet Union and Romania changing the terms for their oil exports to Germany. Russia would now accept only foreign currency as payment, while Romania demanded either foreign currency or a higher price for its oil in marks.[40] Competing demands for scarce foreign currency created shortages in goods ranging from meat, butter, and eggs to oil, rubber, copper, and lead.[41] Economic growth slowed, pushing the economy back into unemployment and jeopardizing rearmament plans, with conditions expected to worsen by year-end.

By the spring of 1936, Hitler's economic and military advisers were scrambling to find solutions. Short-term fixes, such as tapping into grain reserves, were authorized, but the long-term problem appeared intractable as the most obvious options—restricting food or armaments imports—were rejected by the führer. One stopgap measure in particular revealed the degree of desperation for foreign currency: Germany began exporting military matériel to balance its books.[42] But this could not nearly overcome projected deficits. That summer, Göring commissioned a research team under the supervision of Carl Krauch, the number-two executive at IG Farben, to study the problem. By August, the team concluded that only an import-substitution policy could resolve the crisis. Germany would have to quickly build up domestic industries to produce substitutes for needed materials wherever possible to avoid exhausting its currency reserves.[43] Self-sufficiency appealed to Hitler, who endorsed Göring's findings and developed the Four-Year Plan to prepare the economy for war by 1940.[44]

Hitler's Petroleum Deficit

Although several important factors changed from 1933 to 1936, German coercive vulnerability remained low. Understanding the petroleum deficit requires comparing Hitler's strategic goals with his anticipated needs.

The führer came to power with grand ambitions for German territorial expansion. His ultimate goal was to obtain "living space" in the East to encourage population growth among ethnic Germans, whom he viewed as "racially superior" to all other peoples.[45] This was to come at the expense of the Soviet Union, a country that Hitler both reviled and feared.[46] Hitler coveted Russian territory primarily for its abundant agricultural land. He was preoccupied with quasi-Malthusian notions about agricultural productivity as a limit to population growth. Moreover, having lived through the Anglo-French blockade in World War I, which caused widespread starvation, Hitler believed self-sufficiency in food production was paramount to national survival and could be achieved only by acquiring Soviet territory up to the Ural Mountains.

However, in 1936, Hitler knew Germany was too weak to challenge the USSR. Therefore, in the short term, his goal was to strengthen the Reich through economic growth, rearmament, and the incremental conquest of neighboring weak states in Central and Eastern Europe, such as Austria, Czechoslovakia, and Poland. Combining the resources of these states would put Germany on firmer footing to compete with the Soviet Union. Ideally, Hitler hoped to achieve this with coercive diplomacy—threatening military action unless his demands for territory were met. But he was also willing to take territory by force in a series of short wars, if necessary. Each country had a weak military that was small, poorly trained, and nonmechanized. Hitler reasoned that if he could win fast enough, which seemed likely, he could fuel the wars with petroleum stocks alone. As long as the war finished before stocks depleted, he could finesse the flow problem: that the Wehrmacht would likely consume oil at a faster rate than Germany could produce it. After the war, military demand would return to normal levels. Thus, he needed only short-term supply windfalls to fight quick campaigns.

The problem, Hitler understood, was that expansion risked provoking war with Britain and France, which the Reich was unready to fight. If conquering Central and Eastern European countries triggered a conflict, Britain and France would almost certainly impose an embargo and naval blockade on Germany, as they had during World War I with devastating effects. Thus even as Hitler planned for limited wars against minor powers, he sought to postpone any escalation to a European great power war.

The person responsible for compiling military and civilian oil estimates was General Georg Thomas, the key Wehrmacht official on matters of rearmament and economic mobilization. He was also the most outspoken among Hitler's generals in criticizing the blitzkrieg concept of war. Thomas argued that any major European conflict was likely to become a prolonged war of attrition—a "total war"—resembling World War I. He worried Hitler's approach would push Germany into a long war its limited natural resource base could not support. Given this, Thomas advocated immediate and total economic mobilization as the only way forward.[47]

Unsurprisingly, Thomas's office presented the situation pessimistically. In March 1936, it estimated that at current force sizes, Germany would need about three million tons of petroleum annually to wage total war, taking into account both military and essential civilian requirements. If Germany mobilized in 1938, considering plans to expand the military, it would need about five million tons per year. Domestic German oil production, which was increasing, could satisfy 30 percent of 1936 needs and 40 percent of 1938 needs—not insignificant, but not enough.[48] This left a deficit of about two million tons per year that would need to be filled with imports. Thomas did not emphasize, however, that if the military maintained its current force strength through 1938, the Reich would come very close to achieving self-sufficiency.[49]

Annual petroleum consumption was a moot point to Hitler, at least in 1936. He agreed the Reich was poorly positioned for a long war and had no intention of fighting one.[50] His strategy of blitzkrieg economized on resources, especially petroleum, in two ways. First, it aimed for quick victory before the German resource base could be exhausted. Second, its force structure was specifically designed to minimize fuel usage by creating a semi-mechanized army. A small number of divisions were fully motorized into Panzer units designed to rapidly penetrate the enemy front and sever its command, control, and supply tentacles in the rear. The bulk of the army relied on marching and animal power, especially horse-drawn carts, which were tasked with slowly catching up to supply the advance. The result was a two-tiered force structure, "one fast and mobile and the other slow and plodding."[51] The "slow and plodding" portion made up about 80 percent of the German army.[52] The relative weakness of Germany's industrial base also may have played a role in thwarting full motorization of the Wehrmacht, but logic and evidence suggest that, of the two, oil posed the greater constraint. For example, recycling could stretch supplies of crucial materials like steel and rubber, which were collected in scrap drives, but because oil is destroyed when used, recycling as a means of fuel conservation was obviously impossible. Furthermore, the fact that Germany bartered industrial output for Romanian and Soviet oil, discussed below, suggests that the country had at least a small surplus of industrial production but did not enjoy such a margin in petroleum.

Thus the great virtue of the two-tiered blitzkrieg strategy was that it allowed Germany to fight quick wars that minimized petroleum usage.[53] Early in the war, it enabled the Germans to finesse their oil limitations when facing semi-mechanized armies like those of Poland, France, and the Soviet Union. But it ultimately failed against the fully motorized forces of the United States, Britain, and the Soviet Union during the latter half of the war.[54] These armies enjoyed superior mobility compared with the Wehrmacht, particularly once the war bogged down into a campaign of attrition.

Despite resistance from his generals, Hitler remained convinced that a blitzkrieg strategy of quick, successive strikes would enable Germany to defeat an opponent in a matter of weeks or months. From this perspective, the Reich would need far less petroleum than Thomas estimated because it would not be engaged in war for a full twelve months. In fact, given that both the Wehrmacht and German private industry held stockpiles of a few months' supply at any given time, it was potentially possible to fight a blitzkrieg war from stocks alone.[55]

Germany produced modest amounts of oil in 1936, but domestic output was expected to improve considerably. Conventional oil production that year was 445,000 tons, up from 238,000 tons in 1933, which was enough to satisfy only about 15 percent of Thomas's projected needs.[56] But, encouraging signs suggested that the petroleum sector would continue to grow rapidly. First, the industry was finally modernizing its technology, adopting methods that had significantly boosted output in other oil-producing countries. It stood to reason that efficiency improvements would yield similar gains in Germany. Second, the coal-to-oil synthetic fuel technology developed by IG Farben in the 1920s was starting to take off. Synthetic fuel production in 1936 was over six hundred thousand tons—an additional 20 percent of Thomas's projections—and IG Farben executives promised a quick scale-up.[57]

Vulnerability to Import Cutoff

Germany's vulnerability to import cutoff from March 1936 to September 3, 1939, was low for two reasons. First, while Hitler recognized that preying on his weak neighbors could precipitate an Anglo-French intervention in the form of a naval blockade, he viewed the possibility as highly unlikely. Britain and France appeared to have little appetite for fighting another major war, and their credibility was in tatters. Despite their stated commitment to collective defense, they had punished violators of the League of Nations' principles haphazardly, if at all. Benito Mussolini's invasion of Abyssinia in October 1935 stood unchecked. Britain and France also backed down repeatedly when challenged by Germany in 1935 and 1936 on significant provisions of the Peace of Versailles, including reparations payments, limits on German military power, and demilitarization in the Rhineland.[58] Second, although 70 percent of Germany's oil imports originated in the Western Hemisphere, and thus were susceptible to blockade, the remaining 30 percent came overland from continental Europe, primarily Romania and Russia.[59] Romanian exports in 1936 amounted to almost seven million tons, while Russia exported three million tons. The resulting ten million tons available from European sources was more than enough to fill Thomas's projected deficit of two million tons.[60]

All told, Hitler faced low coercive vulnerability from March 1936 until September 3, 1939. The petroleum deficit was small. Hitler's expansionist goals risked military conflict that would boost fuel demand, but only briefly because campaigns were expected to be quick. Hitler also believed it likely that his targets would give up without a fight. The risk to German oil imports was also low. At worst, Germany would lose 70 percent of its prewar oil imports to an Allied blockade, but Romania and Russia could potentially replace them. However, Hitler believed Britain and France would stay on the sidelines. In this situation of low coercive vulnerability, the theory predicts Germany should pursue self-sufficiency, which is just what Hitler did.

Anticipatory Measures: The 1936 Four-Year Plan for Self-Sufficiency

In August 1936, Hitler made up his mind on how to solve the Reich's petroleum and natural resource issues. In an untitled memorandum found in Albert Speer's possession at the end of the war (later known as the "Four Year Plan Memo"), Hitler announced a new initiative to make Germany self-sufficient in raw materials within two to four years and put Göring in charge of the program.[61] The resulting "Four Year Plan" placed special emphasis on achieving self-sufficiency in petroleum, focusing especially on measures like boosting domestic conventional production, investing in alternative fuels, and stockpiling oil in a strategic reserve. Together, the conventional and synthetic oil industries attracted more funding than any other sector—composing over 60 percent of government investment for raw materials under the plan.[62] Increased investment was expected to boost annual petroleum production to six million tons (conventional and synthetic) by 1940.[63] Extensive government subsidies were offered to encourage exploration and nearly doubled the yearly number of oil wells drilled over 1933 totals.[64] More than 1 billion reichsmarks were allocated to construct ten new coal-to-oil synthetic fuel plants; by September 1939, Germany had fourteen plants operating at full capacity and an additional six under construction.[65] Finally, a strategic petroleum reserve of 2.2 million tons had been amassed by the time Germany invaded Poland.[66]

Period III: September 3, 1939–December 1941

The Anglo-French naval blockade, announced September 3, 1939, in reaction to the invasion of Poland on September 1, raised Germany's coercive vulnerability to moderate. This is because the blockade was highly threatening to German imports, cutting off all supplies from the Western Hemisphere.[67] Hitler had miscalculated, finally pushing Britain and France too far.[68] Although Romanian and Russian oil remained accessible, in an unforeseen twist, the export capacity of both countries had fallen. Romanian oil production had peaked in 1936 and was entering a period of decline; as a result, exports decreased to four million tons in 1939. Soviet oil production was expanding, but not enough to keep pace with domestic demand, leaving less than one million tons available for export.

Fortunately for the Germans, the petroleum deficit remained small enough to be met by the lower level of European exports, assuming Romania and the USSR stayed friendly to Germany. Needs changed little, despite the Anglo-French declaration of war. This was "war" in name only; neither Britain nor France launched a substantial ground campaign in Poland's defense (hence the "Phony War" epithet). Meanwhile, the speedy rout of Poland reinforced Hitler's faith in blitzkrieg, and thus his belief that territory could be won quickly and with a small amount of oil. On the "haves" side, Hitler's autarky campaign under the Four-Year Plan had improved Germany's situation. Total oil output (conventional and synthetic) had doubled in three years to 2.2 million tons, equaling 40 percent of all demand in 1939.[69] Thus, although the susceptibility of imports to interdiction was now high thanks to the blockade, coercive vulnerability increased to only moderate because the petroleum deficit remained low.

As the theory predicts, the increase in German coercive vulnerability from low to moderate prompted a major escalation in anticipatory strategy from self-sufficiency to indirect control through alliances. Hitler did not abandon previous self-sufficiency efforts such as coal-to-oil synthetic production, which had yielded success. But these alone no longer sufficed. Hitler thus resolved to keep European oil producers friendly by solidifying economic pacts with Romania and Russia—the only countries whose exports could travel overland, beyond reach of the blockade.

Romania

With an export capacity superior to that of the USSR, Romania emerged as the most important foreign source of oil to Nazi Germany upon imposition of the blockade. Although the country was officially neutral, interference by Germany's great power rivals put access to Romanian oil in jeopardy. Two threats existed. First, Hitler worried that pressure from Britain and France would undermine Germany's oil trade with Romania. The two countries had long-standing influence in Bucharest owing to their dominance of the Romanian petroleum industry. British and French oil companies owned 75 percent of Romania's oil production, whereas German firms owned less than 1 percent—a result of the World War I peace settlement. Now Britain and France were courting closer ties with Romania through arms sales and security guarantees against German aggression.[70] At the same time, they were buying up Romanian oil through advance purchases designed to block sales to Germany.[71] Second, Romania was under threat of Soviet invasion to reclaim Bessarabia, a former Russian territory ceded to Romania after World War I. Bessarabia itself mattered little to Hitler, as it produced no oil. But any Soviet military action against Romania was dangerous because it could cause collateral damage to oil production—even worse, it might lead to Soviet occupation of the entire country. Given that Hitler still considered the USSR to be an enemy, Soviet consolidation of European oil resources would constitute an existential threat.

Hitler had tried to coax Romania into an alignment with the Axis before the blockade, but his efforts took on new urgency, and achieved greater success, from September 1939 onward. On September 17, Stalin annexed eastern Poland (with secret approval from Germany) and massed troops along the Romanian border. Four days later, Armand Calinescu, Romania's president, was mysteriously assassinated.[72] Meanwhile, Romania watched in fear as Britain and France, which had lobbied hard for a security alliance, sat on the sidelines while the Polish drama unfolded.

Terrified of Soviet expansion, and dubious that the Western powers would live up to their security guarantees, Romanian leaders decided to accommodate

German demands in exchange for protection. Negotiations began before the end of September. Through the process, Germany attained cooperation from the Romanian government to defeat interference from Britain and France. A major concession in December 1939 established export quotas to prevent any country from monopolizing Romanian oil sales, thus guaranteeing German access to exports.[73] The Romanian government also cracked down on other creative measures by outside powers to deny oil to Germany—for instance, the French attempt to commission the entire fleet of barges that transported oil to Germany up the Danube.[74] In May 1940, agreement was reached on a weapons-for-oil pact, whereby Romania pledged to deliver two hundred thousand tons of oil to the Reich per month in exchange for armaments.[75]

In June 1940, a crisis erupted as the Soviet Union threatened war against Romania over the Bessarabian dispute. Behind the scenes, Hitler maneuvered assiduously to prevent a Soviet attack, hinting Germany would not stand idly by if military conflict erupted. He worked out a deal with the Soviets, agreeing to force Romania to cede Bessarabia to the Soviet Union in exchange for Soviet military restraint. To obtain Romanian compliance with the deal, Hitler extended a security guarantee to cover the country's pre–World War I territory, which was significantly smaller than its current size. Squeezed between two great powers, Bucharest had no choice but to accept. In addition to supplying arms and a security commitment, Germany sent a military mission to train Romanian forces—and to deter any Soviet change of heart.[76]

Ultimately, Hitler's alliance strategy paid off. Romania became Germany's largest supplier. Its exports to Germany tripled from 450,000 tons in 1938 to 1.3 million tons in 1939, eventually reaching a height of nearly 3 million tons in 1941.[77]

Russia

No stranger to double-dealing, Hitler also pursued an oil-for-weapons alliance with the Soviet Union in the wake of the blockade. This was not a deep friendship but a marriage of convenience; Hitler intended to turn his sights on the USSR once the Western powers were crushed. In August 1939, Hitler and Stalin had signed the Molotov-Ribbentrop Pact; its fundamental value to Germany was that it would solve the two-front war problem that proved so devastating in World War I. The pact also called for a general expansion of trade relations but left all details to be hammered out later.

The Anglo-French blockade set off frantic German attempts to immediately establish trade terms for importing Soviet oil under the pact. This urgency was underscored by Göring in a Reich Defense Council resolution the following day calling for "the further expansion of our economic relations with Russia . . . as quickly as possible."[78] The Germans attempted all manner of diplomatic maneuvers to get petroleum. For example, on September 20, Joachim von Ribbentrop, the German foreign minister, appealed to change the agreed-upon boundaries of the Polish partition to cede an oil region to Germany instead of the USSR, to no avail. On September 28, the Russians budged somewhat by agreeing to provide a "supplementary quantity of petroleum" from USSR-captured Polish fields to be delivered within a year. The Germans hoped to finalize a more extensive agreement within a few weeks, but the Soviets, aware of their superior bargaining position, dragged out talks for four months.[79] Meanwhile, reports from the military continued to highlight Germany's precarious position in fuel. Army chief of staff Franz Halder reported on September 29, 1939, that Germany did not have enough oil stocks to support a Western offensive.[80] In February 1940, a German Foreign Office report stated that Soviet raw materials were "simply irreplaceable" and warned that "the breakdown of a German-Soviet agreement must be avoided at all costs."[81]

A diplomatic breakthrough on February 11, 1940, secured the terms for the first major Nazi-Soviet economic pact. In short, the deal was "gas and grain for coal and cruisers." The Soviets agreed to export 1 million tons of grain, 900,000 tons of oil, and 500,000 tons of metal ore to Germany, among other items. In exchange, the Germans would provide "massive military support" to the Soviet Union, furnishing coal, machine tools, synthetic material factories, gun turrets, mines, ships, combat aircraft including Dornier-115s, Messerschmidt-110s, and Junker-88s, and various other military equipment. Reaching a settlement was a great relief to Hitler, who in a March 8 letter to Mussolini wrote: "The trade agreement which we have concluded with Russia, Duce, means a great deal in our situation!"[82]

By and large, the Nazis honored their export obligations to the Soviets until the last months before the German invasion of the USSR on June 22, 1941. Göring and Hitler pressured German firms to deliver agreed-upon items to Russia in order to ensure that the Soviets would deliver oil as scheduled. German compliance continued even as Stalin repeatedly raised his demands for German manufactures above the agreed-upon terms. Hitler was so eager to please that he confiscated military equipment directly from Wehrmacht divisions and sent it to Russia in hopes of expediting reciprocal oil shipments, much to the consternation of his officers.[83] "It was hurting the Germans to send material to Russia. At a time when military planners . . . were pointing out the need to build up armaments and transportation, industrial output was being exported. Oil was considered more important."[84] By mid-March 1940, Hitler's policy was, in Göring's words, "where reciprocal deliveries to the Russians are endangered, even German Wehrmacht deliveries must be held back."[85] For the rest of the year, Soviet deliveries were to receive "top priority."[86]

Soviet oil was so crucial to the war effort that Hitler prioritized arming Soviet forces over equipping his own military, despite knowing all along that by doing so, he was strengthening a country he planned to invade the following year. Once Hitler launched his war against the Soviet Union, fighting on the eastern front became an "ironic scene. . . . German soldiers fed by Ukrainian grain, transported by Caucasus oil, and outfitted with boots made from rubber shipped via the Trans-Siberian railroad fired their Donetz-manganese-hardened steel weapons at their former allies. The Red Army hit back with artillery pieces and planes designed according to German specifications and produced by Ruhr Valley machines in factories that burned coal from the Saar."[87] The trade pact dramatically increased Soviet oil exports to Germany. In 1939, the USSR had exported a mere five thousand tons of petroleum to Germany; from February 1940 until Hitler's invasion of the Soviet Union on June 22, 1941, Stalin had delivered nearly one million tons of oil to Germany under the auspices of the trade pact.[88]

Period IV: December 1941–May 1945

Finally, from December 1941 until the end of the war, Germany's coercive vulnerability increased to very high. First, the petroleum deficit skyrocketed upon Hitler's realization in early December that the blitzkrieg had failed, miring Germany in a long war of attrition with the Soviet Union. Such a war would require massive amounts of petroleum for an indefinite period—a level of demand clearly beyond the Reich's resources. Second, oil import vulnerability also increased because, by betraying Stalin, Hitler lost access to one of the two sources of oil not jeopardized by the Allied blockade. The invasion of the Soviet Union did not increase vulnerability to high per se because Hitler expected to defeat the USSR quickly, before the loss of Soviet oil would hamper his ability to fight. But in the context of a war that would drag on, the lack of Soviet imports proved devastating. Of the four most crucial materials the Soviets exported to the Reich—petroleum, grain, manganese, and rubber—petroleum was the only loss the Germans could not replace. Grain was pillaged from the populations of Nazi-occupied lands; manganese and rubber stocks remained sufficient thanks to conservation, rationing, and synthetic rubber production. "Oil was the main obstacle."[89]

Indeed, shortages plagued the German military throughout the ill-fated eastern campaign. Poor Soviet roads and muddy conditions translated into a 30 percent increase in fuel demand over prewar estimates by German military planners.[90] As early as July, large portions of the Luftwaffe had to scale back their operations for want of aviation gasoline. By autumn 1941, Luftwaffe bomber squadrons saw their ready rates decline below 50 percent, and all the way down to 32 percent in December.[91] During the same period, oil shortages at the front and throughout the Reich "threatened to bring the operation to a halt," leaving some portions of the invasion force entirely bereft of supplies.[92] Nor could captured Soviet motor fuel eliminate the problem. Soviet gasoline was too low octane to work in German engines without first undergoing a conversion process.[93] Whereas the Germans could feed their troops and solve other supply problems by looting captured Soviet lands, plunder proved inadequate for fueling the Wehrmacht's gas-starved motor vehicles.

At this stage, Hitler had no choice but to pursue oil through direct control, which he attempted to do by opening a campaign in June 1942 to capture the oil-rich Caucasus—against his generals' advice. "The object is to resume the offensive toward the Caucasus as soon as the weather allows," Hitler told the Japanese ambassador on January 3, 1942. "This is the most important direction for an offensive; we must reach the oil fields there and also in Iran and Iraq."[94] Seizing the Baku oil fields, which produced over twenty million tons of oil annually, would have more than made up for the loss of Soviet oil imports.[95] At the same time, the strategic value of petroleum elevated the capture of Stalingrad to an important, if secondary, objective. Seizing the city would have allowed the Germans to cut off Soviet petroleum commerce along the Volga River, the main route through which Caspian oil traveled to the rest of the Soviet Union. The southern campaign, known as Operation Blau, thus offered a double benefit: the opportunity to ensure continued access to Soviet oil while simultaneously denying it to the Red Army.[96] By then, however, it was too late. The Caucasus campaign failed. German fuel requirements soared beyond the Reich's ability to meet them, contributing to its ultimate defeat.

Even as the Wehrmacht muddled through on the eastern front, drastic measures were taken back home to funnel as much fuel as possible to the military. Germany's economy was still primarily fueled by coal, leaving little extra oil to squeeze from the civilian population.[97] Among other factors, this reflected the country's continued low degree of motorization. Nevertheless, the Germans managed to free up additional quantities of petroleum from the home front and send it to war. By the end of 1943, civilian consumption had been cut to one-tenth of prewar levels, and the German armed forces "consumed practically all liquid fuels."[98] This accomplishment was made all the more impressive by the fact that the diversion of oil to the front caused very little disruption to the domestic economy.[99]

Of course, the situation had forced the Germans to get creative. Hundreds of thousands of commercial trucks and civilian automobiles were converted to run on solid fuels such as coal, timber, and charcoal. Conversion entailed attaching a "producer gas" generator to existing engines and was simple enough that many people did it themselves. Major automobile makers in Germany and Nazi-occupied territories, including Volkswagen and Mercedes-Benz, manufactured their new vehicles to run on solid fuels. By the middle of the war, "producer gas became the 'civilian fuel,'" and over 350,000 alternative-fuel vehicles appeared on German roads.[100] As a result of these efforts, the Reich saved five million tons of liquid fuels in 1942 and eight million tons in 1943—numbers equivalent to roughly a year's worth of prewar petroleum consumption.[101] In the meantime, a new network of coal-powered railways was built in the Ruhr to compensate for the loss of motor transportation; and in Silesia, handcarts were used to fulfill deliveries formerly completed by gasoline-driven engines.[102] In efforts reminiscent of Japan's failed pine root oil campaign, "German inventors scoured Europe's flora for fuel substitutes. The acorn harvest . . . was commandeered to produce a usable oil which was capable of fueling haulage vehicles. European nuts were transformed chemically into a good quality fuel to be used in tanks and trucks."[103]

But these cutbacks did not suffice to supply the German military with the petroleum it required. As early as 1942, the Luftwaffe had seriously curtailed pilot training hours to conserve fuel, and the German army relied on producer-gas-powered trucks and tanks for training purposes.[104] Troops fighting in Russia increasingly depended on alternative fuel vehicles for delivering their supplies, and in some cases, "tanks were driven to the front with detachable producer gas units that were then shipped back to the railhead for use on other tanks."[105]

While the Wehrmacht flailed in the east, the situation only worsened in the west, as the Allies finally began a concerted effort to target the German oil industry in May 1944. Previous attempts by the British to bomb German oil facilities early in the war had failed because the Royal Air Force lacked the means to make air attack precise. By 1944, however, the Americans had acquired the capability to strike ground targets with enough accuracy to cause them serious damage. According to the United States Strategic Bombing Survey, "The effect of this campaign on the already tight German oil supply was catastrophic."[106] Allied air assaults on German synthetic fuel plants commenced on May 12, 1944. "On that day," Albert Speer wrote in his postmortem of Germany's military failure, "the technological war was decided."[107] In fact, the possibility of an Allied attack on the Reich's aviation fuel plants "had been a nightmare to us for over 2 years," Speer admitted after the war.[108] Upon surveying the damage on May 19, he reported to Hitler: "The enemy has struck us at one of our weakest points. If they persist at it this time, we will soon no longer have any fuel production worth mentioning. Our one hope is that the other side has an air force General Staff as scatterbrained as ours!"[109] Speer's wish went unfulfilled. A second wave of attacks took place on May 28–29, and a third had begun in mid-June, with devastating effects.

The Allied bombings set off a vicious circle. Destruction of the hydrogenation plants decreased the amount of aviation fuel available to the Luftwaffe precisely

TABLE 5.1 German synthetic oil production (in thousands of tons)

MONTH	TOTAL SYNTHETIC PRODUCTION	MONTH	TOTAL SYNTHETIC PRODUCTION
January 1944	498	September 1944	152
February 1944	478	October 1944	155
March 1944	542	November 1944	185
April 1944	501	December 1944	164
May 1944	436	January 1945	37
June 1944	298	February 1945	13
July 1944	229	March 1945	12
August 1944	184		

Source: United States Strategic Bombing Survey, *Effects of Strategic Bombing*, 79.

for the purpose of defending the plants from Allied strikes. Even with the "extreme measures" the Germans took in their efforts to repair the facilities,[110] rebuilding a hydrogenation plant took six to eight weeks; at that rate, repairs could not keep pace with the Allies' air campaign.[111] At its low point on June 22, 90 percent of synthetic aviation fuel production had been destroyed (see table 5.1).[112]

For several months, Speer made it his personal crusade to get through to Hitler regarding the severity of the Reich's oil situation. The führer, known for his wishful thinking and stubborn predilection to deny unpleasant facts, refused to face reality. Speer arranged for Hitler to meet with petroleum industry experts, who told him on May 24 that the German situation would be hopeless if airstrikes continued.[113] He authored numerous reports foretelling of military doom in the strongest possible terms. In one such report to Hitler dated June 30, 1944, Speer warned that if Allied raids on synthetic fuel plants occurred in July and August at the same rate as they had in May and June, "inevitably by September this year the supply of the amounts necessary to cover the most urgent requirements of the Wehrmacht will no longer be assured; i.e., from this moment on an impossible situation will arise which must lead to tragic results."[114] He repeatedly urged Hitler to devote more airpower to protecting the plants and dedicate as much manpower as possible to rebuilding efforts. Hitler resisted because he did not want to take resources away from military production. "Obviously he had still not grasped the gravity of the situation," a frustrated Speer recorded in his memoirs. "Again and again, I had explained to him that it would be pointless to have tanks if we could not produce enough fuel." Hitler finally acquiesced to Speer's advice, and by late fall 1944, 350,000 skilled workers had been taken off armaments production lines and reassigned to rebuilding the synthetic plants.[115] It was not enough.

TABLE 5.2 German aviation fuel consumption, 1944 (in thousands of tons)

MONTH	TOTAL FUEL CONSUMPTION	MONTH	TOTAL FUEL CONSUMPTION
January	122	July	136
February	135	August	115
March	156	September	60
April	164	October	53
May	195	November	41
June	182	December	44

Source: United States Strategic Bombing Survey, *Statistical Appendix to Overall Report (European War)* (Washington, DC: U.S. Government Printing Office, 1947), 115–16.

According to an estimate by the Strategic Bombing Survey, lost fuel production directly attributable to the Allied bombings totaled about five million tons in the last year of war.[116] This had a disastrous effect on the military, particularly the Luftwaffe. Synthetic fuel plants provided the Luftwaffe with over 90 percent of its aviation fuel. Aviation fuel consumption plummeted in tandem with the destruction of hydrogenation plants (see table 5.2). By the end of the year, aircraft sat idle on runways, and flight training for new pilots was curbed to an hour per week.[117] The dearth of aviation fuel "gave Allied air forces virtual command of the skies, allowing them to attack Germany's meager oil supply lines at will."[118]

By 1945, severely depleted stocks left the Wehrmacht hamstrung. Large portions of the army and air force could no longer be deployed, leaving Germany with "more tanks and planes than she could possibly use."[119] Nearly all domestic transportation within the Reich was powered by generators, which themselves ran on charcoal, peat, lignite, or timber from leveled buildings.[120]

Despite the indisputable difficulties German military forces encountered, especially in the wake of the Allies' air campaign, Hitler refused to surrender no matter how desperate the situation became. The Allies expected as much and pinned their hopes on a military coup by a small group of officers with whom they were negotiating terms for Germany's surrender. The conspirators believed there was no longer any chance of victory for the Reich, and thus continued resistance would be futile. However, the group's attempt to assassinate Hitler on July 20, 1944—shortly after Allied bombings had decimated German fuel supplies—failed. Meanwhile, public opinion remained a nonissue even in the face of military strikes that reduced entire German cities to rubble. Civilians endured the privations of wartime petroleum rationing, in addition to many other hardships, without demanding capitulation from the government. Although the German case constitutes a failure of oil coercion, it demonstrates just how important oil was to military power. Petroleum was a major reason Germany lost the war. Hitler did not surrender as Western leaders demanded, but a more responsible leader may have.

The case of Germany from 1933 to 1945 provides strong evidence for the theory. Hitler's anticipatory strategies changed over time, in tandem with German coercive vulnerability. In the first three years of the period, the need to stabilize the German economy took precedence over measures to secure access to oil. But as the country recovered, Hitler pursued self-sufficiency strategies to compensate for the Reich's low coercive vulnerability, as the theory predicts. Contra present-day understandings, the German oil position from 1936 until September 1939 was strong enough to meet demand through government investment in the oil industry and the creation of a strategic petroleum reserve. This is because the petroleum deficit was small and the susceptibility of oil imports to enemy military power was low. Germany actually did produce about 35 percent of its own oil needs while Hitler's blitzkrieg strategy permitted him to fight short wars without exhausting petroleum supplies. And while Germany depended significantly on oil imports from the Western Hemisphere, Hitler judged an Anglo-French blockade to be unlikely. When his invasion of Poland finally triggered such a blockade on September 3, 1939, German coercive vulnerability increased to moderate, launching Hitler into diplomatic efforts to keep Romania and Russia, Europe's two major oil exporters, friendly to the Reich. This indirect control strategy succeeded in securing overland access to oil that the blockade could not sever. Hitler resorted to direct control only after the blitzkrieg failed to result in quick victory over the Soviet Union. With German forces marooned indefinitely in attrition warfare in the east, coercive vulnerability increased to high. As the theory predicts, Hitler responded with a new plan to conquer the oil fields of the Caucasus—his last, best chance to obtain the oil his war machine desperately needed. The failure of this campaign sealed the fate of the Third Reich.

6

AMERICAN EFFORTS TO AVOID VULNERABILITY

Vast petroleum resources have long distinguished the United States from the other great powers. The country's staggering dominance in oil dates to the earliest days of commercial production, which itself was pioneered in Western Pennsylvania. The United States ranked as the single largest global producer nearly every year from 1860 until 1960; since then, it has never dropped below the top three in output.[1] In fact, American wells have been so prolific as to account for roughly one out of every five barrels ever taken out of the ground—by far the largest contribution by any one country to cumulative output.[2]

A testament to the inexorable link between oil and American life is the profound degree to which petroleum has suffused nearly all aspects of U.S. culture. Oil is ubiquitous in American storytelling, from Upton Sinclair's classic book *Oil!* (1927), to the hit sitcom *The Beverly Hillbillies* (1962–1971), to J. R. Ewing, the memorable villain of *Dallas* (1978–1991), whose ostensible death in the season three finale unleashed the "Who shot J. R.?" furor of the summer of 1980. So rife was the speculation over Ewing's fate that President Jimmy Carter joked at a Texas fundraiser, "I came to Dallas to find out confidentially who shot J.R. If any of you could let me know that, I could finance the whole campaign this fall."[3] That November, over eighty million Americans, at the time the largest ever viewership in television history, watched the episode that revealed the would-be assassin.[4]

Some of the nation's most venerable institutions would not exist but for the wealth bequeathed by petroleum. Oil money from John D. Rockefeller founded the University of Chicago as well as Spelman College, named for the magnate's wife, Laura "Cettie" Spelman Rockefeller, a devoted abolitionist. Oil financed the art collection that would become the J. Paul Getty Museum in Los Angeles. Oil even saturated major sociopolitical movements, including the midcentury emergence of Christian fundamentalism. On the Southwest frontier, the social circles of evangelicals often overlapped with those of wildcatters—individual oil prospectors whose discoveries and misfortunes shaped the booms and busts of the business. *The Fundamentals*, a Christian journal that defined the precepts of modern evangelicalism, was founded by California oil magnate Lyman Stewart. Billy Graham, perhaps inspired by the several oil tycoons among his congregants at the First Baptist Church in Dallas, featured oil as a plot device for his early films *Mr. Texas* (1951) and *Oiltown, USA* (1953), both moralistic tales of "backslidden businessmen appreciating anew the pristine qualities of Christ and capitalism."[5]

Considering the United States' unparalleled petroleum resources and the overwhelming importance of oil to American life, the natural expectation would be that the United States was immune to oil coercion and would have no need for anticipatory strategies. Yet, close examination reveals otherwise. From 1900 until the mid-1970s, the latest period for which ample declassified material exists, U.S. coercive vulnerability fluctuated several times in response to many factors, including changes in output, reserve estimates, U.S. strategic demands, and the rise and fall of oil-producing allies in geographically diverse areas of the world. Consequently, and in contrast to default expectations, the theory predicts that the United States would adopt a variety of anticipatory strategies in tandem with changes in the petroleum deficit and disruptibility of imports. Such predictions are "risky"—they cut against analytical priors, and therefore would strongly confirm the theory if shown to be accurate.[6] Indeed, as the discussion below shows, American decision makers chose self-sufficiency and indirect control, violating what we might call the "null" hypothesis of no anticipation.

The chapter examines the development of U.S. strategic oil policy chronologically from 1900 until the mid-1970s. It divides the case into seven periods corresponding to the major shifts in the petroleum deficit and threat to oil imports. Five of the periods yield testable predictions based on the theory: the late World War I era (1918–1920), the interwar years (1921–1941), World War II (1941–1945), the early Cold War (1950–1968), and the late Cold War (1969–1975). These are the periods referred to as cases. Importantly, the Cold War cases are more about continuity than change. The main drivers of the petroleum deficit and import vulnerability were the same across the 1950–1968 and the 1969–1975 periods: the U.S. commitment to defend Europe, which meant both a larger petroleum deficit and the need to protect Middle Eastern oil, upon which Western Europe and Japan depended. But because the 1970s are often (erroneously) viewed as a significant turning point in U.S. oil vulnerability—and indeed, the U.S. government did a massive review of the country's vulnerability in 1969–1970—the period is considered separately and in depth. It ends with 1975 because the archival record grows thinner toward the end of the decade.

Two additional eras are discussed but not considered proper cases for the qualitative comparative analysis in chapter 7. The immediate post–World War II period, 1945–1950, is too ambiguous for the theory to generate predictions. Whether the United States would commit to the long-term defense of Western Europe—the single most important factor influencing both the petroleum deficit and the disruptibility of imports—remained an open question. With U.S. goals nebulous, the predicted anticipatory strategy is indeterminate. The other era is the baseline observation of U.S. oil policy from 1900 to 1917, the time just before the importance of oil was fully understood. Because it is outside the temporal scope of the theory, it cannot test predictions; but it serves as a useful reference point for changes in U.S. policy once the problem of oil coercion entered policymakers' thinking.

Baseline U.S. Oil Policy before World War I

Before World War I, the U.S. government took no significant actions to ensure the country's access to oil. This was for two reasons. First, few in the government had fully grasped the military significance of petroleum. The U.S. Army did not begin experimenting with motorization until 1906, fully twenty years after the invention of the automobile, and did not recommend complete motorization of the American armed forces until the 1920s.[7] Army experts simply failed to anticipate the role that motor transport would play in future military contests. Simply put, U.S. political leaders had no concept of either the petroleum deficit or the potential strategic threat that would arise should the country one day rely on oil imports. They were not alone. Before 1918, the great powers simply did not understand the threat.

Second, oil abounded on American territory, such that the petroleum deficit almost certainly would have been zero had U.S. leaders thought to measure it. The United States was the world's largest petroleum producer nearly every year from 1860 to 1914.[8] In fact, major discoveries in California and Texas, including the 1901 eruption of Spindletop, the Western Hemisphere's first gusher well, had increased American production to the point of creating a serious oil glut.[9] Such spectacular discoveries reinforced popular assumptions of unlimited American oil plenty.

Only a few officials in the Navy Department seemed to discern oil's importance before 1914. Experiments with oil-burning vessels in the late nineteenth century had unequivocally demonstrated the superiority of petroleum over coal for powering ships, and by 1904 navy experts had recommended full fleet conversion.[10] The advantages of oil were numerous. Oil boosted top speeds and allowed ships to refuel at sea, freeing them from their tethers to coaling stations and thus increasing their range. Petroleum also burned more cleanly than coal, took up less space because it contained more energy per unit of volume, and lowered manpower requirements by eliminating the need for stokers. Moreover, the navy had kept close tabs on Britain's progress in developing an oil-burning fleet and understood this meant that the United States would have to do the same to remain competitive.[11] In strict performance terms, therefore, converting to oil was the obvious choice.

Yet, despite the clear superiority of petroleum and the department's own internal report advocating fuel conversion in 1904, the navy hesitated in switching to oil for nearly a decade. The reluctance reflected concerns among some navy officials as to the security of future oil supplies. Even though the United States currently led the world in petroleum production, naval planners nevertheless found themselves "plagued by the gnawing fear of a supply failure" in the long term, particularly because the new battleships being built were supposed to last for twenty years.[12] Such fears were not entirely baseless. The first attempt at a comprehensive estimate of domestic reserves was made in 1907 by David T. Day, a respected oil geologist at the United States Geological Survey; he concluded that the country might possess as little as eight billion barrels and suggested the possibility that the United States could exhaust its petroleum supplies within a decade.[13]

Although Day's estimates failed to upend the conventional wisdom of American oil abundance, agitation by navy officials eventually convinced the federal government to designate certain public oil lands as naval reserves. Reserves #1 and #2, both in California and together composing over sixty thousand acres, were granted officially in September 1912.[14] Little else was done.

The navy's attempts to secure naval oil supplies briefly grew more ambitious the following year when Josephus Daniels took office as Woodrow Wilson's secretary of the navy in March 1913. Daniels vigorously supported a complete ban on private drilling on federal oil lands and sought to set aside these territories for exclusive military use. Moreover, he argued that the navy should be given authority over the exploitation of federal petroleum reserves and allowed to run its own drilling and refining operations—in essence, putting the navy in the oil business.[15]

These proposals went nowhere. In fact, the Interior Department quickly and thoroughly disabused Daniels of the notion that U.S. oil production was anything but robust. Shortly after Daniels took office, the approval to construct the new battleship *Nevada* had raised the question yet again of whether it was time for the U.S. Navy to convert to oil. Uncertain whether there would be enough oil for the twenty-year life of the battleship, "Daniels carried his problem to the Interior Department which assured him that the supply of oil was ample and that warning of a failure could be given far enough in advance to secure fuel adequate for the life of the oil-burning ships built or in the process of construction. On the basis of this advice, Daniels gave the order to make the *Nevada* an oil-burner."[16]

Indeed, motivations other than availability concerns seem to have driven the bulk of Daniels's policies. In pursuing oil facilities for the navy—much like his British counterpart Sir Winston Churchill, then first lord of the Royal Navy—Daniels was likely motivated more by fears that U.S. oil companies would try to gouge the navy on prices than by worries about future availability. The spike in oil prices from 1912 to 1913 underscored this concern. There is also evidence that the navy sought to control American oil to gain military advantage over potential opponents—quite the opposite logic from worrying about the adequacy of domestic oil resources. "The control of our exports of oil might limit the extent of the adoption of the oil engine by our possible enemies," wrote one navy official. "Under the present law, however, any foreign nation can draw on the production of the oil fields of the United States to an unlimited extent, and can thus accumulate in time of peace a reserve supply." In fact, on the eve of World War I, the German Navy relied on petroleum imports from the United States for some 80 percent of its requirements.[17]

Interestingly, even as the adequacy of American petroleum resources was questioned, the United States passed up multiple opportunities to intervene in Mexico, its oil-rich neighbor whose domestic tumult caused much strife along the southern border. Violence from the Mexican Civil War regularly spilled over into U.S. border towns, causing American casualties. As Navy Secretary Daniels wrote in his diary on April 11, 1913, after a cabinet meeting where the crisis was discussed, "It seems that there are fifteen town[s] in which a street or river only divides the Mexican and American people, and when there is fighting . . . the bullets fly over to American soil and injure, and in some instances, kill American citizens. Only yesterday, an American officer, sitting in his tent, on American soil, had the leg of his chair shot out from under him."[18] But President Wilson, with agreement from his cabinet, was determined to avoid military intervention—despite pressure from the American public, U.S. oil companies, and even the British government to extend some sort of control over Mexican oil. In fact, Wilson regarded the two latter sources of pressure with significant scorn. As Daniels recorded after the following week's cabinet meeting on April 18, 1913, "What to do with Mexico is the great problem and was discussed at length. . . . The general opinion in the Cabinet was that the chief cause of this whole situation in Mexico was a contest between English and American Oil Companies to see which would control; that these people were ready to foment trouble and it was largely due to the English Company that England was willing to recognize Mexico before we did."[19] At the meeting, Wilson and his advisers again sought ways to avoid U.S. involvement. Simply put, the United States had a ready-made pretext to intervene in oil-rich Mexico—either through direct control or indirectly, by installing a pliant regime—but repeatedly declined to take it. The lack of interest in asserting dominance over Mexico and its petroleum suggests that oil security was not viewed as a significant problem by Wilson and his principals.

Case I: Coercive Vulnerability Emerges (1918–1920)

The U.S. government's attitude toward oil shifted dramatically during World War I. A spate of geological studies confirmed Day's earlier, pessimistic findings that American reserves were scarcer than previously imagined, raising the possibility that the United States could one day become a net petroleum importer. Meanwhile, wartime oil demand strained resources enough for the United States to institute civilian fuel conservation programs. For the first time, the United States faced a mild petroleum deficit. Fortunately, the country had a proximate and secure potential source for imports: Mexico produced about 13 percent of global petroleum, which it could export overland, beyond the reach of German U-boats. Therefore, the threat to imports was very low. Put together, the United States faced a low degree of coercive vulnerability.

The prospect of a future petroleum deficit, even a small one, nevertheless shocked policymakers and the American public. The timing of this newfound vulnerability boded poorly for U.S. interests. German submarine warfare against Britain and France had just demonstrated the perils of cutoff in no uncertain terms. Additionally, postwar territorial settlements provoked an intense Anglo-American rivalry over the control of oil resources abroad. In response, the United States embarked on a self-sufficiency strategy to reduce the threat.

Demand generated by World War I significantly strained American petroleum production even before the country entered the conflict. As the main oil supplier to France and Britain, the United States ultimately provided 90 percent of the total oil used by the Western allies. To accomplish this, American oil companies ratcheted up output by over 30 percent in four years, from 728,000 barrels daily in 1914 to 975,100 barrels per day in 1918. Even with such gains, domestic production proved inadequate for meeting demand once the United States began mobilizing its forces. As a result of widespread petroleum shortages beginning in the spring of 1917, the United States was forced to rely on Mexican crude imports to eke through the war.[20] The U.S. government called for civilian rationing through "Gasless Sundays" to conserve fuel.[21] Even President Wilson resolved to walk to church.[22]

In light of such circumstances, it was not long before observers began to worry that the United States was risking the depletion of its own reserves to supply the war in Europe. From 1918 onward, warnings of an impending oil crisis emerged from multiple sources, including the United States military, oil industry experts, petroleum trade publications, and prominent geologists. Echoing Day's earlier findings, geologists estimated reserves at 6.2 billion barrels and predicted the country could run out of oil within a decade.[23] George Otis Smith, the director of the United States Geological Survey, alarmingly declared, "The position of the United States in regard to oil can best be characterized as precarious," and urged drastic government action to obtain future supplies.[24] Meanwhile, continuing shortages after the war threatened the navy's ability to purchase petroleum, prompting a 1919 directive by Secretary Daniels ordering naval personnel to commandeer oil from suppliers if the need arose. Navy officers adhered to his command. Following the Union Oil Company's refusal to deliver oil at the price demanded by the navy, "six destroyers drew up to the San Francisco plant of the Associated Oil Company . . . a few weeks later with orders to seize as much oil as they required." After this incident, suppliers proved much more willing to cooperate in meeting navy fuel needs.[25]

In the context of widespread fears of domestic depletion, aggressive policies undertaken by Britain to dominate Middle Eastern oil concessions heightened the American sense of danger. The British now occupied large portions of the former Ottoman Empire, including many areas speculated to hold vast reserves. What made this new oil predominance threatening to the United States was Britain's clear desire to exclude other nations from negotiating concessions in areas under mandate control. "During the months after the armistice, the British had refused to allow geologists of the Standard Oil Company of New York to investigate its claims obtained in Palestine prior to the war," according to John DeNovo. "Soon they excluded from Mesopotamia American geologists eager to investigate oil possibilities there."[26] This discriminatory policy was codified in the 1920 San Remo agreement, whereby Britain and France divvied up the most promising oil territories and pledged to bar petroleum development by foreign nationals.[27]

From the American point of view, Great Britain's effort to "lock up" Middle Eastern oil reserves was foreboding. Distrust of the British ran high, and remarks from British officials raised suspicions that the country might be willing to use oil for coercive purposes. Sir E. Mackay Edgar, a Canadian oil tycoon based in London, made a variety of ominous statements to the effect that Britain was planning to hoard petroleum reserves and wait for the United States to exhaust its resources.[28] Similarly, Walter Hume Long, as first lord of the Admiralty, reportedly told industry experts in London that British officials sought to control the world's petroleum so "we can do what we like" on the global stage.[29]

At the same time that oil's military value had become indisputable, the U.S. government thus found itself in an unexpected position. The looming possibility of depletion meant the United States might soon face some level of import dependence. Moreover, Britain's uncooperative behavior in the Middle East suggested that even the British could not necessarily be counted on to provide oil should a crisis develop.

The American response to this situation conforms to the expectations of my theory. Official complacency toward petroleum abruptly ended, and the country embarked on an anticipatory strategy of self-sufficiency to lessen vulnerability before coercive threats could emerge. The overarching strategy behind these policies was to preserve domestic petroleum resources for as long as possible. The United States went about this in three ways.

First, more was done to allocate oil supplies to the military. In fact, U.S. policy in this regard began to reflect more serious attitudes about oil soon after the war broke out. In April 1915, the government started setting aside more valuable lands as naval reserves and did so at a greater pace. In a major win for the navy, President Wilson established a new reserve at Teapot Dome, Wyoming, which was estimated to hold one hundred million barrels. The following year, Wilson added tracts of land in Colorado and Utah totaling over 130,000 acres, more than tripling the oil lands designated for the navy. These practices continued into the early 1920s, with the federal government establishing a naval reserve on a large and particularly valuable chunk of Alaskan oil land in 1923.[30]

Second, U.S. policymakers, resentful that so much oil was squandered for a European war of dubious merit, endeavored to preserve American oil resources for as long as possible through a policy of "conservation at home, exploitation abroad."[31] Because oil demand was sure to rise in the future, the only way to stave off depletion of U.S. reserves was to encourage American oil companies to develop new supply sources abroad instead of at home. Policymakers reasoned that the country would be more secure if it drew on overseas petroleum for peacetime consumption and left its own oil underground to be tapped in case of war or national emergency. Strikingly, this means the government actually hoped to *increase* the economy's consumption of imported petroleum because doing so was necessary to preserve domestic oil for national emergencies.

To this end, the United States government extended aid and diplomatic support to American companies seeking oil concessions overseas.[32] While the approach tipped into the foreign policy realm, it nonetheless qualifies as a self-sufficiency measure because the driving logic was to protect homeland oil reserves. Discriminatory policies by the Dutch and British blocked most efforts to establish American footholds in the Middle East and Asia.[33] However, the policy was successful in helping American enterprises penetrate the oil industries of several Latin American countries. Petroleum found in the Western Hemisphere held greater strategic importance because of its proximity to the United States. It was especially advantageous to build up productive capacity in Mexico, as it had helped to meet American military requirements in World War I and its oil could be delivered across the border easily and securely. Thanks to government assistance, American investment in overseas petroleum grew from $75.5 million in 1908 to $872 million in 1935, more than a tenfold increase. Over 70 percent of this new investment occurred in just four Latin American countries: Mexico, Colombia, Peru, and Venezuela.[34] Investment in Venezuela, in particular, paid future dividends when the country emerged as a crucial source of petroleum during World War II and the Cold War.

Case II: Glut and Abrupt Disinterest (1921–1941)

Ultimately, the post–World War I oil scare was short-lived. Several major oil discoveries in the early 1920s discredited the dire earlier forecasts of geologists and reassured Americans of their country's oil abundance. Globally, the petroleum market fell into a glut. The return to petroleum plenty fostered a new sense of complacency within the government. Oil security was neglected, particularly as policymakers focused on handling the Great Depression.

Case III: World War II (1941–1945)

World War II provided the wakeup call that would reshape U.S. foreign oil policy in a lasting way. It illustrated to a new generation of American policymakers that victory in modern warfare would require access to massive amounts of petroleum; yet concurrently, it cast doubt on the adequacy of future domestic output. Interwar complacency about oil meant that as Europe plunged into war, the United States lacked comprehensive estimates of its petroleum reserves and overall production capacity. Meanwhile, the spectacular discoveries of the 1920s fostered perceptions that American petroleum resources were limitless. Even the military took oil for granted, believing "that a mere 'crack of the valve' would provide for all foreseeable war demands." As late as 1941, the U.S. armed forces had "no realistic forecasts of the volume of petroleum that would be required if the Nation became involved in war. Even the military authorities did not foresee the magnitude of the oil supply job and almost until the end of the war consistently underestimated their requirements."[35]

The day after declaring an unlimited national emergency on May 27, 1941, President Franklin Roosevelt established the Office for Petroleum Coordinator for National Defense, later renamed the Petroleum Administration for War (PAW). The organization was tasked with coordinating petroleum supply and demand as needed for the defense requirements of the United States. Among the first actions PAW undertook in support of this goal was a preliminary survey of the American oil position, completed in December 1941. Until the strife in Europe rekindled supply concerns among policymakers, it had been decades since the government had sponsored such a study. The results were sobering. Reserves were estimated at twenty-four billion barrels, but more significantly, the data showed that more oil had been taken out of the ground than had been discovered in 1939 and 1940. This meant that proven reserves had begun to decline. The implication was "that the Nation's productive capacity, although somewhat higher than current production, might not be adequate to meet rapidly rising war demands" unless action was taken immediately to boost discoveries and drilling. A follow-up study completed in May 1942 confirmed the downward trend.[36] Even though the United States was still the world's leading oil producer by a significant margin, the fear was that declining reserves meant it would not be able to produce enough oil in the future to meet its needs.

Meanwhile, wartime demand was massive. In 1943, one-third of all American-produced gasoline was being funneled directly into the war effort—even though the only ground force engaged in active fighting in Europe was the U.S. Seventh Army under General George S. Patton, which had invaded Sicily that July and landed in Italy in September. By 1945, the armed forces of the United States and its Western allies were consuming the majority of American petroleum output. A whopping 85 percent of the oil used by the Allies to win World War II came from American oil fields. This wartime strain created widespread shortages on the home front despite significant rationing and conservation efforts. Emergency measures were taken to boost output, including production in excess of the maximum efficient rates of several oil fields—a practice known to damage oil reservoirs and reduce the total amount of oil that ultimately can be recovered. Despite these efforts, the United States once again had to rely on foreign imports to get through the war, this time from Venezuela.[37]

As the staggering magnitude of military oil demand became increasingly clear, both the government and the oil industry continued to study the American petroleum position extensively. Both concluded that the outlook for American oil was shaky. Exploratory "wildcat" wells were being drilled in record numbers to meet wartime demand, but new discoveries continued a downward trend.[38] The best guess of geologists was now that the country possessed reserves of twenty billion barrels, amounting to just fourteen years of supply at 1939 consumption levels.[39]

These reports generated significant alarm in Washington, particularly within military circles, causing many to worry that domestic supply would not last through another major war.[40] This was particularly the case because military fuel usage for any future world war was expected to significantly exceed current requirements.[41]

Perhaps the most vocal advocate of anticipatory measures to safeguard the United States from oil coercion was Harold Ickes, secretary of the Interior and the head of PAW. Ickes explicitly cited national defense as the most important impetus for government intervention. "If there should be a World War III," he warned in a major article, "it would have to be fought with someone else's petroleum, because the United States wouldn't have it." Unless the U.S. government took anticipatory measures to ensure supply, Ickes argued, "we shall be carelessly exposing ourselves to grave risks," because "no nation can ever surely depend upon another for succor in time of war."[42] Ickes clearly understood that petroleum dependence risked opening the door to political coercion.

Self-Sufficiency, Again

As the first and most important step, the U.S. government sponsored a broad expansion of exploratory drilling in search of additional reserves. In coordination with the Petroleum Industry War Council, a body of private oilmen, Herculean efforts were made to boost output. Significant resources were poured into developing new fields and extracting petroleum as quickly as possible. From mid-1944 onward—in tandem with the Allied invasion of occupied France—the need was so great that the industry continued extracting oil in excess of the marginal efficient rate of production, causing damage to the fields. Despite the problem of declining discoveries, the oilmen succeeded in upping production nearly 25 percent in four years, from 3.8 million barrels daily in 1941 to 4.7 million barrels in 1945.[43] Even this feat was not enough to keep pace with wartime demands.

Second, the government stressed conservation of petroleum products among civilians and within industry to free up as much supply as possible for the war effort. One method was encouraging substitution of other energy sources for oil wherever possible. Beginning in March 1942, the U.S. government individually petitioned power plants, industrial facilities, and other major commercial consumers of fuel oil to convert to coal with government assistance, resulting in a savings of about thirty million barrels nationally by the end of the year. Unfortunately, this amounted to only a week's worth of production, as American wells pumped out four to five million barrels daily. Citizens who used fuel oil to heat their homes were also urged to participate in similar conservation efforts that were voluntary in name only. In practice, those who refused faced the loss of their rations from their local Office of Price Administration boards. As the war waged on, the authorities imposed mandatory civilian rationing on the East Coast in May 1942. The measure was extended to the whole country that November. In the following years, rations grew increasingly strict.[44]

Third, synthetic fuels garnered official attention. Harold Ickes fervently pushed for government subsidization of research into coal-to-oil conversion technologies such as the kind being used to fuel the Luftwaffe in Hitler's Germany.[45] Lacking any prior need for such measures, and given how far the technology was from being profitable, American industry lagged decades behind Germany in development of synthetic fuels manufacturing. Ickes successfully persuaded Congress in April 1944 to allocate $30 million to synthetic fuel research and development.

A more daring attempt to bolster American synfuel manufacturing involved the plunder of German industrial knowledge. The government created the Technical Oil Mission, a group of oilmen who accompanied American troops in Europe for the purpose of interviewing German research scientists and stealing the trade secrets of IG Farben, the firm in charge of Germany's synthetic fuels production. Some of these experts were embedded in the front lines of advancing Allied forces, demonstrating just how important it was to the United States to acquire German synfuel secrets—particularly before Russian troops advancing from the east could beat them to the punch. Perhaps unsurprisingly, "the German scientists—caught as they were between us and the advancing Russians—were terribly helpful in organizing their records and making them available to us," a member of the Technical Oil Mission recalled after the war. In all, the Allies acquired hundreds of tons of IG Farben records from the company's corporate headquarters in Frankfurt and eventually inspected the forty largest synthetic fuel production facilities in Germany.[46] Ultimately, enthusiasm for synthetic production evaporated at the war's end, particularly as increased production in the Middle East caused oil prices to decrease markedly. American industry saw little reason to pursue the expensive and inefficient technology, and files filled with Nazi synfuel secrets were left abandoned in storage.

The Emergence of Official Interest in the Middle East

Although the United States pursued a strategy of self-sufficiency during the war, nascent ideas about establishing strategic relationships in the Persian Gulf first arose in the war's waning days. Even though the Gulf produced only about 5 percent of the global supply before World War II—most of which came from British-controlled Iran—geologists speculated that the region would have strong potential for future petroleum production, potential that was nearly untapped.[47] Mindful of the decline in American oil reserves during the war, Harold Ickes dispatched a team of petroleum experts to study the region. After an exhaustive review of the region's prospects, the delegation confirmed hunches that the region held awesome potential. "The center of gravity of world oil production is shifting from the Gulf Caribbean area to the Middle East—to the Persian Gulf area—and is likely to continue to shift until it is firmly established in that area," the report to Harold Ickes concluded.[48]

In response to the report's findings, Ickes pushed bold proposals to source future U.S. military demand from Saudi Arabia. He championed an effort for government-to-government oil cooperation between the United States and Saudi Arabia with grand hopes of putting Uncle Sam in the oil business. Ickes favored the establishment of the Petroleum Reserves Corporation (PRC), run by the U.S. government, which would take over privately owned American oil concessions in Saudi Arabia and jointly manage them with the Arabian American Oil Company (ARAMCO). Plans included the construction of a pipeline to transport Saudi oil to a deepwater port in the Mediterranean accessible to navy vessels, as well as the creation of a one-billion-barrel military oil reserve on Saudi territory. The proposal further stipulated that in the event of a war, the U.S. military had the right to purchase all petroleum produced by ARAMCO.[49] Ickes also called for the establishment of strategically located military oil stores in Alaska, Hawaii, Guam, the Panama Canal Zone, "those small dots of atolls where our transpacific airliners land and fuel," and "the airfields we may own or possess under lease in all parts of the world."[50]

Although Ickes was the public face of the PRC proposal, "the prime mover in this scheme was not Ickes, but rather the U.S. Navy and the U.S. Army."[51] Cooperative development of the Saudi oil industry was highly sought after by the military, and in fact, the pipeline idea was first proposed by a U.S. Navy captain after a visit to Saudi Arabia.[52] Cordell Hull, Henry L. Stimson, and William F. Knox, secretaries of state, war, and the navy, respectively, all strongly supported the plan, as did the Joint Chiefs of Staff. Even President Roosevelt himself approved of the proposal and pushed for it publicly.[53]

Yet, Harold Ickes's bold proposals never materialized. The ambitious PRC plans were abandoned after heated protest by the petroleum industry, whose leaders had earned significant political clout after partnering with the government to manage wartime production. Obviously, the industry had a profit motive in keeping the government out of the oil business, but it also offered cogent logic for why such a move would be politically untenable. Military involvement in Saudi oil development, industry experts argued, would be viewed as provocative by Britain and the Soviet Union and risked starting a third world war over the control of oil.[54] The costs and risks were substantial and out of proportion with U.S. security needs.

The United States did, however, cultivate diplomatic relations with Saudi Arabia for the first time. As early as the fall of 1942, negotiations with Ibn Saud had resulted in his agreement in principle to an American military presence in his country. The extension of Lend-Lease aid to Saudi Arabia in February 1943 strengthened the relationship and counteracted British attempts to increase their influence in the country. Eventually, the U.S. Navy began purchasing Saudi Arabian oil, though quantities were modest given the country's as-yet small output.[55]

But the U.S.-Saudi relationship at that time fell far short of an alliance. It is widely speculated that, during his famous post-Yalta meeting with Ibn Saud aboard the USS *Quincy* on the Great Bitter Lake on February 14, 1945, the ailing President Roosevelt offered an American military commitment to Saudi Arabia's defense in exchange for guaranteed access to Saudi oil. Indeed, books on U.S.-Saudi relations are nearly uniform in tracing the latter-day U.S.-Saudi alliance to that date. Yet, the principal account of the meeting—from Colonel William Eddy, the U.S. ambassador to Saudi Arabia who acted as the translator and was the only other American present for the private discussion, save Roosevelt himself—mentions no such arrangement.[56] Rather, the question of how to handle Jewish immigration to Palestine dominated the conversation, with the king flatly rejecting any suggestion by Roosevelt that the Arabs accept the establishment of a Jewish homeland there. In Eddy's telling, talk of an alliance went no further than mutual expressions of friendship and support. Notably, Ibn Saud made a point of stressing, with pride, that "his country had never been occupied nor 'protected' as a dependent," and that only on the basis of Saudi independence could he "seek an honorable friendship."[57] Roosevelt and Saud did reportedly discuss the construction of a small U.S. military airbase at Dharan, but its primary role was to serve as a refueling station for U.S. aircraft en route to the Asian theater rather than as an operating base for defending Saudi Arabia. The end of the Pacific War left the airfield a backwater outpost before it was even completed. Thus, there is little evidence to suggest that the U.S.-Saudi security relationship began aboard the *Quincy* in 1945. Thomas Lippman, a noted expert on Saudi Arabia, has concluded that "the supposed 'oil for security' agreement forged between Roosevelt and the King is a myth, extrapolated from subsequent events."[58]

From World War II to the Cold War

Given the wartime uproar over oil, remarkably little high-level strategic oil planning took place from 1945 to 1950. There are several potential reasons why little was done. First, the end of the war created a worldwide oil glut as global demand dropped. Supply scarcity, therefore, was no longer an immediate problem. Second, the U.S. government was undergoing major transitions. Military demobilization consumed the attention of policymakers in the first few years after the war. At the same time, massive institutional reorganization was under way and a new national security bureaucracy was forming. Existing departments were reshuffled as several new bodies, including the Central Intelligence Agency, the National Security Council (NSC), the Joint Chiefs of Staff, and the Department of Defense, were created. Although certain government officials strongly advocated for a comprehensive national oil policy—James Forrestal perhaps being the most prominent—bureaucratic upheaval may have impeded cross-agency initiatives on oil.

Third, Truman may have been reluctant to pursue oil issues after the backlash provoked by his proclamation of September 8, 1945, claiming federal ownership over tidelands oil.[59] The declaration touched off a political firestorm in the United States, drawing the specific ire of powerful members of Congress from Texas and Louisiana, which were directly affected, as well as general disapproval from those who supported the principle of states' rights. The oil industry likewise reacted with predictable hostility. Fourth, the foremost champion of strategic oil policy, Harold Ickes, resigned in February 1946 over conflicts with Truman.[60]

Finally, and most importantly, although the problem of Soviet expansion was recognized early on, the American consensus to balance the USSR by increasing U.S. military capabilities and permanently basing large numbers of troops abroad did not immediately coalesce. Instead, initial U.S. commitments to Europe took the form of economic aid. In March 1947, the Truman Doctrine was announced to provide aid to Greece, Turkey, and potentially any embattled democracy facing Communist insurrection. In June 1947, the United States instituted the Marshall Plan of massive economic assistance to rebuild Europe. Even the publication of George F. Kennan's famous "X" article in the July 1947 issue of *Foreign Affairs*, which advocated for the containment of Soviet influence, left the scope and means of the strategy amorphous.[61]

By the end of the decade, however, military responses loomed larger with the founding of the North Atlantic Treaty Organization (NATO) in April 1949, the first Soviet nuclear test in August 1949, and the outbreak of the Korean War in 1950.[62] In late 1950, with the Cold War order solidified, Truman reelected, and bureaucratic upheaval subsiding, the president and his newly created NSC began serious consideration of the oil problem in future conflicts.

Case IV: Oil Policy in the Early Cold War

The early Cold War period was a crucial time where both causal factors—the petroleum deficit and the threat to imports—shifted dramatically and in lasting ways, creating a new baseline of moderate coercive vulnerability. The petroleum deficit worsened to moderate as needs increased, but haves (U.S. oil supply) appeared insufficient to meet them. Additionally, the vulnerability of imports to coercion also grew as the Middle East emerged as a major productive region. Its proximity to the USSR made it vulnerable to the Red Army, and this raised doubts as to whether its oil would be available if conflict arose. Fortunately, however, Latin American oil production, which was highly secure, compensated for the Soviet threat to the Persian Gulf, at least in the near term.

The Petroleum Deficit: Unanticipated Demand Growth and Uncertainty of Future Output

Five factors conspired to increase American petroleum needs. First and most significantly, American grand strategy underwent a sea change that dramatically increased military requirements. The dawn of the Cold War meant that U.S. military power would have to play a much larger role in the nation's security than in the past, and resultantly, strategic petroleum requirements would be much more extensive than under the traditional stance of isolationism. Before World War II, European multipolarity ensured that no single power could grow strong enough to threaten the United States across distant shores. But the war had decimated Britain, France, and Germany, destroyed the continental balance of power, and raised the possibility of unchecked Soviet expansionism. Troubling signs soon after the war that the USSR would not relinquish control of Eastern Europe, such as the Soviet abrogation of several Three Powers agreements with the United States and Britain, suggested the country harbored aggressive intentions. If the Soviet Union consolidated control over the continent's vast resources and industrial capacity, it would obtain enough power to menace the United States directly. American security would therefore come to rest on the ability to defend Western Europe in a conventional war—or ideally, to deter Soviet aggression in the first place through the credible threat of major war. As World War II had just demonstrated, fighting a major conventional conflict would require massive amounts of petroleum.

Second, there was the issue of whether and how to plan for the needs of the oil-poor NATO allies, whose fate was now deeply entwined with American security. In both world wars, the United States had provided the bulk of Western Europe's oil and would likely be called on to do the same in a future conflict. This raised a difficult set of questions. Should U.S. needs consist only of the amount of oil it required for its own economy and defense? Or, must the United States plan to fuel both itself and its allies for the collective defense of Europe from the Soviet Union, which would require access to much larger quantities of oil?

Notably, although the U.S. commitment to Europe was settled by 1950 and remained firm throughout the Cold War, the question of burden sharing to provide oil security within NATO was never entirely settled. A significant minority of U.S. policymakers argued that European oil needs, and especially essential civilian needs, should not be an American problem. In their view, if the United States had no security commitment to Europe, its deficit would be small enough that even modest investment in self-sufficiency measures could make it autarkic in oil once again. Adherents to this view repeatedly pushed for self-sufficiency measures based on the argument that U.S. oil policy should be based on U.S. oil needs alone. The self-sufficiency crowd lost the big debate: presidents from Truman to Dwight D. Eisenhower to Richard M. Nixon ultimately accepted that the United States must plan to meet Allied or "free world" requirements, as opposed to focusing narrowly on American needs alone.[63] But the faction's influence would prove strong enough to win some of its favored policies, most notably trade protectionism for the domestic petroleum industry.

Third, military technology itself was growing ever more petroleum intensive. This trend was discernible in the massive increase in consumption by U.S. forces in World War II compared with World War I. At the height of World War II, U.S. military gasoline consumption surpassed its World War I peak by a hundredfold while the war economy needed two and a half times the oil required in the previous conflict.[64] Post–World War II projections estimated that U.S. military demand in a future war with the Soviet Union would be twice what it was in World War II because of the widening use of jet aircraft.[65] Although the atomic bomb obviously existed, at this phase in the Cold War, scholars and policymakers did not take for granted that it would significantly lessen military petroleum demand. Even Bernard Brodie, who famously suggested in *The Absolute Weapon* (1946) that nuclear weapons would end wars quickly, argued in a 1947 monograph that military planners should determine oil needs based on the worst-case contingency of a long conventional war.[66]

Fourth, U.S. civilian consumption increased abruptly once rationing was lifted, surprising forecasters who had expected a reversion to prewar levels.[67] Total demand before the war was about 3.9 million barrels per day (see table 6.1). Rationing froze civilian consumption at roughly this level during the war, but overall demand surged to 5.4 million barrels in 1945, the growth driven entirely by the military. Policymakers assumed, quite reasonably, that demobilization would reduce overall demand after the war. Instead, civilian demand jumped 40 percent

TABLE 6.1 U.S. civilian and military petroleum consumption, 1939–1955 (in thousands of barrels per day)

YEAR	CIVILIAN DEMAND	MILITARY DEMAND	TOTAL DEMAND
1939	3,858	33	3,891
1940	3,941	40	3,981
1941	4,300	69	4,369
1942	4,021	272	4,293
1943	3,979	600	4,579
1944	3,907	1,227	5,134
1945	3,747	1,611	5,358
1946	3,881	1,450	5,331
1947	5,526	376	5,902
1948	5,774	369	6,143
1949	5,795	335	6,130
1950	6,523	349	6,872
1951	7,061	402	7,463
1952	7,308	404	7,712
1953	7,499	506	8,005
1954	7,575	540	8,115
1955	8,246	581	8,827

Source: *Petroleum Facts and Figures, Centennial Edition* (New York: American Petroleum Institute, 1959), 209–10, 362.

in 1947, more than offsetting the savings in military consumption. Consumption growth subsequently averaged about 6 percent per year through the mid-1950s.[68]

Finally, growth in European peacetime consumption, the fifth factor that increased the "need" side of the petroleum deficit, was much more dramatic—averaging about 14 percent annually from the close of World War II until the early 1950s.[69] The rapid increase reflected the fact that European countries had long trailed the United States in motorization, even before wartime petroleum shortages forced oil-powered combustion engines to convert to fuels like coal, peat, and wood. Thus, when the Marshall Plan invested heavily in motorization as a means of economic stimulus, there was enormous capacity for demand growth in every area, from the mechanization of agriculture, to the operation and expansion of diesel-driven locomotives, to automotive transportation. Fully 25 percent of Marshall Plan aid—or about $4 billion—was spent on oil or petroleum-related equipment.[70]

While U.S. and Allied oil needs were growing, the American ability to meet demand through domestic production appeared to be faltering. Output exhibited a modest growth of 4 percent annually from 1945 to 1950, not quite keeping pace with demand. In 1948, the United States became a net oil importer, consuming more oil than it could domestically produce—a situation unprecedented in peacetime. Granted, the amount of oil imported was small (fewer than 150,000 barrels per day), but the trend was disturbing.[71] Worse, several factors suggested U.S. output was unlikely to close the gap in the future.

First, the pace of new oil discoveries continued to slow, which indicated that U.S. oil resources were on the decline. Since 1940, most of the growth in U.S. reserves came from revised estimates of known oil fields, not the discovery of new ones, despite the massive exploratory drilling efforts conducted during the war to shore up supplies. Going forward, this meant that more and more exploration would be required just to yield the same rate of replenishment in reserves. At best, this would raise U.S. production costs, assuming additional oil could be found. If it could not, the depletion of known fields, absent the discovery of new reservoirs to replace them, would inevitably cause future output to dwindle.

Second, future U.S. production was also in jeopardy because of new competition from overseas oil that could be produced and sold much more cheaply, which threatened to undercut the higher-cost U.S. domestic oil industry. The price of Saudi Arabian oil in 1946 was forty cents cheaper than the lowest-cost Western Hemisphere producers.[72] The cost differential was driven by the more favorable geology in the Persian Gulf, where oil was closer to the surface and easier to reach, as well as differences in the age of the industry. Whereas the United States had been producing commercial quantities of oil since 1859, with its best oil fields already tapped, Middle East oil was just coming online, with the best fields relatively untouched. If cheap overseas oil drove international prices down—a near certainty—not only would current production suffer but so would the years-long investments required to develop new reserves. Thus, competition from Middle East producers would exacerbate the already worrying trend of declining reserves.

Although these developments stoked reasonable fears about the future, the situation was far from grim when put into proper perspective. According to the Oil and Gas Division of the United States Department of the Interior, in 1947 the United States still held over 30 percent of the world's proven petroleum reserves, by far the largest bounty of any individual country (see table 6.2). Even if reserves dwindled because more oil was extracted than discovered, their sheer size provided a significant cushion.

The Soviet Threat to Allied Oil Imports

The susceptibility of the United States and its allies to the cutoff of oil imports was moderate. On the one hand, Latin America was a major source of oil that

TABLE 6.2 World proven reserves, as of January 1, 1947

	BILLIONS OF BARRELS	PERCENTAGE OF GLOBAL SUPPLY
United States	20.9	31.2
Venezuela	7.0	10.4
Other Western Hemisphere	2.3	3.4
Total Western Hemisphere	30.2	45.0
Middle East	27.3	40.8
Russia	7.6	11.4
Other Eastern Hemisphere	1.9	2.8
Total Eastern Hemisphere	36.8	55.0
World total	67.0	100.0

Source: Committee on Interstate and Foreign Commerce United States House of Representatives, *Fuel Investigation*.

was relatively safe from Soviet military interference. In 1950, the Western Hemisphere, not counting the United States, produced roughly 20 percent of global oil. But it held only about 10 percent of total proven reserves. On the other hand, the most promising sources of future imports lay in the Middle East—uncomfortably close to the Soviet Union and vulnerable to its military power. Although its production was comparable to that of Latin America at the time, the Middle East held some 40 percent of global proven reserves. Clearly, it was the supply of the future.[73]

Western Hemisphere resources were the most secure from Soviet interference for locational reasons. There was no realistic threat of the USSR conquering regional producers like Venezuela or Mexico; the distance alone was forbidding, and the United States would surely intervene, given the long-standing principle of the Monroe Doctrine. Transit routes to the United States were slightly less secure than in the past, however, because there was no major overland source of supply. Mexican production had declined significantly owing to a combination of resource depletion and inept government management following the industry's nationalization in 1938. Whereas Mexican oil fields produced about 175,000 barrels per day in 1918, output fell to about 120,000 barrels per day in 1945. Even as the industry enjoyed an upswing in the late 1940s, production amounted to just 200,000 barrels daily in 1950. Data on Mexican exports during the period are spotty but suggest that the country exported fewer than 40,000 barrels daily—not enough to make up the difference in Allied supplies. Canada, the other potential overland source, was a net importer at this time (see table 6.3).[74]

By contrast, Venezuela churned out 885,000 barrels per day in 1945 and 1.5 million barrels daily in 1950, virtually all of which was exported. This made Ven-

TABLE 6.3 Western Hemisphere petroleum production, 1945–1955 (in thousands of barrels per day)

YEAR	VENEZUELA	CANADA	MEXICO	ALL OTHERS, EXCEPT U.S.*	WESTERN HEMISPHERE, EXCEPT U.S.	UNITED STATES	TOTAL WESTERN HEMISPHERE
1945	885	23	119	227	1,255	4,695	5,950
1946	1,064	21	135	213	1,433	4,860	6,293
1947	1,192	21	154	225	1,592	5,088	6,680
1948	1,343	34	160	231	1,768	5,535	7,302
1949	1,321	58	167	248	1,794	5,046	6,841
1950	1,498	80	198	236	2,012	5,407	7,419
1951	1,705	130	212	283	2,330	6,158	8,488
1952	1,809	168	212	286	2,475	6,274	8,748
1953	1,765	222	198	302	2,487	6,458	8,945
1954	1,895	263	229	314	2,701	6,342	9,044
1955	2,157	355	245	323	3,080	6,807	9,887

Source: Twentieth Century Petroleum Statistics, multiple volumes; American Petroleum Institute, Basic Petroleum Data Book, multiple volumes.
*Specifically, Argentina, Colombia, Peru, and Trinidad, with negligible amounts from Brazil and Ecuador.

ezuela the second-largest petroleum producer in the world after the United States. Russia, the third-largest supplier, produced less than half of these quantities.[75] Prolific production in Venezuela was helpful for the United States, but of course, imports from Venezuela had to cross the Caribbean Sea, which made them at least somewhat vulnerable to Russian naval power. The example of this vulnerability had already been set. During World War II, German submarines sank dozens of oil tankers en route to the U.S. Atlantic coast from the Caribbean and the Gulf of Mexico. In a particularly rough span, from February to May 1942, fifty tankers bound for the East Coast were lost. German submarines also shelled refineries on the islands of Aruba and Curacao, just twenty and forty miles, respectively, off the Venezuelan coast.[76] Over time, however, the United States got better at protecting tankers crossing the Caribbean, curtailing losses significantly. Based on the World War II example, even though overseas transit raised the possibility of Soviet interference, chances were good that the United States could defend against it.[77]

The same could not be said about imports from the Persian Gulf, which dwarfed the Western Hemisphere in productive potential. American officials harbored serious doubts that access to the Middle East could be defended in war.[78] The region was located on the doorstep of the Soviet Union, and the United States would have to project power across oceans to deter and defend against Soviet incursions.

Soviet territorial expansion into the Persian Gulf constituted a very real threat, not only because of the region's proximity but also because the Soviets had a history of violating Iranian sovereignty. During World War II, the Red Army occupied northern Iran while British troops occupied the south. In violation of the Tripartite Treaty, the Soviet Union refused to withdraw from Iran within six months of Japan's surrender, marking one of the very first crises of the Cold War. Additionally, the Soviets had aided Azeri separatists in the 1945–1946 uprising and physically blocked Iranian government forces from subduing the rebellion. Soviet forces eventually departed in May 1946, two months after the deadline, following intense pressure from Britain and the United States and tough negotiations with Iran. Though Stalin claimed the USSR had no interest in expanding into Iran, the tense episode suggested otherwise. In a report to President Truman, Clark Clifford, one of the president's most trusted advisers, warned, "The long-range Soviet aim is the economic, military, and political domination of the entire Middle East."[79] Should Iran fall to the Soviet Union, it would remove a buffer to Soviet expansion in the Saudi Peninsula.[80]

American Coercive Vulnerability Calculus

Although officials at the Department of Defense, the Department of the Interior, and the Joint Chiefs of Staff had advocated the need for a national petroleum program throughout the late 1940s, including a particularly hard press in 1948, the initiative did not make it onto the NSC's agenda until late December 1950. Two factors appear to have made the difference. First, relations with the Soviets had worsened. "During the past two years, the international situation has become increasingly acute," noted James Lay, executive secretary to the NSC, in a memo explaining the president's decision to take up the matter. Second, war plans recently submitted to the NSC indicated that the Allies would face crude production shortages of 500,000 barrels of crude daily and refinery deficits of 1.5 million barrels per day.[81] In light of the new circumstances, President Truman in December 1950 approved NSC 97, which launched a study of Allied oil requirements in the event of war with the Soviet Union, culminating with recommendations for a national petroleum program.

On December 13, 1951, after a year of analysis, the NSC submitted an interim report to the president, who approved its recommendations. The major findings of the report were that "substantial shortages" of oil would occur in the first six months of war, even under the most optimistic assumptions, as a result of five factors: (1) the loss of productive oil regions to enemy control, (2) production losses in areas retained due to enemy attack, (3) "large increases in military requirements," (4) the time needed to put "drastic civilian rationing" into effect, and (5) tanker losses. "It will be impossible for the petroleum industry to fuel an all out [sic] war during the first six months," the report noted, "unless these shortages can be substantially reduced by drastic rationing at the outset of a war, stockpiling, producing crude above maximum efficient rate of production and by reducing losses from sabotage and enemy action." After this period, however, it determined that the government could relieve shortages through crash programs to boost domestic output, which would bring new wells and refineries online beginning at the six-month mark. In the worst case, in which the United States lost all access to Eastern Hemisphere oil, including the resources of the Middle East, the petroleum deficit during the first six months would be 1.3 million barrels of crude per day. Because "a major factor in determining the allied petroleum position in the event of war is whether it is feasible to assure the continued availability of oil from Saudi Arabia, Bahrain, Qatar, and Indonesia," the Department of Defense would conduct a follow-up study to determine whether and at what cost access to oil from Saudi Arabia, Bahrain, and Qatar could be defended.[82] The report also recommended several measures to help the United States weather the first six months of war, including developing military stockpiles; drafting contingency plans to boost drilling in the tidelands oil region and at the Elk Hills Naval Petroleum Reserve, and to quickly expand refinery and tanker capacity, in the event of war; and preparing civilian rationing protocols that could be implemented as quickly as possible. Truman adopted these plans.

Members of the Eisenhower administration continued studying the problem of oil supply in a major war, and with the benefit of new defense studies, they reached slightly different conclusions from the Truman group. They found that "it would be possible—with some severe strains—to get along without Middle East supplies in a war beginning in mid-1953." Again, a deficit would appear in the first six months of hostilities. However, unlike the Truman-era documents, the report identified Soviet attacks on Middle East oil, not increased wartime demand, as the primary cause of the deficit. Severe civilian rationing could hold overall demand (i.e., civilian and military requirements) to roughly prewar levels in the first six months of war, at a level of about 12.4 million barrels daily. Military needs at the onset of war would increase by about 1 million barrels per day, but this could be compensated for by diverting 1 million barrels daily away from civilian purposes. Even at its peak, wartime demand would reach only 13.2 million barrels per day in 1957—just 1 million barrels above prewar levels. "The shortage of crude petroleum in time of war results, therefore, not from a large increase in requirements (provided effective rationing programs are instituted) but from the anticipated loss of, and damage to, important supply areas and facilities." Thus, successfully defending at least some portion of the Middle East in the first six months of war would significantly improve the Allied position. Holding

Bahrain, Saudi Arabia, and Qatar would add 1 million barrels per day to Allied supplies, provided tanker transit routes from the area could be defended. Over time, however, the Allied petroleum position was projected to weaken as Middle East output grew. The report concluded, "It will become increasingly difficult in a war starting after about 1955 to achieve wartime supply balance without Middle East oil. Consequently, the desirability of retaining the Middle East as a source of supply increases with the passage of time."[83]

The Beginnings of Indirect Control in the Middle East

The United States and its NATO allies faced medium vulnerability in the early Cold War. The petroleum deficit was moderate. The United States alone could provide slightly over half of the oil necessary in the first six months of a war (about 6.5 million barrels per day), and the U.S. contribution would increase thereafter as crash oil development programs boosted output. On balance, the susceptibility of imports to Soviet military power was also moderate. On the positive side, about 2 million additional barrels daily could be imported relatively safely from the Western Hemisphere, mostly from Venezuela. However, Middle East production, which also amounted to 2 million barrels daily, was highly insecure. The remaining imports needed to fuel the war would originate in small amounts from scattered sources in the Far East, the security of which fell somewhere in the middle.[84]

The United States responded with a strategy of indirect control through alliances with oil producers. These efforts started with Truman and were strengthened under Eisenhower. Indirect control was pursued primarily in the Middle East, where the United States built security partnerships to bolster the region against Soviet attack.[85] But the strategies tilted toward the lower end of the spectrum—minor basing, few countries, and as disengaged as possible. Saudi Arabia played an especially important role as the one country whose oil concessions were entirely controlled by American companies. Truman signed a Mutual Defense Assistance Agreement with Saudi Arabia in June 1951 and a five-year renewal of the military's lease on the Dharan airfield. The Eisenhower administration broadened the arrangement in June 1953 by increasing defense assistance and establishing the U.S. Military Training Mission. Four years later, in 1957, the United States again extended the lease at Dharan.[86]

The United States also drew up plans for the joint defense of the Middle East by Britain, France, and Turkey in the event of war, and it joined with the British to depose Mohammad Mossadegh, the Iranian leader suspected of Soviet sympathies, in 1953.[87] Later in the decade, Eisenhower attempted to create a "Northern Tier" of allied countries, including Iran, Iraq, Turkey, and Pakistan, as a buffer against Soviet expansion. Indirect control continued through the administrations of John F. Kennedy and Lyndon B. Johnson, but again, the United States tried to resist becoming too entangled in regional disputes. The reticence was made possible by Britain's preference to take the lead, sparing the United States from doing so. Nevertheless, during the Yemen crisis in 1963, the United States deployed fighter jets to Saudi Arabia after the Egyptian air force, active in the Yemeni civil war, bombed Saudi towns along the Saudi-Yemen border. The deployment, known as Operation Hard Surface, consisted of combat patrols to deter Egyptian raids and lasted about six months.[88]

Additionally, both the Truman and Eisenhower administrations recognized the need to protect Western Hemisphere productive capacity while still conserving U.S. reserves as much as possible. Yet, this put American policy on the horns of a dilemma. On the one hand, U.S. officials understood that the maintenance of robust domestic oil production in peacetime was crucial because it determined the baseline amount of oil available at the advent of crisis. Building and mothballing excess capacity was too expensive to be practical, and the fastest that American production could increase was six months, even with massive government investment. On the other hand, officials feared that too much peacetime production would only drain U.S. oil reserves in advance of a war, when they would truly be needed. The result was a tension between the competing objectives of sustaining U.S. oil production and still leaving as much oil as possible underground.

As a solution, both administrations sought to meet growing European demand by encouraging the rapid exploitation of Middle Eastern resources so that the most-threatened supplies would be depleted first. In the words of Interior Secretary Oscar Chapman, who played the dual role of petroleum administrator for defense, it was "indispensable to the security of the free world that Western Europe continue to have the use of Middle East reserves and that the free world have Venezuelan crude available to it, in order that the United States not wholly deplete its own reserves before the advent of an all-out war in trying to supply the entire free world."[89] In practice, this meant providing diplomatic support to American oil companies operating in the region. American firms were also valuable because they possessed the most advanced technology, which meant they could extract oil at even higher rates than their British counterparts and maximize the availability of exports from the Middle East.[90]

In 1957, Eisenhower took the further step of imposing voluntary import restrictions on oil entering the United States, a measure designed to protect the high-cost U.S. petroleum industry from competition by cheaper oil producers abroad. Quotas were designed to favor imports from Western Hemisphere countries, especially Canada and Venezuela, which from a security perspective were the next-best oil sources to domestic U.S. supply. Any policies that could harm these countries' oil industries would be counterproductive to American interests.

Accordingly, the U.S. government also encouraged the development of oil industries in countries throughout the Western Hemisphere. U.S. investment in the Canadian oil industry was especially massive, growing 1,400 percent from 1946 to 1959.[91] Because voluntary restrictions were not always honored, the import controls became mandatory in 1959.

Embargo? What Embargo? The 1960s Lull

From the standpoint of U.S. oil security, the years after Eisenhower were relatively quiet with no major changes to anticipatory strategies. The political and economic fundamentals underlaying the petroleum deficit and disruptibility of imports changed little from the 1950s, and the mild shifts that did occur happened gradually and in a positive direction, without much notice from policymakers. American oil fields produced steadily with capacity to spare, thanks to watchful regulation of output by the Texas Railroad Commission. Globally, oil producers faced a glut that pushed already-low prices down by about 30 percent between 1953, that decade's peak, and 1969.[92] As late as 1967, world oil supply exceeded demand by roughly 1.5 million barrels per day, and some 5 million barrels per day of spare capacity existed in the market, much of it in Texas.[93] In practical terms, this meant that oil producers could quickly provide an extra 6.5 million barrels daily—quite the supply cushion.

Perhaps no better indicator of the slack market of the 1960s exists than the failed attempt by Arab oil producers to use the "oil weapon" in 1967. Much like its reprise some six years later, the embargo was triggered by a regional war that pitted Israel against a coalition of Arab states headed by Egypt and Syria. On day two of what is now known as the Six-Day War, several Arab oil producers—led by Iraq but also including the moderate, generally pro-West kingdoms of Saudi Arabia and Kuwait—agreed to embargo oil to the United States and Britain in protest. Whether, and to what extent, individual oil producers *actually* embargoed oil is unclear; Libya, Kuwait, and Saudi Arabia evidently cheated by secretly selling some oil to the United States and United Kingdom (UK).[94] But the embargo was not entirely illusory. Some oil commerce was certainly disrupted. Saudi Arabia, cheating aside, actually exported less oil in the short run because of trouble diverting output to other sources. Saudi exports during the war fell from 2.7 million to 1.1 million barrels per day, a forfeiture of profits on the order of $30 million over just five days. Syria also ceased its modest oil production entirely.[95]

Yet even though significant quantities of oil were removed from the market, the embargo had no discernible effect on the United States politically or economically. Texas producers alone added 344,578 more barrels of daily output almost immediately and could have increased production far higher.[96] In fact, the degree to which the embargo barely registered with policymakers is striking. The most important strategy documents between 1967 and 1973 mention the episode only in passing and quickly label it an abject failure. In fact, the mild-to-nonexistent consequences of the 1967 embargo were used to argue that the Arab "oil weapon" had no teeth. As a result, policymakers continually discounted its danger in documents leading up to the 1973 embargo.

By mid-July, just five weeks since its imposition, Saudi and Libyan leaders concluded that the embargo had backfired, hurting only themselves, and they resumed normal exports. The embargo officially ended in mid-August under a deal whereby the Arab oil states pledged to use export profits to help rebuild the defeated belligerents. Some 20 percent of Arab oil profits that year, chiefly from Libya, Kuwait, and Saudi Arabia, went to Egypt and Jordan.[97]

The 1960s also represented somewhat of a lull in U.S.-Mideast relations, except perhaps in the Arab-Israel conflict, where the United States drifted from even-handedness under President Eisenhower to a robust pro-Israel stance under President Johnson. In the main, however, the United States remained unengaged in the region to the point of "neglect" in the eyes of internal critics.[98] Perhaps neglect was inevitable given that Vietnam was already distracting Johnson from his main policy objectives: advancing civil rights and reducing domestic poverty. In the shadow of Vietnam and the Great Society, Middle East policy was low priority, and the absence of major shocks impacting coercive vulnerability ensured that it would remain of tertiary concern at best.

Case V: 1969–1975—A Reckoning?

Toward the end of the 1960s, after several years of calm, emerging trends were subtly suggestive of a change in the petroleum deficit and disruptibility of imports. The trends themselves did not capture policymakers' attention enough to force a reevaluation of the anticipatory strategies currently in place. But as lurking background factors, they magnified the effects of acute shocks soon to come.

Two countervailing forces had the potential to alter the petroleum deficit in unpredictable ways. First, domestic oil demand was expanding at a remarkable rate, squeezing out excess production capacity in American oil fields.[99] Because the oil import restrictions imposed by Eisenhower artificially constrained oil supply in the United States, not enough foreign oil could be brought in to keep prices steady. Therefore, prices in the United States surged, diverging ever more significantly from the global market price. Yet, at the same time, high domestic prices were potentially expanding U.S. oil reserves—and long-run output—by making new, higher-cost sources of oil economical to produce.

Perhaps the most important area for prospecting was the Alaskan frontier. On December 26, 1967, exploratory drillers discovered the most massive North American oil field ever found, at Prudhoe Bay on Alaska's North Slope. It was expected to come online within three years and was projected to produce, at its peak, some two million barrels per day. Other finds rapidly followed, including the continent's second-largest oil field of all time, Kuparuk, also on the North Slope, discovered in 1969.[100] These two countervailing forces—increased demand and new discoveries—made the petroleum outlook increasingly nebulous.

Import disruptibility was also in flux. But unlike the case of the petroleum deficit, which had cross-cutting pressures, threats to imports were trending in one direction: up. Beginning in the late 1960s and continuing into the early 1970s, intelligence reports warned of a growing Soviet influence in the region, the significance of which was difficult to interpret. Optimists acknowledged the plain truth that the USSR had turned to the region with new vigor, as evidenced by, among other things, increases in Soviet aid and arms sales to the region.[101] But, they viewed the degree of Soviet penetration as tolerable, if concerning. Optimists reasoned that Soviet ambitions would be constrained by local nationalism and by the desire to keep relations with the United States, which were improving, on a positive track. To pessimists in the intelligence community, however, recent Soviet forays presaged the emergence of a "dominant position" in the region within ten to twenty years, which analysts argued could translate into Soviet control over Persian Gulf oil.[102]

Not only was the Soviet threat growing; it was changing in nature. Since the mid-1940s, the United States perennially worried about the possibility of direct Soviet intervention in the Middle East, as either a standalone action or an accompaniment to conventional attack in Europe—hence the importance of "buffer states" between the USSR and the Gulf (i.e., the Central Treaty Organization [CENTO], formerly known as the Baghdad Pact). That threat remained, of course. But layered on the traditional threat was the increasing realization that the United States also had to worry about more insidious forms of Soviet penetration: the cultivation of regional proxies sympathetic, or even beholden, to Moscow.

Indeed, the Soviet proxy threat intensified throughout the 1960s as British and French colonial power gradually collapsed. Nasserism, the Arab nationalist movement with a decidedly Marxist tinge, had continued to fester in Egypt and Syria, both longtime Soviet client states. In addition to that old thorn, pro-Soviet regimes replaced Western colonial rule in Algeria in 1962, Aden (renamed South Yemen) in 1967, and Libya in 1969. Soviet-Iraqi ties, already cordial, also strengthened. Iraq had transformed from British bastion to Soviet arms purchaser after the 1958 coup that deposed the British-backed monarchy. Yet relations with Moscow did not deepen until the 1967 Arab-Israeli War, followed by the resumption of the Kurdish rebellion in 1968, drastically increased Iraqi needs for Soviet weaponry.[103] The 1968 coup that installed pro-Soviet Ba'athists also contributed to Iraq's stronger lean toward the USSR. When added to Iraq, the realignment of Algeria and Libya against the West meant that, by 1970, roughly one-third of Mideast–North African oil production occurred in Soviet-leaning states (Algeria, Libya, and Iraq), compared with one-fifth of regional output in 1960 (solely from Iraq).[104] Pro-Soviet regimes now encircled the three major Western-aligned Arab oil producers: Saudi Arabia, Kuwait, and the Trucial States. Soviet political reach had already jumped the CENTO land buffer formed by Iran and Turkey when Iraq succumbed; now it had made it onto the Arabian Peninsula courtesy of the new government in South Yemen. By the late 1960s, then, the political outlook in the Mideast had dimmed considerably.

The Petroleum Deficit: An Impetus to Reevaluate

Against this backdrop, two catalyzing events directly spurred the study phase of the causal logic. The first catalyst, which launched a reexamination of the petroleum deficit, was soaring demand that led to a series of price increases announced by American oil companies in early 1969, just after Nixon assumed office. The increases caused public outcry against the oil import controls that had long been controversial for keeping U.S. oil prices above the global oil price. By the late 1960s, domestic U.S. prices under the quota scheme were estimated to be about 65 percent higher than they would have been in the absence of quotas, costing U.S. taxpayers some $5 billion annually. American manufacturers, and their allies in Congress, complained that U.S. businesses faced a competitive disadvantage because they paid higher oil prices than competitors abroad.[105] Questions were also raised in op-eds, on the Hill, and in the White House about the fairness of making U.S. consumers pay a premium to ensure adequate Free World oil production in an emergency, while consumers in Japan and NATO countries, who would also benefit from U.S. productive capacity in a crisis, bought oil at the substantially lower market price.

Public pressure caused by increased demand and high prices induced the newly inaugurated president Richard M. Nixon to impanel a special task force to review, for the first time, the mandatory oil import restrictions established by Eisenhower in 1959. Though the task force sought to answer a relatively narrow question—namely, whether oil import restrictions were still necessary on national security grounds, and if so, what form they should take—its study was sweeping. The key consideration was the fear that if imports were allowed to grow and the domestic oil industry permitted to shrink, "a substantial volume of such foreign oil might be cut off to our military, political, or economic detriment; or a cutoff might be threatened in order to influence our foreign policy."[106]

To assess the threat posed by imports, the task force required interested departments and agencies, including the Departments of State, Defense, Interior, Treasury, and Commerce, the Central Intelligence Agency, and the NSC, to submit reports on whether or how an increase in imports—and the consequent shrinking of the high-cost domestic petroleum industry—might make the country militarily, politically, or economically vulnerable. In the course of preparing their reports for the president's committee, the agencies assessed the availability of oil supplies from domestic production as well as from international sources, and they examined potential threats to those sources, chiefly from the Soviet Union, but also the possibility that Arab states could attempt to embargo oil to the United States, most likely over the Arab-Israeli conflict.

Perhaps unsurprisingly, given the diversity of agencies consulted in the process, the president's task force did not return a unanimous set of recommendations. Instead, it produced a split report, which itself papered over deep divisions behind the scenes. Nevertheless, two of the report's key findings appeared to command general agreement: first, that some level of import restrictions would have to continue for the sake of national security, and second, that preference should be given to Western Hemisphere producers, whose supplies were deemed the most secure.

The oil import review found that if the quotas were removed, the ability of the United States to deal with security contingencies would be significantly compromised. In the absence of quotas, the wellhead price in the United States would drop from the current price of $3.30 to the world price of $2.00. While good for consumers, who would save $5 billion to $8 billion a year, the oil industry would be seriously hurt. U.S. oil reserves would shrink dramatically because some erstwhile reserves would no longer be economical to extract at the lower price. Reserves in the lower forty-eight states would be halved over six years; Alaskan reserves would also shrink, but by a much lesser sum. By 1980, domestic oil production would decrease by 30 percent—from an estimated 13.5 million barrels per day to just 9.5 million barrels per day. The country would have to rely on imports for over 50 percent of its oil needs, as compared with about 27 percent of its oil needs if the quotas remained. This meant that, in a contingency in which access to Mideast and Latin American oil was lost, the United States and Canada would face a deficit of 4.7 million barrels per day. If only Mideast oil was lost, the deficit would be about 0.8 million barrels daily. By contrast, if quotas remained, North America could lose access to all imports and face no deficit at all.[107] Notably, these numbers omitted the needs of U.S. allies in Western Europe and Japan.

As the report concluded:

> **Total abandonment of all import controls might on present evidence be deemed to threaten security of supply.** We are unable on present

evidence to rule out the possibility that abandonment of all import controls would result in an inability to satisfy our essential oil requirements by acceptable emergency measures in response to certain conceivable supply interruptions. Whether such conceivable interruptions are "reasonably possible" is a matter on which judgments may vary. Our estimates indicate that a one-year supply crisis in 1980 would leave about 21% of the United States and Canadian demand unmet if North America received no Eastern Hemisphere or Latin American oil. . . . In case of such an interruption, military and essential civilian demand could be met only by severe and perhaps intolerable rationing. . . . Although the probability of such an extreme interruption is small, these considerations and the uncertainty of our estimates render the Task Force unable to say that complete abandonment of import controls at this time would be consistent with the national security.[108]

Second, the report recommended, with broad agreement among the agencies, that Canada and Mexico be exempted from restrictions because "Canadian and Mexican oil is nearly as secure politically and militarily as our own" and that other Western Hemisphere countries, such as Venezuela, whose oil had been "delivered without interruption over the years," should get preferential treatment for security reasons.[109]

Beyond these general points, deep cleavages existed over the perceived likelihood of supply disruptions and the question of whether allies' needs should be included for emergency planning, as opposed to just U.S. needs. State, Commerce, and the task force chairman, whose interpretation dominated the report, were adamant that the allies be left to their own devices and viewed serious, sustained disruptions as almost laughably unlikely. Thus, they favored drastic reductions in import controls. Those who were more pessimistic about the prospects of disruptions and who believed allies' security was intrinsically tied to the United States'—officials at the Department of Defense and the White House Office of Emergency Preparedness (OEP), run by retired brigadier general George A. Lincoln—favored higher import restrictions. To placate Defense and OEP, language was inserted to indicate that the findings were provisional and that no full determination could be made. Defense and OEP, then, believed they still had a strong ability to influence the final policy, which was enough to get them to sign on to the final report. The secretary of defense penned a pointed dissent. Though he paid lip service to the idea that import restrictions could be loosened (albeit not eliminated), his comments and suggestions, if followed, would essentially require the maintenance of at least the present level of quotas.[110]

In light of the divisions among his committee and concerns about domestic politics, Nixon equivocated by calling for further study and consultation with allies before any changes were made.[111] The president did not want to endanger the electoral prospects for Republican candidates in oil-producing states, such as Texas and Louisiana, in the 1970 midterm elections. Ambiguity in the report's findings left wiggle room for Nixon to accommodate electoral interests, or at the very least, do them no harm. Ultimately, the president made a nondecision to punt the question past the next election to avoid potential backlash.

Strikingly, the potential price effects of supply disruptions were absent from the report—nowhere did the analysis attempt to model how much economic damage might be done to the U.S. economy if prices skyrocketed because of disruption. This indicates that national security, rather than economic growth, was the overwhelming concern.

The Redcoats Are Not Coming: The British Withdraw from the Gulf

The second and more significant shock, which caused U.S. officials to reconsider oil import disruptibility, was Britain's announcement in January 1968 that it would withdraw all military forces from the Middle East by the end of 1971. For decades, the UK had acted as a stabilizing force to maintain the flow of Persian Gulf oil to the West.[112] The United States had encouraged this role, gladly free riding on British efforts to check Soviet influence and to dampen security competition between local powers while avoiding unnecessary involvement in regional disputes.[113] The removal of the British pacifier could create a power vacuum that Soviet proxies—or Moscow itself—might be tempted to fill. Anything that intensified Soviet influence over the region's oil producers had the potential to jeopardize Western oil access in a crisis.

Despite the significance of the announcement, the United States' reaction was muted at first, consisting mainly of unsuccessful backchannel efforts to persuade the British to stay.[114] Why was the initial U.S. response so mild? The simple explanation is that President Johnson had essentially "checked out" on Middle East matters by early 1968. Though he had yet to disclose it publicly, Johnson had decided as far back as September 1967 not to run for reelection.[115] He spent his remaining time in office hopelessly wrapped up in Vietnam, with little energy to spare even for the domestic programs he most cared about, let alone the goings-on in the remote Persian Gulf region.

Thus it fell to the incoming Nixon administration to respond. In the early months of the administration, the NSC commissioned cascading studies on the Persian Gulf, beginning with basic questions about U.S. interests and Soviet threats and then narrowing to the more specific question of what to do about British withdrawal.[116] The review culminated in two key reports: a longer study, "Future U.S. Policy in the Persian Gulf,"[117] which outlined the problem of British withdrawal in depth and considered in detail the pros and cons of several options; and a condensed final report by the Senior Review Group within the NSC, titled "U.S. Policy Options toward the Persian Gulf," dated October 19, 1970, and included as a tab in Kissinger's memo of October 22, 1970, to President Nixon outlining the "Twin Pillars" strategy, which the president initialed to approve its recommendations.[118]

AN OPPORTUNITY FOR DIRECT SOVIET "MISCHIEF-MAKING"?

The NSC reports suggested that Britain's exit would exacerbate the existing Soviet threat to Middle East oil in two interrelated ways. First, it would increase the (albeit unlikely) possibility that the USSR might attempt to conquer regional oil exporters. Given that Britain had successfully "excluded unfriendly major powers from the Gulf proper" during its tenure as a regional security provider, its absence could create a power vacuum that the USSR would be tempted to fill. Soviet interest in the Gulf was long-standing, the reports argued. Russian ambitions there dated back to czarist times, when strategists viewed it as a toehold for intercepting British sea lines of communication to India. Britain's departure seemed to have piqued this interest anew. Forebodingly, "several Soviet naval squadrons have already visited the Gulf since the British withdrawal announcement, the first Russian warships to show the flag there in over sixty years," one report notes. The reports also offered a potential motive for Soviet expansion—the Communist bloc might soon depend on Persian Gulf oil. Recent intelligence suggested that Soviet oil fields might deplete in as few as fifteen years, raising the "distinct possibility" that the Warsaw Pact countries might seek to import large amounts of Gulf oil within the decade.[119]

Yet, although the probability of Soviet conquest would increase once the British retreated, the overall likelihood of it was still recognized as small. Various mitigating factors independent of U.S. policy would reduce the danger. For instance, the burgeoning need for Persian Gulf oil might reinforce, rather than undermine, the Soviet stake in maintaining a stable status quo. Moreover, the reports argued, the Soviets lacked the capabilities to project significant naval power into the region, and the political prospects for locating Soviet naval bases to ease deployments to the Gulf were poor. Local proxy leaders understood that a Soviet military footprint in their territory would provoke public backlash against their regimes. Nevertheless, policymakers could not entirely discount the threat of Soviet adventurism. As one report pointed out, "Short-sightedness or opportunism might draw the Soviets into mischief-making in the Gulf no matter how clearly *we* can see that it would only complicate Soviet policy."[120]

THE GRASP OF UNFRIENDLY HANDS: AN EXPANSION OF SOVIET INFLUENCE

However, the "main worry" triggered by Britain's retrenchment was the spread of Soviet political influence. "It is virtually certain that the USSR will seek to increase its presence in the Gulf after the British leave," one report warned.[121] Policymakers believed that greater Soviet political penetration would "affect the East-West geopolitical balance" by "increasing Soviet pressure on Iran and Turkey and—although there is debate over how this would work out in practice—by increasing the potential for Soviet control over the disposition of Persian Gulf oil."[122]

The reasoning went as follows. Without Britain acting as a regional stabilizer, Marxism and radical Arab nationalism would be more likely to expand into the conservative oil-exporting monarchies traditionally aligned with the West. If so, one or more of those countries—Saudi Arabia, Kuwait, Bahrain, Qatar, and the Trucial States—could fall under Soviet sway. That would undermine the U.S. indirect control strategy to keep as much Gulf oil in friendly hands as possible. Moreover, Moscow could potentially use its influence to coerce these regimes into reducing or suspending oil deliveries to the West. Coercion works better against allies, especially inferior ones, than adversaries.[123] Because Europe and Japan, which depended heavily on Gulf oil, would feel the impact of a cutoff more immediately and acutely than the United States, which had its own domestic supplies to fall back on, the Soviets could sow internal division within NATO and potentially rupture the alliance. American policymakers understood that oil was a wedge issue that could throw NATO into political disarray, above and in addition to the problems that oil shortages would cause for economic and military effectiveness.

Importantly, American policymakers also understood that the most realistic way that a denial threat could materialize was with Soviet backing. Oil exporters benefited too much from oil sales to the West for unilateral action to be desirable.[124] Such states, even unfriendly ones, had every incentive to keep selling to the international market—that is, unless Moscow made them a better offer. U.S. officials feared that the Soviets could bribe oil-rich proxy regimes to stop exporting oil to any nation outside the Communist bloc. Whether through cash, credit for arms purchases, or some other side payment, the USSR could simply compensate the producers, using its own economic wherewithal to absorb the loss.[125] Thus, the only serious Mideast embargo scenarios were those linked to Soviet sponsorship.

Radical Arab Marxism could spread to the conservative monarchies through two main pathways, both widened by Britain's departure. First, conquest by Soviet proxies would be more likely without Britain acting as a deterrent. With the

British gone, the costs and risks of Arab nationalist leaders conquering oil-rich countries in the Western orbit would decrease—perhaps enough to make invasion a gamble worth taking.[126] If conquest succeeded, Soviet beneficiaries would control more oil fields, which in turn could then be denied to the West. The natural targets were the small Gulf states that had relied on "formal British protection [and] tutelage," namely, Bahrain, Kuwait, Qatar, and the seven Trucial States.[127]

The usual suspects—Egypt, Syria, Iraq, and South Yemen—were voted most likely to aggress.[128] Each had recently demonstrated revisionist interests and exhibited a certain coziness with the Soviets. Shortly after the withdrawal announcement, South Yemen extended material support to Marxist rebels in Dhufar who were fighting in an insurgency against the central Omani government.[129] The following year, South Yemeni forces invaded and briefly occupied the Saudi border town of al-Wadiah, the subject of a long-running territorial dispute. Egypt had also behaved aggressively in the recent past. In 1969, Nasser launched the War of Attrition, a series of low-level attacks on Israeli positions in the occupied Sinai Peninsula.[130] In early 1970, he welcomed thousands of Soviet military advisers into Egypt to operate, and eventually train the Egyptians to use, dozens of new SA-3 missiles and MiG-21 fighters provided by Moscow for the effort.[131] Syria also seemed eager for a fight; in September 1970, it intervened in Jordan to defend the Palestine Liberation Organization (PLO) from King Hussein's campaign to expel the militant group from his country. Both Kissinger and Nixon attributed the move to Soviet encouragement.[132]

The most obvious flashpoint for post-British conflict, however, was the territorial dispute between Iraq and Kuwait. Baghdad had long contended that Kuwait rightfully belonged to Iraq because it was administered as part of Basra under Ottoman rule and all of Basra was meant to pass to Iraq.[133] The claims went beyond mere bluster. In July 1961, just after Kuwait formally declared independence from Britain, an Iraqi invasion appeared imminent as British intelligence detected signs of troop movements toward the border in conjunction with threatening rhetoric from General Abd al-Karim Qasim, Iraq's leader. At Kuwait's request, Britain rapidly deployed some three thousand troops to defend Kuwait under Operation Vantage, which appeared to thwart a potential invasion.[134] Whether Baghdad would move against Kuwait after the British defense commitment ended was uncertain; unlike 1961, Kurdish uprisings supported by Iran had bedeviled Iraqi leaders for years and pinned down large portions of the military in the far north by 1970. Then again, if internal upheaval—a coup, for instance—distracted the Kuwaitis, Iraq could quickly overrun Kuwait with the small military forces based nearby in the south.[135] All things equal, external threats to Kuwait and the other small Gulf states would worsen without the backstop of British military power.

The second pathway for increased Soviet political penetration was through the subversion of Western-leaning conservative regimes. British intelligence services and policing had played a crucial role in suppressing pro-Soviet domestic dissidents that might otherwise threaten the Gulf monarchies from the inside. British forces successfully stamped out the Marxist National Liberation Front in Bahrain. They also trained, funded, and officered the Trucial Oman Scouts (TOS), a gendarmerie 1,400 strong, to prop up the Gulf sheikhdoms.[136] These regimes would struggle to approach British competence in such tasks. Even Saudi Arabia, an American ally, would suffer increased domestic threats. The Saudis indirectly benefited from British policing in the Gulf sheikhdoms insofar as a tamping down of radicalism in neighboring states prevented contagion to the Saudi regime. The discovery in 1969–1970 of a plot by Saudi air force officers to overthrow the regime underscored this concern.[137]

Furthermore, diminished policing and intelligence capabilities in the Gulf following the British withdrawal would embolden radical Arab and Soviet efforts to foment unrest. Syria and South Yemen already broadcast radio propaganda against the Gulf monarchies and would almost certainly increase funding to nationalist subversive groups. The much-advertised Soviet interest in supporting national liberation movements in the Third World, including the Arab world, likewise unsettled Western leaders. Unless ongoing efforts to forge a political federation of Gulf states succeeded, enabling the sheikhdoms to pool resources for domestic security provision, analysts feared the TOS would collapse—along with "one or more of the governments in, say, three to five years."[138]

Moreover, Britain's absence would revive security concerns that governments friendly to the West had vis-à-vis one another, which in turn would hinder the security cooperation necessary for regional stability post-withdrawal, particularly across the Arab-Persian divide. With the British gone, Iran would emerge as the preponderant power—a frightening reality for the small Gulf states, several of whom had unresolved territorial disputes with Tehran. British security guarantees had ensured that the shah would not violate the sheikhdoms' borders. Without them, Iranian land grabs were all but inevitable (and indeed came to pass in November 1971, when the shah occupied Abu Musa and the Tunbs islands, claimed by Sharjah and Ras al-Khaimah, respectively).

Nor did the Saudi Arabians relish the coming Iranian regional hegemony. King Faisal, like most leaders in the region, distrusted the shah's intentions and feared his superior military capabilities. Iran's friendly relations with Israel, which Faisal suspected of communist sympathies based on the old forgery *The Protocols of the Elders of Zion*, certainly did not help.[139] In fact, Faisal, who "never tired of telling his American interlocutors that the Zionists and the Communists were conspiring together," was so consumed by fictitious plots that he warned Nixon that Vietnam War protesters were secretly agents of a "Zionist-Communist global conspiracy."[140]

In sum, Britain's departure raised the likelihood that Soviet-aligned groups could depose a petrostate monarch and, consequently, withhold oil from the West in a superpower crisis.

Recommendations and Outcome

Ultimately, the reports concluded that the United States should intensify its indirect control measures to counter the heightened threat of Soviet political penetration caused by Britain's withdrawal. Indirect control was still the optimal strategy—as it had been since the start of the Cold War—but should be pursued more vigorously. Thus, this was a change in degree rather than a change in kind. The strategy of keeping oil in friendly hands—and, perhaps more to the point, *out* of hostile hands—would suffice to protect NATO oil access in a crisis; it would simply require more effort. To buttress the pro-Western regimes against rising Soviet pressure, then, the United States would have to deepen its existing alliances and forge new relationships with the small Gulf states for which British protection was about to expire.

The reports also considered, but thoroughly rejected, the idea of replacing the British. As one report warned, the United States should not "assume ourselves the UK role in modern dress," which would necessitate "a meaningful naval presence" and "the establishment of what would, in effect, be a US 'base' on the Arab side of the Gulf." Although that level of indirect control verging on direct control would strongly guarantee Western oil access, it was "not clear that the protection of our interests requires such action." Because the United States was only moderately vulnerable to Soviet-inspired oil coercion, the benefits of a more aggressive strategy simply were not needed. In other words, a modest decrease in vulnerability would suffice to make Western oil access secure, so why pay the costs for an extreme strategy that provides more benefits than needed? And, indeed, the diplomatic fallout of replacing Britain would be highly costly. The Saudis and the shah would bristle at any hint that the United States might establish itself as a nouveau colonial regime in the region. The basing of significant U.S. forces would inflame sentiment in the radical Arab states and risk a diplomatic confrontation with the Soviet Union. Moreover, the United States would get drawn into local disputes and rivalries. And, while the budgetary costs would be "modest," prevailing attitudes in Congress "would make it difficult . . . to mount the additional military, naval, and diplomatic effort that would be needed."[141]

Erecting the Pillars

The reports' positive recommendations, codified as National Security Decision Memorandum (NSDM) 92 on November 7, 1970, consisted of two main components. First, and most important, the United States should designate Saudi Arabia and Iran as joint stewards of the Gulf and encourage cooperation between them—a plan that would become known as the "Twin Pillars" policy.[142] The idea, consistent with the Nixon Doctrine already being practiced in Vietnam, was to strengthen allies' military capabilities so that they could defend themselves from aggressors without American combat troops on the ground. The plan also sought to deputize those allies as guardians of the regional status quo.

Iran would take the lead here. As the preponderant regional power, Iran alone possessed the military wherewithal to intervene in regional contingencies—for instance, if one or more Gulf states succumbed to radicalism or if Iraq threatened Kuwait. Indeed, Iran had already demonstrated both the capabilities and the will to assist pro-Western regimes; during the aforementioned al-Wadiah conflict between Saudi Arabia and Yemen in late 1969, the shah airlifted emergency military supplies to help repel the attack and pledged to send its air force to help defend against any future Yemeni incursions.[143]

However, an overreliance on Iran would provoke a negative reaction likely to strengthen the influence of radicals in friendly Arab states, given the Persian-Arab cultural schism and the shah's friendly ties with Israel. Thus, the plan would need an Arab pillar to act as a counterweight. Saudi Arabia was the logical choice. Though too weak to deal with military contingencies, it possessed the political capital that Iran lacked, especially with the small Gulf states.[144] Moreover, its military, traditionally kept weak because the Saudi royal family doubted the loyalty of its officers, gravely needed American assistance.[145]

In truth, "Twin" was a misnomer, for it implied an equality between pillars that did not actually exist; NSDM 92 officially recognized Iran as the primary U.S. instrument and relegated Saudi Arabia to the role of junior partner. Although each would receive substantial amounts of American weaponry for self-defense, arms sales to Iran would be far larger and more technologically sophisticated than what was offered to the Saudis. From 1969 to 1974, roughly Nixon's tenure in office, American weapons deliveries to Iran totaled $7.6 billion, compared with $612 million in deliveries to Saudi Arabia.[146] Iran also enjoyed unparalleled access to the best American military hardware. To the shock of several of his subordinates, Nixon agreed in May 1972 to provide Iran with "all available sophisticated weapons short of the atomic bomb," including scores of F-14s and F-15s, precision-guided munitions, Maverick missiles, and as many as twenty thousand U.S. military technicians—the same number of Soviet technical personnel then in Egypt.[147]

The Twin Pillars approach also entailed close diplomatic cooperation between the United States and its proxies, but again, Nixon coordinated much more closely with the shah than with King Faisal on matters both diplomatic and martial. Partly this reflected Nixon's high personal esteem for the shah, whom he had considered a friend since the early 1950s. But more importantly, Iran's superior capabilities simply meant that it could devote more and better resources to scheming with Washington.

And scheme they did, with the shared goal of blocking Soviet encroachment in the Gulf. Particularly noteworthy were the contingency plans hatched over the summer of 1973 by Kissinger and the shah for Iranian military intervention if Kuwait or Saudi Arabia was threatened by rebellion or attacked by a Soviet proxy, such as Iraq.[148] The two also discussed Iranian intervention if Syria or Iraq attacked Jordan, which both viewed as such a crucial military ally of the Gulf monarchies that, in the shah's estimation, "if Jordan goes, there is no future for Kuwait or Saudi Arabia."[149] Details about these contingency plans have not yet emerged on the American side, as countless archival documents are still being withheld from declassification on national security grounds. But according to Iranian sources, the contingency plans for Saudi Arabia included using the Iranian military "to secure Saudi Arabia's oil fields and restore the Al Saud to their throne if the Saudi monarchy were ever threatened."[150]

Perhaps the most striking privilege the Nixon administration offered to its pillars was to condone, and even to assist, their drive for greater oil profits—even at the expense of American consumers and U.S. oil companies operating in Saudi Arabia and Iran. On several occasions from 1970 through 1973, Nixon personally assured the shah and his ambassador, Ardeshir Zahedi, that Iran could go after the oil companies to raise prices and share a greater portion of their profits without incurring official American wrath. "Tell the Shah you can push [us] as much as you want [on oil prices]," Nixon told Zahedi on May 14, 1970.[151] That stance alone was remarkable, for it meant that the president secretly authorized the shah to jack up prices at the pump—in an election year, no less.

Equally striking is that, at the time, the shah was one of the two OPEC antiheroes pressuring the oil companies the hardest to renegotiate revenue sharing. The other was Colonel Mu'ammar Gadhafi, the brash new leader who had just overthrown the pro-Western Libyan monarchy—strange company indeed for Nixon's closest Mideast ally. Predictably, greenlighting the shah would (and did) set off incessant rounds of "leapfrogging" negotiations, whereby OPEC nations competed to outdo each other in demanding better and better deals from the companies, often with the threat of expropriation looming in the background.[152]

The Nixon administration also supported the Saudis as they wrested majority control of ARAMCO from a consortium of four U.S. oil corporations, even though this obviously hurt the companies' interests. Kissinger, deeply involved in the negotiations, had no sympathy for the oil companies' plight, describing their CEOs as "people whose political acumen is not up to their income to put it mildly," "stupid bastards," and "politically irresponsible . . . idiots."[153] His rhetoric, and the administration's behavior more broadly, belie the notion, prevalent at the time, that U.S. oil policy acted at the behest of Big Oil.

Acceding to higher prices furthered Nixon and Kissinger's strategy in two ways: first, it bought them goodwill with the shah and the Saudis that they hoped to later trade for favors, and second, it enabled Iran and Saudi Arabia to finance the vast expenditures on American-made weapons necessary for the Twin Pillars strategy to work. This practice, an example of what is sometimes called petrodollar recycling, meant that a decent portion of the wealth transferred to the Gulf through high oil prices actually reentered the American economy as payments to arms manufacturers, somewhat compensating for the loss.[154]

The second broad component of the strategy articulated in NSDM 92 focused on building new ties to the small states of the Gulf—Kuwait, Bahrain, and the Trucial States—that previously fell within the United Kingdom's security purview. Britain had historically discouraged the United States from diplomatic and military coordination with these regimes for fear that American influence might compete or interfere with vital British interests there. Resultantly, as of late 1970, the United States had no permanent diplomatic presence in the lower Gulf. NSDM 92, therefore, recommended that the State Department establish diplomatic posts and develop programming to expand commercial, educational, and cultural ties. Traditional economic aid, a standard diplomatic lever, was unnecessary given the countries' oil wealth, but plans to offer technical assistance were to be drawn up. More importantly, for the first time, the United States would consider selling military equipment to Kuwait and other interested Gulf states—another practice previously avoided so as not to irk the British. Finally, it was decided that MIDEASTFOR, the symbolic U.S. naval presence that consisted of two destroyers and a seaplane tender homeported at British facilities in Bahrain, would remain in place. The force held "little military value" and might not be "welcome or useful for very long in the future," but U.S. officials judged that its removal would unnecessarily alarm the Bahrainis.[155]

The 1973 OAPEC Embargo

The 1973 oil crisis is commonly viewed as a turning point in U.S. history, an event that supposedly revealed a newfound U.S. vulnerability to the whims of a small cadre of Middle Eastern oil producers. But from the point of view of the theory, very little changed. The petroleum deficit and the threat to oil imports remained tied to U.S. perceptions of the Soviet menace—both to Europe and to the Middle East.

The Arab oil producers' use of the oil weapon was prompted by U.S. support for Israel during the Yom Kippur War. On October 6, 1973, just two days before several OPEC countries were to meet with five of the oil majors in Vienna to renegotiate oil profit sharing, Egypt and Syria launched a surprise attack on Israel.[156] The military situation looked very bad for Israel for the first several days of war; in the north, the Syrians breached Israeli lines in the Golan Heights, while in the south, the Egyptian army pushed several miles into the Israeli-occupied Sinai Peninsula. Within the first seventy-two hours of battle, Israel lost some ninety tanks and forty to fifty planes, about one-tenth of its air force.[157] Pleas for U.S. assistance from Israeli leaders, who warned the country was running dangerously low on munitions, combined with the Soviet decision to massively resupply Egypt and Syria, convinced U.S. officials to undertake an urgent airlift to Israel. It was meant to be a secret mission, with U.S. planes arriving and departing in the dead of night on Saturday, October 13. However, to the Nixon administration's chagrin, crosswinds at a refueling base in the Azores delayed the mission and the C-5A cargo planes "came lumbering out of the sky on Sunday during the day, October 14, their immense white stars visible for all to see."[158]

The spectacle, delivered to the world's capitals through television footage of the landings at Tel Aviv airport, proved unbearable for the Arab oil producers, who had warned throughout the summer of 1973 that they would consider resorting to the oil weapon if progress was not made in settling the Arab-Israeli dispute. At roughly the same time, the Vienna oil talks collapsed and the Persian Gulf delegates (including Iranians) decamped to Kuwait City to confer on next steps. On October 16, they announced a unilateral 70 percent hike on posted prices—dismaying to the international oil companies, but not exactly a surprise.

Then, on October 17, came the news: OAPEC leaders (less Iraq—and Iran, of course, being non-Arab) announced a 5 percent production cut and vowed to continue cutting output by 5 percent each month "until an Israeli withdrawal is completed and until the restoration of the legal rights of the Palestinian people."[159] Over the next four days, the coercive pressure escalated as the participating countries sought to outdo each other in demonstrating their concern for the Palestinians' plight. On October 18, Saudi Arabia doubled its production cuts to 10 percent while Kuwait and Abu Dhabi announced a total embargo on oil shipments to the United States. On the 19th, in response to Nixon's request that day for congressional approval of a $2.2 billion military aid package for Israel, Saudi Arabia also ceased all oil deliveries to the United States. Libya announced its own embargo on the United States the same day. By October 21, eight countries had completely embargoed oil to the United States: Saudi Arabia, Kuwait, Abu Dhabi, Dubai, Qatar, Bahrain, Libya, and Algeria.

Over the course of the next several weeks, Henry Kissinger, the double-hatted secretary of state and national security advisor, in cooperation with the Soviets, negotiated a ceasefire that led to a January 1974 disengagement plan between Israeli and Egyptian forces in the Sinai Peninsula. Even before the diplomatic breakthrough, however, the oil weapon was faltering. Without explanation, the Saudis announced a halt to the production cuts on December 4, 1973; on Christmas, the Arab oil ministers agreed to increase production by 10 percent, signaling the effective end of the crisis.[160] Officially, the embargo against the United States did not end until March 1974, but by then, the real tumult had passed. In the end, the oil weapon had utterly failed to change U.S. policies toward Israel. "The lack of results is so striking," Roy Licklider notes, "that some scholars have argued that perhaps the Arabs did not really *want* to influence the policies of the target states."[161]

The oil weapon had no real effect on the petroleum deficit faced by the United States. It neither changed the amount of oil the United States could produce domestically, nor did it affect U.S. needs. The United States continued to produce two-thirds of its own oil; Europe continued to need the U.S. defense commitment through NATO.

The threat to imports also did not meaningfully change for the simple reason that trade cessation is generally ineffective as a means of cutoff. Despite the ubiquitous media images of long lines at American gas stations, no true shortages developed. At its height, the production cuts removed some 3.1 million barrels of oil per day from the *global* market, roughly 5 percent of supply, but it is not at all clear that oil shipments to the *United States* actually declined. As Blake Clayton notes, the production cuts "failed to dent commercial inventories. Private inventories of crude oil held in the United States were all but unchanged between July and December 1973."[162] Even if the United States had received less oil, the amount would have been easily offset by the two months of inventories routinely kept by private companies. In fact, the consensus among economists was that the difficulties ordinary Americans had in obtaining oil were the fault of bad policy—specifically, that price controls Nixon had enacted early in his presidency to rein in inflation made it impossible for markets to adjust cleanly. Finally, it is true that the actions taken by the Arab oil producers in October 1973 caused oil prices to spike, which many believe caused significant economic damage—particularly to Western Europe and Japan, which depended most heavily on Mideast oil, but also to the United States. But a significant portion of the price spike resulted from panic buying and market speculation, not the Arab production cuts or price hikes per se.

Because the petroleum deficit and the threat to imports did not shift in any meaningful way, the theory predicts that the United States should retain its indirect control strategy. It did. The United States remained aligned with the Saudis, despite the obvious tension caused by King Faisal's embrace of the oil weapon. Relations with Iran also continued to be strong, despite the shah's role in driving up global oil prices.

The United States enjoyed the unique luxury of being one of the world's most prolific oil-producing countries from the mid-nineteenth century throughout the twentieth century. Resultantly, when World War I demonstrated the strategic value of oil in no uncertain terms, the United States found itself far better off than the other great powers. Because its remarkable strength in oil suggests that the United States would be immune to oil coercion and refrain from strategic anticipation, the U.S. cases are unlikely ones for the theory. If even the United States, the largest producer in global history, experienced periods of vulnerability and followed anticipatory logic, then those cases constitute persuasive evidence in support of the theory because they cut against the grain of initial assumptions.

Indeed, as the chapter showed, the historical record contradicts the default assumption of U.S. oil security. In fact, the state was vulnerable to oil coercion and its vulnerability fluctuated significantly, prompting U.S. leaders to not only adopt anticipatory strategies but also adjust them accordingly. The policies chosen ranged from self-sufficiency to indirect control, depending on the threat posed to oil imports and the size of the petroleum deficit.

A few recurring issues stand out across the U.S. observations. Over and over, American policymakers struggled with the dilemma of how to maintain robust domestic production without unduly depleting the country's oil reserves. The core problem arose because productive capacity could not expand quickly in response to a crisis; instead, it would require several months to bring new wells online, even in the context of an emergency crash program. This was not a problem unique to the United States. Because the problem derives from the physical properties of oil, all great powers would be stuck with whatever the peacetime level of output was for the first several months of an oil crisis. If a state must produce eight million barrels per day to sustain its objectives from day one of a crisis, then it must produce eight million barrels per day under regular circumstances. Unfortunately, however, maintaining the crisis level of output would deplete domestic oil fields more quickly than if the country relied on imports to meet peacetime requirements. With these forces in tension, U.S. policymakers sometimes erred on the side of resource conservation by promoting overseas oil development; other times, they erred on the side of high domestic production in case of emergency, even at the cost of depletion—most notably during World War II.

Second, U.S. officials evinced deep ambivalence about fulfilling allied oil requirements while planning crisis scenarios. How necessary was it for U.S. security that Europe and Japan be able to meet their requirements—especially their *civilian* requirements—in an emergency? And just how much should the American taxpayer have to pay to ensure adequate supplies not just for the United States but for the entire Free World? The question had enormous consequences for the petroleum deficit. Studies found that the United States could meet its own essential military and civilian needs through self-sufficiency strategies, but it could not meet the needs of its allies without resorting to indirect control, which meant ensuring that at least some Persian Gulf oil could reach the Free World in an emergency.

The essential issue of burden sharing divided U.S. officials throughout the Cold War. Principals who believed that the United States could be secure even if Europe and Japan did not have enough oil favored self-sufficiency strategies, arguing that allies needed to make their own provisions for emergency oil. During the Nixon administration, for example, officials at the Department of Commerce and the Department of State fell into that category. By contrast, officials who saw allied security as fundamental to U.S. security—which typically included Defense Department officials, the Office of Emergency Preparedness, and the Joint Chiefs—advocated for indirect control to prevent the USSR from dominating the Middle East. Perhaps unavoidably, this schizophrenic/divided opinion led to the adoption of some self-sufficiency strategies during the Cold War even though the bulk of U.S. anticipatory efforts centered on indirect control in the Persian Gulf. Those self-sufficiency measures mainly consisted of the Eisenhower oil import quota system, designed to protect the U.S. petroleum industry from foreign competition, and Congress's decision, at the urging of Nixon, to fast-track the construction of the Alaskan oil pipeline in late 1973 despite environmental concerns.

7
EMPIRICAL TESTS WITH FUZZY-SET QCA

The three previous chapters assessed the validity of the theory's predictions through congruence testing and process tracing and found strong support for the theory across a large number of cases. This chapter continues the testing with fuzzy-set methods, which test for necessary and sufficient causal relationships using the logic of set theory.

The chapter begins by further explaining the fuzzy-set qualitative comparative analysis (fsQCA) method, which is still relatively uncommon compared with the ubiquity of regression-based work. The two techniques operate according to fundamentally different views of causality, so readers whose expectations derive from their familiarity with regression methods may come to the table with assumptions that do not match the assumptions of fsQCA. Then, the chapter lays out the standards for scoring cases according to their membership in the three primary sets: the set of great powers with large petroleum deficits (D), the set of great powers whose oil imports are highly threatened (T), and the set of great powers that adopt extreme strategies (S). Next, the chapter uses fsQCA to test whether a large petroleum deficit and high disruptibility are necessary causal conditions to produce extreme strategies. Then it uses standard truth table analysis to test whether the causal conditions are sufficient causes of extreme strategies.

About the Method

Qualitative comparative analysis (QCA), developed by Charles Ragin, uses set theory to express and test complex causal relationships according to the logic of necessary and sufficient conditions. Fuzzy-set QCA is the ideal method to use when testing a theory that is conjunctural in nature, as is the case in this book.[1] Conjunctural causation postulates that "the effect of a single condition unfold[s] only in combination with other, previously specified conditions."[2] In other words, the logic suggests that both causal factors should be present to generate the outcome; if only one factor is present, the outcome should not be observed.

Recall that the theory echoes the logic of expected values: the petroleum deficit is the magnitude of harm caused by oil cutoff, and import threat is the probability that a disruption of oil might occur. If either term—magnitude or probability—is zero, the expected value is zero. Ergo, if either the petroleum deficit or disruptibility is zero, coercive vulnerability is zero, and the great power will not invest in costly and risky anticipatory strategies. As argued in chapter 1, it would not make sense for a great power to engage in anticipatory strategies if it had no petroleum deficit, regardless of whether potential oil imports would be highly disruptible. Likewise, if a country has a large petroleum deficit but there are no realistic threats to its imports—for instance, if it is the only great power in the system, as the United States is today—there would be no reason for anticipatory strategies.

Conjunctural causation differs from the standard "net effects" view of causation implicit in correlational, regression-based analysis, which assumes that "each variable, by itself, is capable of influencing the level or probability of the outcome."[3] In other words, with correlational methods, the presence of both causal factors is not strictly required to generate a hypothesized effect. Instead, the effect can result from the presence of a single causal factor; the addition of another causal factor simply strengthens the effect.

Thus, regression analysis would test the theory based on the questionable assumption that the petroleum deficit could trigger strategic anticipation on its own even if import disruptibility was zero. As a result, regression analysis would be an inappropriate tool because its foundational assumptions violate the logic of the theory.

Fuzzy-set methods are also superior to regression in the current context for other reasons. The lens of necessary and sufficient conditions employed by QCA provides a more fine-grained understanding about the nature of the causal relationship being observed. Additionally, as a practical point, regression-based methods are less conducive to testing phenomena in intermediate-N studies (i.e., studies with ten to fifty cases). QCA, originally designed for small-N and intermediate-N research, has no such limitation.[4]

Fuzzy-Set Scoring of Causes and Outcomes

In QCA, instead of "coding variables," the researcher establishes a framework for scoring the degree of membership in a set according to firm benchmarks. The researcher sets these benchmarks based on deep knowledge of the cases (i.e., by qualitatively identifying the boundaries that represent meaningful variation according to the substance of the theory) rather than by deriving benchmarks inductively from a sample or population distribution, as regressions do.[5] There are two types of scoring systems: crisp-set scoring systems and fuzzy-set scoring systems. This study uses the latter because it is better suited to political science inquiry.

In crisp-set analysis, scores take on the value of 1 or 0, whereby 1 indicates that the case qualifies as a full member of the set and 0 indicates that the case qualifies as a full nonmember of the set. A crisp-set scoring scheme is most appropriate when the phenomena of interest are inherently binary. An example might be voting behavior. A person either casts a ballot in a given election or does not; there are no outcomes in between voting and not voting.

In practice, however, few political phenomena are so cut and dry. The extent to which a country qualifies as "democratic" is widely understood to be a matter of degree, for example. Present-day Canada might be unambiguously democratic, while present-day North Korea is unambiguously nondemocratic, but countries such as Turkey and Iran fall somewhere in between. They are neither full members of the set of democratic countries nor full nonmembers of the set of democratic countries.

When dealing with sets in which membership is not strictly binary, as is the case for most, if not all, causal factors of interest to political scientists, fuzzy-set analysis is the more appropriate tool. It allows scholars to score partial-membership cases as such, rather than requiring researchers to apply labels of "full member" and "full nonmember" that may not really fit. It accomplishes this by setting standards for scoring cases as partial members of a set according to intrinsically qualitative judgments. Note that qualitative is not the same as subjective: they are objective standards that must be explicitly specified and adhered to by the researcher. Qualitative means that these standards are inherently nominal-categorical rather than quantitative-numeric.

The most basic scale for a fuzzy set has three categories: full membership, scored as 1.0; full nonmembership, scored as 0.0; and the crossover point, representing the threshold at which membership is maximally ambiguous, which is scored as 0.50. The cut points in the scale transform qualitative gradations to numerical increments.

Criteria for Scoring the Sets

I employ a fuzzy-set scale with four possible membership scores: fully included in the set (1.0), more in than out (0.67), more out than in (0.33), and fully excluded from the set (0.0). The four-category scale conveys more information about degree of membership than the three-category scale but does not require excessively fine-grained distinctions to sort membership.

It merits emphasis that fuzzy scores are *not* probabilities. Membership scores can be confused with probabilities because both measures are expressed along a range from 0 to 1. Assigning a score of 0.33 to a particular case, for example, means that the case falls closer to nonmembership (closer to 0) than membership. This is a measure of certainty, not likelihood. It does not mean that there is a 33 percent chance that the case falls within the set.

Testing the theory with QCA starts with specifying the three basic fuzzy sets. The first two correspond to the two causal factors, the petroleum deficit and the threat to imports, while the third set corresponds to the outcome, strategic anticipation. Below, I construct each of the three scales and explain the reasoning behind them.

Scoring the Petroleum Deficit

The first causal set represents the petroleum deficit—a country's capacity for home-territory oil production compared with expected demand for oil in an emergency scenario. In earlier chapters, I outlined in detail the many factors that can affect both productive capacity and oil demand. All these factors combine to determine the degree of petroleum deficit. Here I set basic scoring principles to indicate set membership in the simplest possible terms.

The petroleum deficit set (D) consists of "all great powers with large petroleum deficits." To count as a full member of the set, a country must have an expected crisis demand that far exceeds domestic productive capacity. To operationalize this, I calibrate scoring based on the expected level of oil rationing a country would require in a realistic crisis scenario (see table 7.1). The scoring reflects the assumption that, in times of grave national emergency, military oil supplies receive the highest priority because they are most closely tied to survival, the foremost goal of states. That is, a state will impose serious limits on military consumption only when all other prospects for rationing are exhausted.

Consequently, severe military rationing unambiguously signals a large deficit. So, too, does an expected or actual plunge in military effectiveness clearly attributable to shortages of oil, regardless of whether the government announces official military rationing. In either case, the fact that military demand is not ade-

TABLE 7.1 Fuzzy-set scoring of great powers with large petroleum deficits (D)

SCORE	MEMBERSHIP CRITERIA
1.00	Military needs unmet / military rationing
0.67	Military needs met with severe civilian rationing
0.33	Military needs met with mild to moderate civilian rationing
0.00	Military and civilian needs met without rationing

quately met clearly indicates that the state is a full member of set D and should be scored as 1.0. It should be clear that all great powers that lack commercial-scale oil resources unambiguously belong to set D. Allow me to stress that military rationing does not *cause* the deficit; it merely *indicates* the existence of a deficit.

The next increment down from full membership in set D is "more in than out," scored as 0.67. This score is assigned when military needs can be adequately met, but only through severe civilian rationing. Severe civilian rationing jeopardizes the continued operation of the war economy and threatens loss of life among civilians, for instance, by diverting diesel fuel from agricultural production to war fighting, which risks hunger and starvation. Mild military rationing designed to economize on oil consumption may also exist at this membership threshold, but only if it does not degrade effectiveness.

Countries that can fulfill their essential crisis needs through mild to moderate civilian rationing are scored as 0.33, more out than in. The score indicates that there is some truth to the claim that "the country has a large petroleum deficit," but the statement is more untrue than true. Limited civilian rationing impinges on citizens' quality of life but does not cripple a war economy nor does it threaten civilian life. Military needs and essential civilian needs are fully met.

Finally, a country that can meet all emergency oil needs without military or civilian rationing qualifies as a full nonmember of the set D (0.0). The statement "the country has a large petroleum deficit" is clearly false if the state can weather a serious emergency without imposing a rationing system. Ergo, to have any degree of membership in set D, at least some level of crisis rationing must be anticipated by policymakers.

Scoring the Vulnerability of Imports

The second causal set represents the susceptibility of the country's oil imports to disruption by enemies. The determinants of the threat to imports are numerous. The goal here is not to reiterate those factors but to state explicit thresholds that indicate varying degrees of set membership.

CHAPTER 7

The import threat set (T) is defined as "all great powers with highly threatened imports." Recall from chapter 1 that physical interdiction tends to be more threatening than trade cessation. Because oil is a fungible commodity, it is equally useful regardless of where it originates; states can obtain it from third parties that buy and resell petroleum, not just from producer countries. Therefore, peaceably disrupting oil access necessitates near-global cooperation, which is difficult to achieve. Thus, the most important indicators of threat relate to physical vulnerability, not market-related vulnerability.

Scoring set (T) membership is somewhat more complicated because there is no single indicator that can sort cases into membership increments (unlike the petroleum deficit, where rationing is a straightforward metric). Instead, membership score depends on the answers to a series of questions depicted in

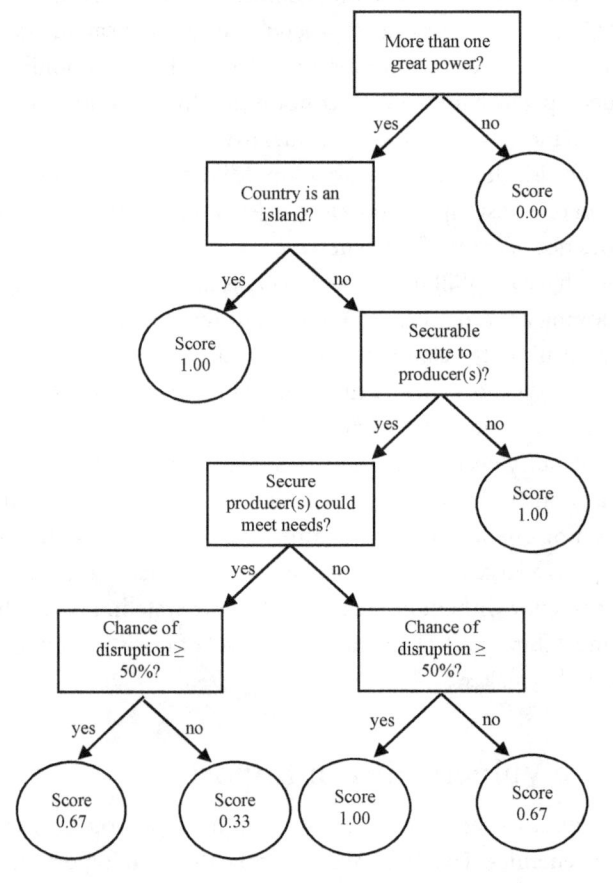

FIGURE 7.1. Membership in set of great powers with highly threatened imports (T)

the flowchart in figure 7.1. These questions, in turn, reflect several underlying assumptions.

First, I assume that if there is only one great power in the system, that country's imports are not threatened. A minor power simply cannot disrupt large amounts of a great power's oil in the face of military resistance from the great power. As a result, a lone superpower qualifies as a full nonmember of set (T), receiving a score of 0.0. Only the United States since the collapse of the Soviet Union in late 1991 fits this description.[6]

Second, in a bipolar or multipolar world, where anarchy reigns and offensive military power exists, there is no such thing as perfect invulnerability of imports. Imports are inherently physically vulnerable, which is why countries highly value self-reliance.[7] Consequently, no country qualifies as a full nonmember of set (T) when there are two or more great powers in the system.

Third, I assume that oceangoing oil imports are more susceptible to military disruption than imports traveling overland, ceteris paribus. Ergo, the imports of countries with land routes to major local producers are less threatened than the imports of self-contained island countries, which can obtain oil only by sea. That said, ceteris is rarely paribus. The ability to defend seagoing imports varies across countries according to their relative military capabilities. Also, if a country gets at least some of its imports overland, it is much less taxing to defend the seagoing portion of imports than if all imports are oceangoing. Thus, not all oceangoing imports are inherently insecure; it depends on the context. But all countries that rely *only* on oceangoing routes are less secure than those that have both land and sea options.

Fourth, any state sharing a land border with another state can obtain oil through "oil laundering"—that is, buying petroleum (often in secret) from a neutral neighbor that has imported it from an overseas supplier—but I assume that the quantity of oil obtainable from laundering is small. This is because laundering puts neighbors in a diplomatic bind. On the one hand, open laundering risks retaliation from the countries attempting to sever oil access. On the other hand, secret laundering in hopes of avoiding external pressure limits the quantities that can be transferred without raising suspicion. Sudden, large increases in oil imports are an obvious sign of laundering; the inelasticity of oil demand means that noncombatants' consumption virtually never increases drastically, even when oil prices are low. Since abrupt increases are a dead giveaway, laundering countries can buy and transfer only small amounts of excess oil on a gradual basis if they hope to avoid negative repercussions.[8] Therefore, though oil laundering is difficult for a blockader to curtail completely, it does not relieve much pressure on a vulnerable country's supplies, and therefore it does not substantially change the overall blockade susceptibility of any country. As a result, countries whose only

TABLE 7.2 Fuzzy-set scoring of great powers with highly threatened imports (T)

SCORE	MEMBERSHIP CRITERIA
1.00	Multiple great powers, island; or multiple great powers, not an island, but transit routes cannot be secured; or multiple great powers, not an island, routes securable, needs unmet, cutoff chance ≥ 50%
0.67	Multiple great powers, not an island, routes securable, needs unmet, cutoff chance < 50%; or multiple great powers, not an island, routes securable, needs met, cutoff chance ≥ 50%
0.33	Multiple great powers, not an island, routes securable, needs met, cutoff chance < 50%
0.00	No other great powers

potential method for circumventing a blockade is to launder oil through land neighbors are highly vulnerable to cutoff and qualify as a full member of set (T).

Finally, I assume that countries take expectations of the likeliness of disruption—and the probability it will actually impinge on import flows—into account when gauging threat. Oil imports are much more threatened if a disruption has already occurred or appears likely to occur soon. Successfully imposing a blockade requires formidable military effort and commitment; it is not a decision states make unless they have compelling reasons to do so. Therefore, if there is no strong reason to believe a blockade is imminent, vulnerability to disruption will be lower than if a blockade has a 50 percent or greater chance of occurring. This leads to the following questions, depicted as a flowchart in figure 7.1 and summarized in table 7.2.

> Is there more than one great power in the system? If the answer is no, the lone great power is scored as 0.0 for set (T) membership. If the answer is yes, proceed to the next question.
> Is the country a self-contained island (meaning it shares no land borders with other countries)? If the answer is yes, the country is scored as 1.0, a full member of set (T). If the answer is no, proceed to the next question.
> Does the country have secure routes to major producers? Proximity to those producers matters but is not determinative of security. All else equal, shorter supply lines are easier to defend and thus are considered more secure than long supply lines. Then again, if the country is very powerful, it may be able to defend long routes. If there are no secure routes, the country is scored as a full member (1.0). If at least some transit routes are secure or at least reasonably defendable, proceed to next question.
> Could the producers with secure routes provide enough oil to meet total demand? If the answer is yes, proceed to the question on the left. If the answer is no, proceed to the question on the right.

Is the threat of disruption 50 percent or higher (including 100 percent), based on the state's read of other states' intentions and capabilities? If yes, the country is scored as 0.67, more in than out of the set. If the answer is no, the country is scored as 0.33, less in than out.

Is the threat of disruption 50 percent or higher (including 100 percent), based on the state's read of other states' intentions and capabilities? If yes, the country is scored as 1.0, a full member of set (T). If the answer is no, the country is scored as 0.67, more in than out.

Scoring the Outcome Set: Degree of Strategic Anticipation

The outcome set (S) represents the phenomenon to be explained: the degree of strategic anticipation pursued by great powers. The truth statement representing full membership in the set is "all great powers that pursue extreme anticipatory strategies." Recall that each strategy—self-sufficiency, indirect control, and direct control—is defined by its costs, risks, and benefits, which vary in tandem from strategy to strategy. Direct control, the most extreme strategy, is at once the costliest, riskiest, and most potentially beneficial option that great powers can choose. Indirect control entails moderate cost, risk, and benefit, while self-sufficiency ranks lowest on the cost-risk-benefit scale. Although they are distinct strategies, they nevertheless fall on a single continuum: their degree of membership in the "extreme strategies" set.

Color theory is an apt metaphor to explain how anticipatory strategies can be categorically distinct yet exist on a single continuum. Individual colors like red, yellow, and blue exist along a unified color spectrum defined according to the wavelengths of light they emit. These colors gradually blend from one to the next— for example, red to orangish-red to reddish-orange to orange—yet, we can still discern six distinct categories of light along that spectrum: red, orange, yellow, green, blue, and purple. The exact boundaries between each category are fuzzy, but most of the time the viewer does not need to know precisely where the boundaries are to distinguish red from orange from yellow.

Similarly, direct control, indirect control, and self-sufficiency are analytically distinct, yet they occupy the same conceptual spectrum defined by the combined level of cost, risk, and benefit. There can also be significant variation within strategic categories just as variation exists within color categories. The hue known as red denotes a family of colors such as crimson, scarlet, vermillion, and ruby; the strategy of indirect control includes a family of behaviors such as military aid, alliances, proxy relationships established through covert intervention, security guarantees, basing, and many others.

TABLE 7.3 Membership in set of countries with extreme anticipatory strategies (S)

SCORE	MEMBERSHIP CRITERIA
1.00	Direct control
0.67	Indirect control
0.33	Self-sufficiency
0.00	No strategic anticipation

Scores within the fuzzy set of extreme anticipatory strategies (S) correspond to the three categories used throughout the book. Direct control strategies count as full members of set S and are scored as 1.0. Indirect control strategies register as 0.67, more in than out. Self-sufficiency strategies rank as 0.33, more out than in. Finally, the absence of anticipation corresponds to full nonmembership in the set, scored as 0.0 (see table 7.3).

Fuzzy-Set QCA

Table 7.4 displays the fuzzy-set data that result from the above scoring criteria. Additionally, it contains two columns of operations combining the two causal factors. Set (D·T) is the logical intersection of set (D) and set (T), which represents the Boolean logical AND. Intersections operate according to a "weakest link" logic—that is, the score for each case in the intersection is only as strong as its weakest membership score across *both* sets. Thus, the intersection score is calculated by taking the minimum score of either set (D) or set (T). Set (D+T) is the union of set (D) and set (T), representing the Boolean logical OR. A case's membership in the union set is calculated using the maximum score across the conjoined sets. The logic here is like Jiffy Lube guidance: a car needs an oil change *either* when it hits 7,500 miles *or* when six months have elapsed, whichever comes first.

Analysis of Necessary Conditions

The first step of the fuzzy analysis is to use the data in Table 7.4 to test for necessary conditions. Necessary conditions are causes that must be present for the outcome to occur. The causal relationship is asymmetric: if the cause is absent, the outcome is also absent; but the presence of the cause does not guarantee that the outcome will occur. Formally, a condition X is necessary for Y if $X \geq Y$ for all cases. Stated differently, in a relationship of causal necessity, the outcome Y is a subset of the cause X.

TABLE 7.4 Fuzzy data on great powers with extreme strategies

	CAUSAL CONDITIONS				OUTCOME
CASE	LARGE PETROL DEFICIT (D)	HIGH IMPORT THREAT (T)	LOGICAL AND (D·T)*	LOGICAL OR (D+T)	EXTREME STRATEGY (S)
Britain 1918–45	1.00	1.00	1.00	1.00	1.00
Germany 1933–36	0.33	0.33	0.33	0.33	0.00
Germany 1936–39	0.33	0.33	0.33	0.33	0.33
Germany 1939–41	0.33	0.67	0.33	0.67	0.67
Germany 1941–45	1.00	1.00	1.00	1.00	1.00
U.S. 1918–20	0.33	0.33	0.33	0.33	0.33
U.S. 1920–41	0.00	0.33	0.00	0.33	0.00
U.S. 1941–45	0.33	0.33	0.33	0.33	0.33
U.S. 1950–69	0.67	0.67	0.67	0.67	0.67
U.S. 1970–75	0.67	0.67	0.67	0.67	0.67
Japan 1941–45	1.00	1.00	1.00	1.00	1.00

*The intersection of the set of high petroleum deficit great powers and the set of high import threat great powers is also known as the set of great powers with high coercive vulnerability, a macro-condition.

In fsQCA, two parameters quantify how well the data fit the model: consistency and coverage. Because real-world social science is messy—some amount of randomness and error in the data is expected—perfect set relations are rare. Usually, one or more cases contradict the subset. Consistency scores determine whether the data approximate a set relation closely enough to claim that a necessary condition roughly exists. In fuzzy sets, consistency for a necessary condition is the sum of all correct fuzzy-set scores for cases where the outcome is present divided by the total fuzzy set score for cases where the outcome is present.[9] A consistency closer to 1 is better, but the standard cutoff to sustain the claim that a necessary condition exists is a consistency score of 0.90 or higher.[10] The consistency column of table 7.5 shows that having a high petroleum deficit or a high threat is necessary for a country to adopt an extreme strategy.

Consistency alone cannot sustain the argument that the causal factors are necessary conditions, because it does not account for the number of cases tested. Intuitively, in a hypothetical situation where two out of two cases passed the threshold, consistency would be perfect, but because the N would be so small, the finding would not constitute grounds for strong confidence in generalizable causal necessity. Therefore, I use Ragin's procedure based on a binomial probability test to assess the significance of the consistency score.[11] The test asks how likely we would be to observe a consistency value as high as we did if the underlying set-theoretic relationship were weaker. If we assume that the underlying set-theoretic relationship had a consistency of only 0.4, for example, the probability of calculating the above

TABLE 7.5 Analysis of necessary conditions for extreme strategies (S)

CONDITION TESTED	CONSISTENCY	CONSISTENCY IS SIGNIFICANT?	COVERAGE
High deficit (D)	0.94	No	0.94
High threat (T)	1.00	Yes	0.90
High deficit AND high threat (D·T)	0.83	No	0.94
High deficit OR high threat (D+T)	1.00	Yes	0.90

Note: Significant with $\alpha = .05$ and benchmark of 0.65 ("usually" necessary)

consistency values from a sample of our size is vanishingly small. In fact, the lowest benchmark value of true consistency that is consistent with the observed consistency at the 0.05 confidence level is 0.65. This is what Ragin calls "usually" necessary to generate the outcome.[12] Thus, the results demonstrate with high confidence that the causal conditions are necessary to cause the outcome *at least* 65 percent of the time. In fact, the underlying causal relationship may be much stronger.[13]

Once consistency is established, coverage indicates how relevant or trivial a cause is in producing an outcome. While the consistency analysis showed that the causal pathways involving high deficit and high threat led to extreme measures, the coverage column in table 7.5 shows that there are few ways to get extreme measures without high deficit and high threat. That is, high threat and high deficit explain a lot of the appearance of extreme strategies in the world.

Analysis of Sufficient Conditions

A sufficient condition always generates the outcome when the cause is present, but the absence of the cause does not guarantee the absence of the outcome. It represents one possible path—but not the only path—to the effect. Formally, a condition X is sufficient for Y if $Y \geq X$ for all cases. In other words, in a relationship of causal sufficiency, the cause X is a subset of the outcome Y.

In QCA, sufficient conditions are analyzed using a truth table, which displays all possible combinations of the causal conditions. Table 7.6 features four rows because my theory uses two causal conditions: the petroleum deficit (D) and the threat to imports (T). Following Ragin, I use a consistency cutoff of 0.85 for determining whether a causal pathway is sufficient to cause the outcome.

The final row of the table indicates that the causal combination of high petroleum deficit but low threat (1,0) is a logical remainder. There are no cases in the sample that contain this combination of factors; thus we lack empirical evidence to test whether this combination is sufficient to generate the outcome. This is an

TABLE 7.6 Truth table derived from fuzzy data on great power strategies

(D)	(T)	NUMBER OF CASES IN PATH	CONSISTENCY*	OUTCOME	CASES
1	1	5	0.944908	1	UK, Ger4, US4, US5, Jap
0	1	1	0.778524	0	Ger3
0	0	5	0.456221	0	Ger1, Ger2, US1, US2, US3
1	0	0	n/a	n/a	n/a

*Cutoff of 0.85 used for scoring outcome as consistent with subset relation, following Ragin, *Redesigning Social Inquiry*, 136.

example of limited diversity, which is "essentially omnipresent" across all social science analysis, whether quantitative or qualitative.[14]

How should we interpret this limited diversity? There are a few possible interpretations. First, the absence of a case fitting the causal pathway could be random, an artifact of the relatively small N, which suggests that the row would be populated if the N were larger. Five cases existed where T was 0.33 (which rounds to zero in the truth table), but none of these cases happened to have a petroleum deficit of 0.67 or higher.

Second, the nature of the cases selected may partially explain the empty pathway. Recall that the import threat to a great power is scored as 0.00 only when there are no other great powers in the system. All of the cases that were examined occurred during bipolarity or multipolarity, which meant that T was never 0.00. This decreases the number of opportunities for cases of high deficit and low threat to arise.

Finally, the empty row could suggest that a systematic relationship exists between the petroleum deficit and the import threat, meaning that while the two are distinct concepts, they covary to some extent.[15] Unlike in regression analysis, the fsQCA method does not require that causal conditions be independent of each other to draw causal inferences (a stipulation of large-N work that may be unrealistic and is oft violated in any case).

Table 7.7 presents the solution using the standard analysis of the truth table algorithm, which solves for causal sufficiency.[16] It shows that there is only one pathway sufficient to produce the outcome: the intersection of the set of great powers with large petroleum deficits and the set of great powers with high threats to oil imports (D·T). Both causal conditions must be present to cause the outcome. This means that only the combination of high deficit and high threat will propel a country to adopt extreme strategies. A petroleum deficit by itself, even a large one, will not induce the adoption of an extreme strategy. Likewise, even a large threat to imports will fail to generate the adoption of an extreme strategy.

TABLE 7.7 Results of standard analysis

SOLUTION	CONSISTENCY	CONSISTENCY IS SIGNIFICANT?	COVERAGE
D·T → S	0.9449	Yes	0.9433

Note: Significant with $\alpha = .10$ and benchmark of 0.65 ("usually" necessary)

Note that the consistency and coverage of the solution surpass 94 percent, which means that the solution appears to closely fit the data. To determine whether the claim of causal sufficiency is generalizable, I use the same binomial probability test conducted above to assess statistical significance, which in this case reaches the 0.10 level. The high coverage score indicates that the causal pathway is nontrivial. That is, high threat combined with high deficit is sufficient to account for most instances of extreme strategies.

Summary Interpretation of Results

Altogether, the findings from the fsQCA strongly support the theory at standard levels of statistical significance. The data confirm the hypothesis that both the petroleum deficit and the threat to imports must be substantial to trigger anticipatory strategies.

Thus, the fsQCA results reinforce the findings from the qualitative chapters that coercive vulnerability, as determined by the petroleum deficit and import disruption threat, spurs great powers to adopt anticipatory strategies to reduce the danger of coercion. Moreover, the severity of the strategy chosen is consistent with the level of coercive vulnerability faced by the state. The more extreme the deficit and import disruption threat, the more extreme the strategy chosen; the less extreme the deficit and threat, the less extreme the strategy chosen.

Beyond empirical reinforcement, this chapter provides systematic evidence that a general social phenomenon is at work. For many social scientists, one out of one, two out of two, or three out of three randomly drawn or representative test cases that conform to a theory's predictions are not enough to reject the null hypothesis that no relationship exists between causes and an outcome. But using the binomial probability test, the chapter demonstrates with statistical significance that the joint values of the petroleum deficit and threat to imports are sufficient to generate anticipatory strategies.

Conclusion
OIL AND THE FUTURE OF GREAT POWER POLITICS

Oil's importance for both economic and military power casts a long shadow over world politics. Since the emergence of mechanized warfare in the early twentieth century, oil has played a crucial role in the capacity of nations to wage war. Because of its uniquely high energy density and naturally liquid state, oil offers superior performance when it comes to mobility and transportation. Great powers are hardwired to worry about oil supplies, lest they be vulnerable to coercion in a conflict or crisis. The power to deprive a nation of its ability to defend itself in war—even a hypothetical future war—presents a potent opportunity for exercising political leverage. Because of this potential, states have a healthy fear of the "oil weapon," and those nations most vulnerable to oil cutoffs do not sit idly by waiting for enemies to coerce them. Instead, they pursue strategies of self-sufficiency, indirect control, and direct control, according to their degree of coercive vulnerability.

Concerns about coercive vulnerability drove a good deal of competition and conflict among the great powers throughout the twentieth century in ways often overlooked. Unrestricted submarine warfare targeting oil tankers en route to Britain nearly knocked that country out of World War I. The superiority of oil-fueled engines meant that Britain had no choice but to convert its fleet from coal to oil, a material it did not possess. Fearing this left the country vulnerable to politically motivated supply disruptions in the future, Britain launched a successful last-ditch offensive during World War I to capture Mesopotamian oil lands before hostilities ceased. In interwar Germany, the Nazis worried that the Reich's dearth of oil could become its Achilles' heel, given expectations of an Allied blockade in the coming war. With strategic anticipation, Hitler first invested heavily in the highly unprofitable domestic synthetic fuels industry; negotiated economic alliances with Romania and the Soviet Union to exchange German military equipment for oil, despite plans to invade the USSR the following year; and ultimately diverted Wehrmacht forces south to capture the Caucasus oilfields once Barbarossa had stalled—against the advice of his generals. During the Cold War, even the oil-rich United States worried that the Soviets might coerce the West by overrunning the Persian Gulf and cutting off its exports, rendering NATO unable to win a conventional war in Europe. To deter the Soviets, the United States took an indirect, alliance-based approach, offering security guarantees to friendly Middle Eastern producers like Iran and Saudi Arabia.

How will oil affect great power politics in the twenty-first century? The growing realization that fossil fuel emissions are causing devastating harm to the planet's climate has spurred efforts to transition away from oil and toward cleaner energy technologies. In the transportation sector—by far the most important consumer of oil—that transition seems increasingly likely to occur through the spread of electric and hybrid vehicles. Advances in battery technology that improve vehicle range and performance, coupled with the declining prices of electric cars, have generated optimism that the "electric car revolution" is finally under way.[1]

Does the rise of new technology imply that oil will lose its strategic importance in the coming decades? Sadly, the answer is no. Rumors of oil's demise are greatly exaggerated, however discouraging that fact is from an environmental point of view.

Even optimistic forecasts predict that world oil demand will *increase* through at least 2040. The "New Policies Scenario" (NPS) modeled in the International Energy Agency's annual *World Energy Outlook* report, used in the analysis below, makes projections based on "where today's policy frameworks and ambitions, together with the continued evolution of known technologies, might take the energy sector," as opposed to estimating demand based solely on laws currently in effect. The most recent version of the NPS at the time of writing assumes that all policy goals announced by August 2018 will be achieved, including the pledges made by signatories to the 2015 Paris Climate Accords, European Union targets to increase fuel efficiency by 32.5 percent by 2030, and Chinese efforts to improve air quality by encouraging electric cars, among other proposals.[2]

The NPS predicts that even if all of the above policy promises are kept, global oil demand will increase by roughly 10 million barrels per day (mb/d) from about 95 mb/d in 2017 to 106 mb/d in 2040, with nearly the entire demand increase coming from developing countries such as India and China. That is the optimistic scenario. Limiting the increase in demand to such a small rise over the next twenty years would represent a staggering policy achievement; to hit those numbers, the number of electric cars in use would have to increase more than ninety-fold, from about 3.3 million vehicles today (or roughly 0.3 percent of a global fleet of 1,100 million cars) to 300 million by 2040 (roughly 15 percent of a projected fleet of 2,000 million cars). Absent the promised policy interventions, oil demand would instead increase by 26 mb/d to reach 121 mb/d over the same period.[3]

How likely are countries to meet the aspirational targets articulated in the Paris Agreement and elsewhere? There is ample reason for pessimism, not least because Donald Trump has committed to pulling the United States, currently the world's largest oil consumer, out of the treaty altogether. Dealing with climate change is a nightmare from the point of view of international cooperation. Compliance with emissions-reducing international agreements is costly, states have strong incentives to free ride off the climate policies of others, and no enforcement mechanism exists to punish states that cheat. It is a safe bet that the probability that states will fully adhere to stated promises—especially now that the United States has shrugged them off—is zero.

Future oil consumption, therefore, will almost certainly surpass projections made by the NPS. Because the NPS understates future demand, the analysis in this chapter, which is based on that scenario, represents the lower bound of the strategic problems facing petroleum-deficit states. We can be relatively confident that future petroleum deficits will be *at least as bad* as the estimates made below.

Setting aside peacetime consumption, oil will continue to be incredibly important for military forces. Whereas civilian oil demand per capita has decreased in developed countries since the 1970s, military requirements per soldier have steadily increased. In World War II, each U.S. soldier consumed an average of one gallon of petroleum daily, but by Vietnam that number had jumped to about eight gallons, and by 2007, long after major combat operations officially ceased, American troops in Iraq were burning about twenty-two gallons of oil per soldier per day.[4] Notably, the U.S. Department of Defense has experimented with alternative fuels and green energy technologies, partly to reduce the need for fuel convoys in combat areas, which are among the operations most vulnerable to enemy attack, and partly to support the social goal of lessening fossil fuel emissions by encouraging research and development into eco-friendly fuels with spin-off potential in the civilian economy. Thus far, however, the DoD has invested very little on alternative fuels and has used them only for demonstrations and military exercises rather than combat operations.[5] Given all that we know about the superiority of oil for military transportation, it is difficult to imagine that militaries will end their oil dependence anytime soon.

Clearly, oil will remain strategically important for at least the next few decades—a time frame that coincides with the expected rise of China as a great power. How will China protect its access to oil? Will the country need to adopt anticipatory strategies to guard against oil disruptions, and if so, which strategies should it pursue? Might China use force to obtain oil, as Britain, Japan, and Nazi Germany ultimately did in the first half of the twentieth century? Will it forge alliances with oil-exporting countries to keep oil in "friendly hands" as the United States did in the Persian Gulf during the Cold War? Or, will the country meet its petroleum needs peacefully through self-sufficiency measures, as the United States did in the early twentieth century before Washington made its defense commitment to Europe?

The answer depends on China's degree of coercive vulnerability, which is a function of its future petroleum deficit and the disruptibility of its imports. China's future petroleum deficit cannot be definitively ascertained because several of the factors influencing it are not made public by the regime. This is particularly true for the "need" side of the deficit, which reflects a country's military doctrine and its strategic ambitions, among other factors. An expansionist great power would require greater supplies of oil to pursue its objectives than a status quo state would, for example. In the case of China, we simply do not know whether the state harbors expansionist or status quo intentions; indeed, the nature of China's intentions is arguably the most important strategic question of the twenty-first century. Relatedly, we have no insight into Chinese government estimates of the country's emergency oil consumption requirements. How big a supply shortfall could China absorb and still meet essential civilian and military demand? If rationing is necessary, how much oil do policymakers believe could be squeezed out of the nonessential civilian economy?

Although China's strategic petroleum needs are unknown, rigorous projections of its future peacetime needs, as well as its future domestic output levels, do exist—and those numbers suggest that China will almost certainly face a massive petroleum deficit. Even under the optimistic assumptions of the NPS, by 2040, China will emerge as the largest net petroleum importer ever, with foreign oil composing about 80 percent of normal peacetime consumption. Despite massive government efforts to promote hybrid and electric cars, Chinese oil demand will reach nearly 16 mb/d, while production will decline to roughly 3 mb/d. That would leave a yawning gap of 13 mb/d to be filled by imports—a situation notably worse than China's unenviable oil position today. In 2017, China imported about two-thirds of its oil needs, or 8 mb/d, out of a total consumption of 12 mb/d.[6]

When it comes to the threat to imports, the picture improves somewhat. About 80 percent of China's oil imports travel by sea across the Indian Ocean and through the Strait of Malacca maritime choke point, which makes them highly vulnerable to disruption by the U.S. Navy.[7] Indeed, Chinese military strategists have long worried that the United States could sever oceangoing energy imports and other crucial materials "so as to cut off the lifeblood of China's economy."[8] India also poses a major threat, as Chinese oil tankers must pass by its entire coastline to even approach the Malacca route.

Chinese relative power weakness affords the state little hope today of protecting the sea lines of communication (SLOCs) on which its oil imports rely. Despite nearly twenty years of intense modernization, the People's Liberation Army Navy (PLAN) has only just begun to acquire a blue water navy capable of operating far from Chinese shores—the type of force necessary to protect oil shipments across the Indian Ocean.[9] The PLAN launched its first domestically built aircraft carrier in April 2018, bringing the fleet's total number of carriers to an underwhelming two. The other carrier, the *Liaoning*, is a refurbished Soviet-built ship previously owned and discarded by Ukraine, which sold it for $20 million to a Chinese businessman under the false pretense that it would become a floating casino.[10] By contrast, the United States Navy currently has eleven supercarriers, complete with carrier strike groups, which are both larger than and qualitatively superior to anything China possesses. Of course, China's rapid naval modernization aims to close that gap over the next few decades.

China's proximity to major oil-producing states tempers its relative power disadvantage in securing SLOCs from U.S. intervention. Immediate neighbors Russia and Kazakhstan combined account for over 8 percent of the world's proven oil resources, an estimated 136 billion barrels. In 2017, the two produced a combined total of 13 mb/d, some 9.5 mb/d of which were exported—more than enough to meet China's 8 mb/d import demand that year.[11] Most of that oil went to countries other than China, but actual exports are less important for gauging vulnerability than potential exports are. What matters is that, theoretically, Russia and Kazakhstan could divert their oil exports to meet Chinese demand. Thus, even though China's current petroleum deficit is probably high, the threat to its imports is relatively low, meaning that its coercive vulnerability is probably moderate today.

But what of the future? Chinese vulnerability to oil coercion will likely worsen over the next few decades. The NPS estimates that China will need to import about 13 mb/d in 2040, while Russia, Kazakhstan, and the other Soviet successor states in Central Asia will produce 12.6 mb/d and export 8.4 mb/d in total, leaving China with a 4.6 mb/d supply gap. Thus, by 2040, Russia and Central Asia could meet, at maximum, around two-thirds of Chinese foreign oil demand.[12]

Fortunately for China, it lives on the same supercontinent as the Middle East, albeit far away.[13] Nevertheless, the Eurasian landmass could theoretically function as an extended land bridge for Middle Eastern oil exports to reach China while avoiding the U.S.-dominated seas. Middle Eastern producers could easily fill the Chinese supply gap; the region is expected to export nearly 27 mb/d in 2040.[14] Although Persian Gulf producers are not exactly close, the potential exists for China to secure its oil imports by land corridor. If significant quantities of

Persian Gulf oil could be realistically transported overland, away from U.S. naval interference, then the future threat to Chinese imports would remain low. Combined with a petroleum deficit that is likely to be large, Chinese coercive vulnerability could be held to a moderate level.

Moderate coercive vulnerability should induce China to pursue indirect control as it emerges as a great power. Thus, the theory predicts that China is likely to eventually forge alliances with major oil-producing countries and transit states to keep oil in "friendly hands." As yet, China is too militarily weak to shield friendly oil-producing states from interference by the United States or other potential rivals, but the beginnings of an alliance-based strategy appear to be taking shape under the auspices of the Belt and Road Initiative (BRI), described by some analysts as a nascent framework for twenty-first-century Chinese grand strategy.[15] Though Chinese officials insist that the BRI has solely peaceful intentions, emerging evidence increasingly suggests that the BRI could act as a vehicle for establishing Chinese military dominance over resource-rich portions of Eurasia.

First announced in a speech by Chinese president Xi Jinping in 2013, the BRI has morphed from vague development ambitions to a $1 trillion effort to forge a grand economic bloc—centered on China—that would extend through Central Asia to Europe and the Middle East. A formal statement of the project emerged in 2015 with the release of a major policy document called "Vision and Actions on Jointly Building Silk Road Economic Belt and 21st-Century Maritime Silk Road." According to the World Bank, some sixty-five countries have signed on to the initiative's stated mission to boost economic development by funding infrastructure projects like ports, railways, roads, and pipelines.[16] Xi has cloaked the initiative in benevolent, if not utopian, terms, describing it as a plan to build a "community of common destiny," imbued with a "Silk Road spirit," that will foster trade, investment, and peace.

But many speculate that ulterior motives lurk behind the platitudes, that the BRI may be a front to establish and codify Chinese hegemony under the guise of public goods provision. The direct involvement of top Chinese leadership, including Xi himself, in overseeing the BRI suggests that it is no mere construction project but rather a major priority for the regime. The initiative strikingly resembles the historical Chinese tributary system through which imperial China dominated large swaths of Eurasia until the mid-nineteenth century. Military protection of vassal states in exchange for taxes and trade privileges was the core of that system. The BRI appears to draw on Western strategic thinking as well. Commenting on the Mackinder-esque purview of the project, Nadège Rolland notes, "This is the region that Western geopoliticians have identified as the Eurasian 'heartland,' an area whose control would supposedly enable world domination. Not coincidentally, this vast expanse corresponds to the current geographic scope of the BRI."[17]

Cynical interpretations of China's true motives naturally arise when the magnanimous gloss projected externally does not match the language used internally. Chinese-language publications regularly refer to the endeavor as the Belt and Road *Strategy*, but the regime expressly decided that the English-language version of the "Vision and Actions" document must replace "strategy" with "initiative" because the latter term was deemed more innocuous. The BRI is the concrete realization of a strategy to "March West," articulated by Wang Jisi, a dean at Peking University and close associate of Hu Jintao's, to avoid encirclement by the United States and its allies in East Asia, as well as the Indian navy, by turning toward the Eurasian interior. The BRI is not just a development plan "but a strategic concept meant to break through US attempts to 'strangle' China."[18] China also shrouds the terms of its deals with BRI countries in great secrecy, which is another source of suspicion over what China's true motives are.

Bolstering Chinese energy security is a major goal of the BRI, and oil factors heavily into its endeavors. The BRI coevolved with a major push to boost energy security following a 2014 Chinese government report that concluded China would have to import 75 percent of its oil by 2030. Many of the coping measures recommended by the report—including the diversification of oil imports and the goal of rerouting oil shipments away from the Strait of Malacca choke point—are being realized as BRI projects. The program devotes large tranches of investment to developing new oilfields in Russia, Kazakhstan, Azerbaijan, and Iran—prime components of what BRI documents call the "21st century strategic energy and resource base"—and transporting their petroleum bounty to China via port, pipeline, road, and rail.[19]

The Belt and Road strategy envisions the creation of six main economic corridors linking China to the rest of the continent. Each involves energy-related investments, but the three corridors most pertinent to oil security are the China-Pakistan Economic Corridor (CPEC), the Bangladesh-China-India-Myanmar Economic Corridor (BCIMEC), and the China-Central Asia-West Asia Economic Corridor (CCWAEC).

Far and away the most developed corridor is CPEC. As of 2017, China has loaned over $62 billion to Pakistan to build roads, rails, and a 1 mb/d pipeline linking the port of Gwadar, Pakistan, located just 30 miles from the Iranian border and 250 miles from the mouth of the Persian Gulf, to the city of Kashgar in western China. The initiative also includes funds to convert Gwadar into a major deepwater port. Shipping Persian Gulf oil to Gwadar by tanker and then delivering it overland to China would not only bypass the Strait of Malacca choke point but also shorten the supply line to 1,600 miles from 6,200 miles.[20] Shortening the SLOCs and avoiding Malacca would significantly lessen, though not eliminate, the naval threat from India and the United States. As for overland passage, though energy security experts have focused primarily on the pipeline, the massive new network of highways and railroads could prove just as important for transporting oil. Moving oil by rail is slightly costlier than shipping it by pipeline, but rail offers more flexibility, and companies regularly use it when oil production booms exceed local pipeline capacity.[21] Indeed, Gwadar is so close to the Iranian border that it could be feasible to eliminate the oceangoing leg of the route entirely by extending pipeline, highway, or railway spurs from CPEC directly into Iran.

The BCIMEC, for its part, includes a 2016 deal to build a deepwater port at Kyaukpyu, Myanmar, at the mouth of new roads, railways, and a 0.44 mb/d oil pipeline connecting Kyaukpyu to Kunming, the capital of China's Yunnan Province. China possesses a fifty-year lease on the port, with the option to extend for an additional twenty-five years.[22] Shipping oil from the Persian Gulf to the port at Kyaukpyu, and then moving it by land corridor, offers China yet another option to avoid the Malacca route, where the U.S. Navy would be most likely to focus blockade efforts in the event of a major conflict.[23] However, the oil would still have to cross the entire length of the Indian coast.

Finally, the CCWAEC aims to expand land routes to oil-rich countries in Central Asia and the Middle East, especially Kazakhstan and Iran. The corridor includes a new cargo railway linking Almaty to Xi'an, a city of twelve million in north central China, which would reduce travel between the two cities to just six days instead of twenty-six days by road. It also includes a railway running from Aktau port on the Caspian Sea—where the Kazakh oil industry is centered—to Kashgar to link with the existing Chinese rail network. The Chinese have also pursued equity investments in the Kazakh oil industry, notably receiving an 8.33 percent stake in Kazakhstan's largest oil field, Kashagan. China and Iran also jointly built the first freight train linking their two countries. The line, which opened in 2016, runs all the way from Tehran to Yiwu in highly populated eastern China.[24] Chinese financing to develop Iranian oil fields is extensive and increasing. In late 2018, the Chinese state oil company Sinopec reportedly offered Iran $3 billion to further develop the Yadavaran oil field, which Sinopec is operating, with the goal of doubling output of the field.[25]

Observers worry that China is using the BRI to engage in predatory lending practices—extending huge, high-interest-rate loans to countries likely to default on them—to tighten Beijing's political grip on BRI countries by putting them in hock to the Chinese regime. For example, Sri Lanka received massive Chinese loans to build a deepwater port of dubious economic value—a "port to nowhere"—in Hambantota, a small fishing town on the thinly populated southeastern coast. After the Sri Lankan government fell behind on its debt payments, China used its windfall of leverage to obtain a ninety-nine-year lease for control of the port and some fifteen thousand acres surrounding it, which many suspect will be converted into a naval base. Hambantota's isolated nature, while bad for its commercial fortunes, would offer valuable privacy for operations. If the port is militarized, Sri Lanka would have unwittingly allowed China to circumvent Colombo's resistance to any deals that threatened India, Sri Lanka's much more powerful neighbor. The episode reportedly convinced U.S. and Indian officials that catching Sri Lanka in a "debt trap," and subsequently using it to pressure Colombo into actions against its own interests, was China's goal all along, and that similar traps are being set to ensnare additional countries.[26]

Will China's cooperation with oil exporters such as Iran and Kazakhstan, and transit countries such as Pakistan and Myanmar, evolve into the oil-for-security military alliances that characterize indirect control? If China's dramatic economic rise continues over the next few decades, will it build military forces capable of defending such allies and transit routes from likely competitors such as the United States and India?

It remains to be seen, of course, but China's current trajectory suggests that an alliance-based oil security strategy could be in the cards. Though the PLA navy remains far behind that of the United States, China is moving quickly to increase its military capacity in the Indian Ocean region. In 2017, China opened its first-ever overseas naval base in Doraleh, Djibouti, on the Bab-al-Mandeb Strait linking the Indian Ocean to the Red Sea. The base is expected to house as many as ten thousand Chinese troops, along with ammunition stores, maintenance facilities, a midsize airfield, and other logistical support materials.[27] The location is noteworthy because the Bab-al-Mandeb is a choke point for oil shipments from Yanbu, a port on the Saudi Red Sea coast where in 2012 the Chinese state oil company Sinopec obtained a 37.5 percent equity stake in a joint refinery-building venture with Saudi Aramco.[28]

Additionally, China is building a network of at least eight, and possibly as many as eighteen, dual-use ports in the Indian Ocean capable of accommodating commercial and military vessels. Conflicting reports suggest that one or more of these ports could evolve into Chinese bases. Multiple sources close to the Chinese military have confirmed that the PLAN will build a new naval base at the Gwadar port complex in Pakistan, for example, and bases in Oman and the Seychelles could soon follow.[29] Deepwater ports that do not become full-blown bases nevertheless help China project naval power in the Indian Ocean through port of call relationships. In recent years, PLAN ships have docked at dual-use ports in Pakistan, Sri Lanka, Bangladesh, Myanmar, Maldives, Malaysia, and the Seychelles, much to the alarm of India.[30] Even if the PLAN trails U.S. naval might, Chinese investments in naval capabilities have deterrent value because they would raise the cost of American interference in SLOCs.

China also appears to be boosting military cooperation with BRI countries important to Chinese oil interests—most notably Pakistan. In late 2018, the *New York Times* broke the news that China and Pakistan concluded a secret deal in early 2018—just two weeks after Donald Trump suspended U.S. aid to Pakistan—to use Belt and Road funding to establish a special economic zone for the joint manufacture of next-generation fighter jets. The development marks a significant shift, because "with its plan for Pakistan, China is for the first time explicitly tying a Belt and Road proposal to its military ambitions—and confirming the concerns of a host of nations who suspect the infrastructure initiative is really about helping China project armed might."[31] From 2011 to 2016, China doubled its weapons sales to Pakistan and has given it access to the military applications of Beidou, China's homegrown satellite navigation system modeled after the U.S.-created GPS (global positioning system). Beidou would allow Pakistan to improve the precision of missile guidance and military navigation systems on a platform not easily monitored by the United States. Moreover, China has been exporting anti-ship missiles and high-speed boats, two essential components of its A2/AD capabilities, to Pakistan and Iran, helping them raise the costs of U.S. naval intervention in their territorial waters.[32]

The expanded Chinese presence in the Indian Ocean has touched off a security dilemma with India, which sees in the BRI a strategy of encirclement.[33] Most Indian oil imports also travel along the maritime routes from the Persian Gulf, thus steps taken by China to secure the SLOCs also threaten India's oil access. In response to China's buildup, India is underwriting the construction of a deepwater port at Chabahar, Iran, about one hundred miles from Gwadar. It is also negotiating agreements to build dual-use and some dedicated military facilities in Oman, the Seychelles, Djibouti, and the northernmost islands of Mauritius.[34] Thus far, India's blue water capabilities outclass those of China; the Indian aircraft carrier program dates back decades, and its navy has fought in multiple naval engagements, whereas the Chinese navy has not been battle-tested.[35]

The above analysis suggests that China and Pakistan will likely deepen their military ties as the latter emerges as a crucial alternative route for Chinese imports of Persian Gulf oil. The ongoing tensions between India and Pakistan potentially threaten to draw Chinese involvement to protect its designs for the CPEC. The importance of Iran for China's indirect control strategy likewise could prompt a Sino-Iranian alignment whereby China helps protect Iran from the United States, which has threatened Tehran repeatedly over its nuclear program. Such possibilities may seem unlikely today, but if the future resembles the past, alliances in which China offers security guarantees to BRI countries in exchange for cooperation on oil may emerge as a core feature of the twenty-first century.

Notes

INTRODUCTION

1. Jerome B. Cohen, *Japan's Economy in War and Reconstruction* (Minneapolis: University of Minnesota Press, 1949), 134; Bruce M. Russett, *No Clear and Present Danger: A Skeptical View of the United States Entry into World War II*, Harper Torchbooks (New York: Harper & Row, 1972), 45–49, 53–54; Scott D. Sagan, "The Origins of the Pacific War," *Journal of Interdisciplinary History* 18, no. 4 (1988): 897–98, 904–8, 911–13; Masataka Chihaya, "Some Features Concerning Changes in the Japanese Fleet Organization during the War," in *The Pacific War Papers: Japanese Documents of World War II*, ed. Donald M. Goldstein and Katherine V. Dillon (Washington, DC: Potomac Books, 2004), 286–87; Marquis Koichi Kido, "Extracts from the Diary of Marquis Koichi Kido," in Goldstein and Dillon, *Pacific War Papers*, 119–21; Kichisaburo Nomura, "Diary of Admiral Kichisaburo Nomura, June-December 1941," in Goldstein and Dillon, *Pacific War Papers*, 199–200, 208–13.

2. Ivan L. Pearson, *In the Name of Oil: Anglo-American Relations in the Middle East, 1950–1958* (Eastbourne, England: Sussex Academic Press, 2010), 64.

3. Hugh Thomas, *Suez* (New York: Harper and Row, 1967), 37; Memorandum by the Secretary of State for Foreign Affairs: Suez Canal, July 28, 1952, PRO CAB 129/54, accessed February 7, 2013, http://discovery.nationalarchives.gov.uk/SearchUI/Details?uri=D7656747; Cabinet Secretary's Notebook: Minutes and Papers: Suez Canal, July 27, 1956, PRO CAB 195/15/18, accessed February 7, 2013, http://discovery.nationalarchives.gov.uk/SearchUI/Details?uri=D7739563.

4. Jimmy Carter, "The State of the Union Address Delivered before a Joint Session of the Congress." January 23, 1980, The American Presidency Project, accessed February 7, 2013, https://www.presidency.ucsb.edu/node/249681.

5. Charles Ragin, *Fuzzy-Set Social Science* (Chicago: University of Chicago Press, 2000), 229.

6. Political science theories are best understood as probabilistic, rather than deterministic, models of causation. Because they explain extraordinarily complex phenomena that are subject to idiosyncratic or "random" variation, no political science theory can predict outcomes with 100 percent accuracy. A few errant cases, therefore, are to be expected and do not necessarily disprove the theory. Standard statistical benchmarks enable us to objectively determine what threshold of failed tests should result in the rejection of a probabilistic theory.

7. See, for example, Kenneth N. Waltz, *Theory of International Politics* (New York: McGraw-Hill, 1979), 152–56; Richard Rosecrance, *The Rise of the Trading State: Commerce and Conquest in the Modern World* (New York: Basic Books, 1986), chap. 1; Dale C. Copeland, "Economic Interdependence and War: A Theory of Trade Expectations," *International Security* 20, no. 4 (1996): 5–41; Robert O. Keohane and Joseph S. Nye, *Power and Interdependence* (New York: Longman, 2001).

8. Sean Mirski, "Stranglehold: The Context, Conduct and Consequences of an American Naval Blockade of China," *Journal of Strategic Studies* 36, no. 1 (2013): 389.

9. In September 2013 alone, China inked $100 billion worth of energy deals to refine and transport Central Asian oil. More strikingly, in October it concluded an unprecedented

$85 billion equity agreement with Russia to import Siberian oil for the Chinese market. Wayne Ma, "Russia Lets Down Guard on China; Deal by Oil Giants to Jointly Explore Siberia Reserves Follows Spate of Chinese Inroads around Globe," *Wall Street Journal*, October 18, 2013; Frank Ching, "China Leads in Race for New Silk Road in Central Asia," *Business Times (Singapore)*, October 9, 2013.

10. Geoffrey Kemp, *The East Moves West: India, China, and Asia's Growing Presence in the Middle East* (Washington, DC: Brookings Institution Press, 2010), 175.

11. Simon Denyer, "China Charting Two New 'Silk Roads,' Bypassing U.S.," *Washington Post*, October 15, 2013. By comparison, the Strait of Hormuz, the major choke point for Persian Gulf oil, is twenty miles wide at its narrowest passage.

12. Rosemary A. Kelanic, *Oil Security and Conventional War: Lessons from a China-Taiwan Air War Scenario*, Council on Foreign Relations Energy Report, October 2013, http://www.cfr.org/china/oil-security-conventional-war-lessons-china-taiwan-air-war-scenario/p31578.

13. Notably Daniel Yergin, *The Prize: The Epic Quest for Oil, Money & Power*, with a new epilogue (New York: Free Press, 2009).

14. Important work from the 1970s and 1980s includes Stephen D. Krasner, "Oil Is the Exception," *Foreign Policy*, no. 14 (1974): 68–84; Robert L. Paarlberg, "Food, Oil and Coercive Resource Power," *International Security* 3, no. 2 (1978): 3–19; David A. Deese, "Energy: Economics, Politics, and Security," *International Security* 4, no. 3 (1979/1980): 140–53; Robert Lieber, "Energy, Economics and Security in Alliance Perspective," *International Security* 4, no. 4 (1980): 139–63; G. John Ikenberry, *Reasons of State: Oil Politics and the Capacities of American Government*, Cornell Studies in Political Economy (Ithaca, NY: Cornell University Press, 1988). More recent work does attempt to generalize. See Rosemary A. Kelanic, "The Petroleum Paradox: Oil, Coercive Vulnerability, and Great Power Behavior," *Security Studies* 25, no. 2 (April 2016): 181–213.

15. Michael L. Ross, "The Political Economy of the Resource Curse," *World Politics* 51, no. 2 (1999): 297–332; "Does Oil Hinder Democracy?," *World Politics* 53, no. 3 (2001): 325–61; James D. Fearon and David D. Laitin, "Ethnicity, Insurgency, and Civil War," *American Political Science Review* 97, no. 1 (2003): 75–90; Philippe Le Billon, *Fuelling War: Natural Resources and Armed Conflict* (London: Routledge for the International Institute for Strategic Studies, 2005); Cullen Hendrix, "Cold War Geopolitics and the Making of the Oil Curse," *Journal of Global Security Studies* 3, no. 1 (2018): 2–22. Interestingly, the resource curse does not appear to hold in Latin American countries. Thad Dunning, *Crude Democracy: Natural Resource Wealth and Political Regimes* (Cambridge: Cambridge University Press, 2008).

16. Michael L. Ross, *The Oil Curse: How Petroleum Wealth Shapes the Development of Nations* (Princeton, NJ: Princeton University Press, 2012).

17. John Orme, "The Utility of Force in a World of Scarcity," *International Security* 22, no. 3 (1997/1998): 138–67; Thomas F. Homer-Dixon, "Environmental Scarcities and Violent Conflict," *International Security* 19, no. 1 (1994): 5–40; Michael T. Klare, *Resource Wars: The New Landscape of Global Conflict* (New York: Owl Books/Henry Holt, 2002); Michael T. Klare, *Rising Powers, Shrinking Planet: The New Geopolitics of Energy* (New York: Metropolitan Books, 2008); Michael T. Klare, *The Race for What's Left: The Global Scramble for the World's Last Resources* (New York: Picador, 2012).

18. Emily Meierding, "Dismantling the Oil Wars Myth," *Security Studies* 25, no. 2 (2016): 258–88; Omar Bashir, "The Great Games Never Played: Explaining Variation in International Competition over Energy," *Journal of Global Security Studies* 2, no. 4 (2017): 288–306.

19. Blake C. Clayton, *Market Madness: A Century of Oil Panics, Crises, and Crashes* (Oxford: Oxford University Press, 2015); Roger Stern, "Oil Scarcity Ideology in US Foreign Policy, 1908–97," *Security Studies* 25, no. 2 (2016): 214–57.

20. Michael T. Klare, "From Scarcity to Abundance: The Changing Dynamics of Energy Conflict," *Penn State Journal of Law and International Affairs* 3, no. 2 (2015): 10–41.

21. Jeff D. Colgan, "Oil and Revolutionary Governments: Fuel for International Conflict," *International Organization* 64, no. 4 (2010): 661–94; Colgan, "Fueling the Fire: Pathways from Oil to War," *International Security* 38, no. 2 (2013): 147–80.

22. Michael L. Ross and Erik Voeten, "Oil and International Cooperation," *International Studies Quarterly* 60 (2016): 85–97.

23. Cullen Hendrix, "Oil Prices and Interstate Conflict," *Conflict Management and Peace Science* 34, no. 6 (2017): 575–96.

24. Colgan, "Fueling the Fire."

25. Charles L. Glaser and Rosemary A. Kelanic, eds., *Crude Strategy: Rethinking the U.S. Military Commitment to Defend Persian Gulf Oil* (Washington, DC: Georgetown University Press, 2016); Charles L. Glaser, "How Oil Influences U.S. National Security," *International Security* 8, no. 2 (2013): 112–46; Doug Stokes, "Blood for Oil? Global Capital, Counter-insurgency, and the Dual Logic of American Energy Security," *Review of International Studies* 33, no. 2 (2007): 245–64; John S. Duffield, *Over a Barrel: The Costs of U.S. Foreign Oil Dependence* (Stanford, CA: Stanford University Press, 2008); Keith Crane et al., *Imported Oil and U.S. National Security* (Santa Monica, CA: RAND Corporation, 2009); Eugene Gholz and Daryl G. Press, "Protecting 'The Prize': Oil and the U.S. National Interest," *Security Studies* 19, no. 3 (2010): 453–85; Michael A. Levi, "The Enduring Vulnerabilities of Oil Markets," *Security Studies* 22, no. 1 (2013): 132–38; Eugene Gholz and Daryl G. Press, "Enduring Resilience: How Oil Markets Handle Disruptions," *Security Studies* 22, no. 1 (2013): 139–47; Steve A. Yetiv, *Myths of the Oil Boom: American National Security in a Global Energy Market* (Oxford: Oxford University Press, 2015).

26. Robert D. Blackwill and Meghan L. O'Sullivan, "America's Energy Edge: The Geopolitical Consequences of the Shale Revolution," *Foreign Affairs* 93, no. 2 (2014): 102–14; Meghan O'Sullivan, *Windfall: How the New Energy Abundance Upends Global Politics and Strengthens America's Power* (New York: Simon & Schuster, 2017). For a more skeptical view, see Michael A. Levi, *The Power Surge: Energy, Opportunity, and the Battle for America's Future* (Oxford: Oxford University Press, 2013).

27. Barry Posen, "Command of the Commons: The Military Foundation of U.S. Hegemony," *International Security* 28, no. 1 (2003): 8. Hughes and Long discuss the implications of command of the commons for oil security. Llewelyn Hughes and Austin Long, "Is There an Oil Weapon? Security Implications of Changes in the Structure of the International Oil Market," *International Security* 39, no. 3 (2014/2015): 152–89.

28. Caitlin Talmadge, "Closing Time: Assessing the Iranian Threat to the Strait of Hormuz," *International Security* 33, no. 1 (2008): 82–117; Joshua R. Itzkowitz Shifrinson and Miranda Priebe, "A Crude Threat: The Limits of an Iranian Missile Campaign against Saudi Arabian Oil," *International Security* 36, no. 1 (2011): 167–201.

29. Angela Stent, "An Energy Superpower? Russia and Europe," in *The Global Politics of Energy*, ed. Campbell and Price (Washington, DC: Aspen Institute, 2008): 76–95; Ariel Cohen, *Europe's Strategic Dependence on Russian Energy* (Washington, DC: Heritage Foundation, 2007), 12; Marshall I. Goldman, "The Russian Power Play on Oil, Natural Gas Reserves," *Boston Globe*, August 23, 2008; Michael T. Klare, *Rising Powers, Shrinking Planet*, chap. 4; Daniel W. Drezner, "Allies, Adversaries and Economic Coercion: Russian Foreign Economic Policy since 1991," *Security Studies* 6, no. 3 (1997): 65–111; Adam L. Stulberg, "Strategic Bargaining and Pipeline Politics: Confronting the Credible Commitment Problem in Eurasian Energy Transit," *Review of International Political Economy* 19, no. 5 (2012): 808–36.

30. Ziv Rubinovitz and Elai Rettig, "Crude Peace: The Role of Oil Trade in the Israeli-Egyptian Peace Negotiations," *International Studies Quarterly* 62 (2018): 371–82.

31. Andrew Cheon and Johannes Urpelainen, "Escaping Oil's Stranglehold: When Do States Invest in Energy Security?," *Journal of Conflict Resolution* 59, no. 6 (2015): 953–83.

32. *BP Statistical Review of World Energy*, 67th ed. (London: BP Amoco, 2018), 47, accessed February 1, 2019, https://www.bp.com/content/dam/bp/business-sites/en/global/corporate/pdfs/energy-economics/statistical-review/bp-stats-review-2018-full-report.pdf.

33. John S. Duffield, *Fuels Paradise: Seeking Energy Security in Europe, Japan, and the United States* (Baltimore: Johns Hopkins University Press, 2015); Llewelyn Hughes, *Globalizing Oil: Firms and Oil Market Governance in France, Japan, and the United States* (Cambridge: Cambridge University Press, 2014).

34. OAPEC is a political coalition of Arab oil producers that overlaps with, but does not perfectly coincide with, the membership of the more widely known cartel the Organization of Petroleum Exporting Countries (OPEC). At the time of the embargo, OAPEC consisted of the same ten members that are active today: Algeria, Bahrain, Egypt, Iraq, Kuwait, Libya, Qatar, Saudi Arabia, Syria, and the United Arab Emirates. Tunisia joined OAPEC in 1982 but deactivated its membership in 1986. OAPEC: Organization of Arab Petroleum Exporting Countries, "History—The Definition of the Organization," accessed January 30, 2019, http://www.oapecorg.org/Home/About-Us/History.

35. Thomas C. Schelling, *Arms and Influence* (New Haven, CT: Yale University Press, 1967), 69–91.

36. Consequently, the definition excludes events like the British boycott on Iranian oil sales from 1951 to 1953 and attacks on petroleum exports during the Iran-Iraq War. Coercive threats to deprive an oil exporter of revenue may spur anticipatory behavior by producers, but the strategies adopted would be very different.

37. For an analysis of this possibility see Mirski, "Stranglehold."

38. On market adaptation, see Gholz and Press, "Protecting 'The Prize.'"

39. John J. Mearsheimer, *The Tragedy of Great Power Politics* (New York: Norton, 2001), 45.

40. For excellent analyses of Iran's capabilities and intentions in the strait, see Caitlin Talmadge, "Closing Time"; Joshua Rovner, "After America: The Flow of Persian Gulf Oil in the Absence of U.S. Military Force," in *Crude Strategy: Rethinking the U.S. Military Commitment to Defend Persian Gulf Oil*, ed. Glaser and Kelanic (Washington, DC: Georgetown University Press, 2016), 141–65; Eugene Gholz, "Threats to Oil Flows through the Strait of Hormuz" (unpublished manuscript 2011).

41. Jeff Colgan's *Petro-Aggression: When Oil Causes War* (Cambridge: Cambridge University Press, 2013), one of the most important books on oil in international relations, limits its scope to the post-1973 world. *The Oil Curse* (2012), a hugely influential book on the comparative politics of oil by Michael Ross, explains a phenomenon that appears only in the 1970s and after.

1. A THEORY OF STRATEGIC ANTICIPATION

1. On a practical level, it would be impossible to produce obviously "better" estimates of the petroleum deficit and import threat when states can put far greater resources into the effort. Great powers regularly commission large teams of experts to study the coercive vulnerability problem, sometimes over the course of years. Moreover, those experts can use the authority of the state to collect sensitive data from companies, the military, the intelligence community, and other restrictive sources inaccessible to scholars.

2. Clayton, *Market Madness*; Stern, "Oil Scarcity Ideology."

3. Refinery capabilities are less important than oil resources in determining the "have" side of the deficit and are excluded to increase theoretical leverage. Great powers can build and reconfigure refineries as needed to produce their desired petroleum products but cannot quickly expand their recoverable oil reserves.

4. For this reason, economists consider oil supply to be highly inelastic in the short term: even a large increase in oil prices will not cause an immediate expansion in quantity supplied to the market. In the long term, the price is more elastic as producers adapt by scaling investment up or down as appropriate.

5. The one exception is Saudi Arabia, whose state-owned oil company ARAMCO has deliberately produced below capacity since the mid-1980s, when it adopted its role as "swing producer" to moderate prices. The country is uniquely equipped to maintain excess capacity because its resources are massive and its production costs are the lowest in the world. Conventional wisdom holds that Saudi Arabia derives political influence from its singular position as price moderator, but the proposition is difficult to test empirically.

6. Technically, it is possible to exceed maximum capacity in the short term by pushing extraction beyond the marginal efficient rate of production. The option is unattractive, however, because the increase is slight and the process irrevocably damages oil fields, reducing ultimate petroleum recovery. See Robert O. Anderson, *Fundamentals of the Petroleum Industry* (Norman: University of Oklahoma Press, 1984).

7. The following discussion applies only to conventional oil production. This is justified because practically all oil produced during the nineteenth and twentieth centuries was conventional oil, except for synthetic oil produced by Germany and Japan under World War II–era self-sufficiency programs. In the middle of the first decade of the twenty-first century, countries such as Canada and the United States began producing unconventional oil from tar sands and shale. Even at the height of the "fracking boom" in the mid-2010s, however, unconventional output was small relative to conventional oil, which makes up the vast majority of the global market. Unconventional oil is costlier to exploit because it is less liquid in its natural form and requires extra processing.

8. If the forces are sufficiently strong, the result is the iconic "gusher well" famous in American popular culture.

9. As reserves are developed into active fields, petroleum engineers gain better information that allows them to more accurately judge the size of recoverable reserves. Because initial resource estimates are usually conservative, they often understate the promise of fields. Therefore, as information improves, proven reserves tend to rise.

10. I take state goals as given, bracketing questions about their content and origins. This likely introduces some endogeneity because states probably take oil availability into account when formulating their goals. The problem is not unique to my theory. Endogeneity is almost always present in means-ends calculations; at the very least, means influence ends by limiting the universe of realistic goals.

11. Cohen, *Japan's Economy*, 143.

12. United States Strategic Bombing Survey, *The Effects of Strategic Bombing on the German War Economy* (Washington, DC: U.S. Government Printing Office, 1945), 40, 67, 77.

13. Carl von Clausewitz, *On War*, ed. Michael Eliot Howard and Peter Paret (Princeton, NJ: Princeton University Press, 1984), 119–20.

14. "Embargo" is also commonly conflated with "boycott," which describes the peaceful refusal to *purchase* a country's goods.

15. Although the 1973 OAPEC incident included an embargo, this is not what imposed economic damage on the United States. Rather, damage resulted from the simultaneous production cuts OAPEC members adopted, which reduced the total amount of petroleum available on the international market, as well as poorly managed oil rationing policy in the United States.

16. On coordination problems and other collective action issues, see Mancur Olson, *The Logic of Collective Action: Public Goods and the Theory of Groups* (Cambridge, MA: Harvard University Press, 1965).

17. Arthur Jay Klinghoffer, *Oiling the Wheels of Apartheid: Exposing South Africa's Secret Oil Trade* (Boulder, CO: Lynne Rienner), 7–8.

18. Ibid., 21.

19. The case is coded as a failure even in optimistic studies on the effectiveness of sanctions. Gary Clyde Hufbauer, Jeffrey J. Schott, and Kimberly Ann Elliot, *Economic Sanctions Reconsidered: History and Current Policy* (Washington, DC: Institute for International Economics, 1985), 351–56. For an opposing view, see Audie Klotz, *Norms in International Relations: The Struggle against Apartheid* (Ithaca, NY: Cornell University Press, 1995).

20. Robert A. Pape, *Bombing to Win: Air Power and Coercion in War* (Ithaca, NY: Cornell University Press, 1996), 4. Following Pape, "coercion," as I define it, is thus equivalent to what Thomas C. Schelling calls "compellence." Schelling, *Arms and Influence*, 69–91.

21. Attacks specifically designed to damage the target's war economy also qualify as denial, because economic might is the basis of military might and thus harming the war economy constrains the target's material capabilities to resist.

22. Pape, *Bombing to Win*; Max Abrams, "Why Terrorism Does Not Work," *International Security* 31, no. 2 (2006): 42–78.

23. Pape, *Bombing to Win*.

24. Keir A. Lieber, *War and the Engineers: The Primacy of Politics over Technology* (Ithaca, NY: Cornell University Press, 2005).

25. George H. Quester, *Offense and Defense in the International System* (New Brunswick, NJ: Transaction Publishers, 2003), 3, 16, 90.

26. John J. Mearsheimer, *Conventional Deterrence* (Ithaca, NY: Cornell University Press, 1983), 31.

27. Ibid., 26.

28. Lance Edwin Davis and Stanley L. Engerman, *Naval Blockades in Peace and War: An Economic History since 1750* (New York: Cambridge University Press, 2006), 3.

29. Saudi Arabia is the lone exception. Because government subsidies keep local Saudi oil prices artificially low, significant amounts of petroleum are used to generate electricity. Demand is so high that the Saudi domestic economy consumes about 30 percent of the country's oil output. If subsidy policies remain in place and demographic trends continue, domestic consumption will reach 100 percent of total Saudi production as early as 2025. Thomas W. Lippman, "Saudi Arabian Oil and US Interests," in *Crude Strategy: Rethinking the US Military Commitment to the Persian Gulf*, ed. Charles L. Glaser and Rosemary A. Kelanic (Washington, DC: Georgetown University Press, 2016), 115–16.

30. On average, one barrel of crude oil contains 5.8 million Btus (British thermal units) of energy and weighs about 0.13 metric tons. It requires twice the weight of coal (about 0.26 metric tons) to yield the same amount of energy. Exact numbers vary depending on the API gravity (density) of the crude oil and the type of coal being used (e.g., bituminous, lignite, anthracite). API gravity was developed by the American Petroleum Institute (API); hence the name. See the Energy Information Administration website for energy conversion tables.

31. National Research Council, *Producer Gas: Another Fuel for Motor Transport* (Washington, DC: National Academy Press, 1983), v, 2, 3, 12, 17, 25.

32. Richard J. Overy, *Why the Allies Won* (New York: W. W. Norton, 1996), 231.

33. National Research Council, *Producer Gas*, 8, 24; John Fuller Ryan, *Wartime Woodburners: Gas Producer Vehicles in World War II—An Overview* (Atglen, PA: Schiffer Military History, 2009), 11.

34. Kate Van Dyke, *Fundamentals of Petroleum*, 4th ed. (Austin: University of Texas, 1997), 318.

35. Yergin, *Prize*, 366.

36. States can shift to more extreme measures within the same category; typically, within-strategy escalation results from minor increases in coercive vulnerability, while across-strategy escalation results from major increases in coercive vulnerability.

37. On covert action and plausible deniability, see Lindsey A. O'Rourke, *Covert Regime Change: America's Secret Cold War* (Ithaca, NY: Cornell University Press, 2018), 49–50.

38. Waltz describes internal balancing thinly as "moves to increase economic capability, to increase military strength, to develop clever strategies" in response to external threats. Waltz, *Theory*, 118.

39. A common misconception is that petroleum has no general substitutes. In fact, the substitution problem applies specifically to transportation. Coal, wind, and natural gas closely substitute for oil in many nontransit activities, including electricity generation, heating, and industrial use.

40. Arnold Krammer, "Technology Transfer as War Booty: The U.S. Technical Oil Mission to Europe, 1945," *Technology and Culture* 22, no. 1 (1981): 69; Overy, *Why the Allies Won*, 233.

41. The United States could not actually withdraw the entire supply of SPR oil *within* four and a half months, however. The maximum drawdown rate is about 4.4 million barrels per day, which means it would take at least five months to physically empty the reserve. U.S. Department of Energy, "SPR Quick Facts and FAQs," accessed June 21, 2018, https://www.energy.gov/fe/services/petroleum-reserves/strategic-petroleum-reserve/spr-quick-facts-and-faqs.

42. Eugene Gholz, "US Spending on Its Military Commitments to the Persian Gulf," in *Crude Strategy: Rethinking the US Military Commitment to Defend Persian Gulf Oil*, ed. Charles L. Glaser and Rosemary A. Kelanic (Washington, DC: Georgetown University Press, 2016), 167.

43. External balancing consists of maneuvers "to strengthen and enlarge one's own alliance or to weaken and shrink an opposing one." Waltz, *Theory*, 118.

44. Louis Wesseling, *Fuelling the War: Revealing an Oil Company's Role in Vietnam* (London: I. B. Tauris, 2000), 165–68.

45. "Kuwait, US in Fuel Payment Row," *al-Jazeera (English)*, March 16, 2005; United States Department of Defense Office of the Secretary of Defense, *Report on Allied Contributions to the Common Defense* (Washington, DC: Office of the Secretary of Defense, 1992), appendix C.

46. Thomas J. Christensen and Jack Snyder, "Chain Gangs and Passed Bucks: Predicting Alliance Patterns in Multipolarity," *International Organization* 44, no. 2 (1990): 137–68; Pape, *Dying to Win*.

47. Pearson, *Name of Oil*, 14–39.

48. Waltz, *Theory*, 142, 155.

49. This claim rests on the assumption that great powers are seeking security, not that greedy states are pursuing expansion as an end in itself. This assumption is quite standard but not universal in the international relations theory literature. If a state were motivated by greed, prestige, or other nonsecurity goals, it might still get a positive benefit from high-cost actions like conquering oil. The benefit would not be security; rather, it would be the wealth or political prestige that controlling oil could provide.

50. I explain in chapter 3 why this does not cause endogeneity problems.

51. One exception might be tall trees for the British navy.

52. Mancur Olson famously demonstrated how the British were able to compensate for food imports lost to naval blockades by adjusting domestic food production. Mancur Olson, *The Economics of the Wartime Shortage: A History of British Food Supplies in the Napoleonic War and in World Wars I and II* (Durham, NC: Duke University Press, 1963).

53. "Oil Production—Barrels," subset of "Statistical Review of World Energy—All Data, 1965–2018," BP Statistical Review of World Energy, accessed September 11, 2019, https://www.bp.com/en/global/corporate/energy-economics/statistical-review-of-world-energy.html.

54. R. J. Forbes, "Oil in Eastern Europe," in *Oil's First Century; Papers,* Centennial Seminar on the History of the Petroleum Industry, Harvard University, 1959 (Cambridge, MA: Harvard Graduate School of Business Administration, 1960), 5.

55. Kendall Beaton, "Founders' Incentives: The Pre-Drake Refining Industry," in *Oil's First Century; Papers,* 9.

56. Paul H. Giddens, "The Significance of the Drake Well," in *Oil's First Century: Papers,* 23.

57. Ibid.

58. Joseph Stanley Clark, *The Oil Century, from the Drake Well to the Conservation Era* (Norman: University of Oklahoma Press, 1958), 49, 52, 73.

59. Ibid., 53.

60. Anderson, *Fundamentals,* 37.

61. Steve LeVine, *The Oil and the Glory: The Pursuit of Empire and Fortune on the Caspian Sea* (New York: Random House, 2007), 11.

62. Forbes, "Oil in Eastern Europe," 3.

63. Beaton, "Founders' Incentives," 9.

64. Yergin, *Prize,* 79.

65. Fiona Venn, *Oil Diplomacy in the Twentieth Century* (New York: St. Martin's Press, 1986), 2.

66. Ibid., 3.

67. Some credit the invention of the automobile to Karl Friedrich Benz, who in 1885 created a three-wheeled vehicle driven by a gasoline engine. Others attribute it to Gottlieb Daimler for his invention of the first four-wheeled gasoline-powered motorcar in 1886.

68. Commercial aviation did not develop until the 1920s. Venn, *Oil Diplomacy,* 4.

69. Robert Gilpin, *War and Change in World Politics* (Cambridge: Cambridge University Press, 1981), 224.

70. Venn, *Oil Diplomacy,* 2. On the coal production of the great powers, see Paul M. Kennedy, *The Rise and Fall of the Great Powers: Economic Change and Military Conflict from 1500 to 2000* (New York: Random House, 1987), 200, 210, 233.

71. American Petroleum Institute, *Petroleum Facts and Figures, Centennial Edition* (New York: American Petroleum Institute, 1959), 432–37; DeGolyer and MacNaughton, *Twentieth Century Petroleum Statistics,* 40th ed. (Dallas: DeGolyer and MacNaughton, 1984), 4–11; "Oil Production—Barrels."

72. Anderson, *Fundamentals,* 10.

73. Mearsheimer, *Tragedy,* 33.

74. Waltz, *Theory,* 142.

2. OIL AND MILITARY EFFECTIVENESS

1. Waltz, *Theory of International Politics,* 127–128; Barry R. Posen, "Nationalism, the Mass Army, and Military Power," *International Security* 18, no. 2 (1993): 81–86.

2. William McNeill, *The Rise of the West: A History of the Human Community* (Chicago: University of Chicago Press, 1991), 223.

3. Larry H. Addington, *The Patterns of War since the Eighteenth Century* (Bloomington: Indiana University Press, 1994), 48.

4. McNeill, *Rise of the West,* 253. Martin Van Creveld disputes this conventional view, arguing that Prussia's use of railroads in 1866 "could hardly be regarded as a resounding

success," while the contribution railroads made to the Prussian victory over France in 1871 "has been grossly overestimated." Martin Van Creveld, *Supplying War: Logistics from Wallenstein to Patton*, 2nd ed. (Cambridge: Cambridge University Press, 2004), 84, 104. For a critique of Van Creveld, see John A. Lynn, "The History of Logistics and Supplying War," in *Feeding Mars: Logistics in Western Warfare from the Middle Ages to the Present*, ed. John A. Lynn (Boulder, CO: Westview Press, 1993), 9–27.

5. Lieber, *War and the Engineers*, 52.

6. John A. Lynn, "Modern Introduction," in *Feeding Mars: Logistics in Western Warfare from the Middle Ages to the Present*, ed. John A. Lynn (Boulder, CO: Westview Press, 1993), 184.

7. Addington, *Patterns of War*, 48.

8. Lieber, *War and the Engineers*, 57.

9. Ever studious, the German General Staff learned from this experience. To correct the problem, the military intervened in the railroad industry so that future lines would serve strategic interests rather than merely commercial ones. "After 1870–1871," as a result, "no new line could be built without General Staff approval, and many new lines were laid out with a purely military object." This consolidated German railway advantage over the French, who continued to allow rail lines to grow organically according to business imperatives. Alan Henniker, *Transportation on the Western Front, 1914–1918* (London: H.M. Stationery off., 1937), xx.

10. Lieber, *War and the Engineers*, 54.

11. Van Creveld, *Supplying War*, 85, 105.

12. Ibid., 112–13.

13. Ibid., 84, 91, 160.

14. Lynn, "Modern Introduction," 184.

15. Quoted in Lieber, *War and the Engineers*, 52.

16. Ibid., 52, 53.

17. Van Creveld, *Supplying War*, 95, 129, 157.

18. Jon Sumida, "British Naval Administration and Policy in the Age of Fisher," *Journal of Military History* 54, no. 1 (1990): 11.

19. William Engdahl, *A Century of War: Anglo-American Oil Politics and the New World Order* (London: Pluto Press, 2004), 19.

20. Anderson, *Fundamentals*, 326–27.

21. Clausewitz, *On War*, 119–20.

22. Lynn, "Modern Introduction," 184.

23. J. F. C. Fuller, *Armament and History: The Influence of Armament on History from the Dawn of Classical Warfare to the End of the Second World War* (New York: Da Capo Press, 1998), 180.

24. Harold F. Williamson, Ralph L. Andreano, Arnold R. Daum, and Gilbert C. Klose, *The American Petroleum Industry: The Age of Energy, 1899–1959* (Evanston, IL: Northwestern University Press, 1963), 283.

25. Railroads were much more efficient and economical than motor transit beyond the two-hundred-mile range because they had a much greater cargo capacity relative to the amount of fuel they required to travel. Van Creveld, *Supplying War*, 143.

26. Ian Malcolm Brown, *British Logistics on the Western Front, 1914–1919* (Westport, CT: Praeger, 1998), 145.

27. Anderson, *Fundamentals*, 327.

28. Venn, *Oil Diplomacy*, 3.

29. Max E. Fletcher, "From Coal to Oil in British Shipping," in *The World of Shipping*, ed. David M. Williams (Aldershot, England: Ashgate, 1997), 158.

30. Engdahl, *Century of War*, 19.

31. Leo J. Daugherty, *The Allied Resupply Effort in the China-Burma-India Theater during World War II* (Jefferson, NC: McFarland, 2008).
32. Fletcher, "Coal to Oil," 159.
33. Jon Sumida, "British Naval Operational Logistics, 1914–1918," *Journal of Military History* 57, no. 3 (1993): 461.
34. Ibid., 464n58.
35. Ibid., 462, 468–469.
36. Daniel R. Beaver, "'Deuce and a Half': Selecting U.S. Army Trucks, 1920–1945," in *Feeding Mars: Logistics in Western Warfare from the Middle Ages to the Present*, ed. John A. Lynn (Boulder, CO: Westview Press, 1993), 253.
37. Henniker, *Transportation on the Western Front*, ix.
38. Jon Sumida, "Forging the Trident: British Naval Industrial Logistics, 1914–1918," in *Feeding Mars: Logistics in Western Warfare from the Middle Ages to the Present*, ed. John A. Lynn (Boulder, CO: Westview Press, 1993), 217.
39. Hubert C. Johnson, *Breakthrough! Tactics, Technology, and the Search for Victory on the Western Front in World War I* (Novato, CA: Presidio, 1994), 127.
40. The received wisdom is that European leaders expected a short war, but revisionist histories of the conflict challenge this view. According to some historians, German military officials correctly predicted the conflict would settle into a protracted war of attrition. See Keir A. Lieber, "The New History of World War I and What It Means for International Relations Theory," *International Security* 32, no. 2 (2007): 178–83.
41. German leaders understood the hazards of relying on railways to supply armies in foreign territories but had not come up with a viable alternative before invading Belgium. Ibid. The British and French were also unprepared for the logistical challenges ahead, having only a "rudimentary" grasp of military transportation in 1914. M. G. Taylor, "Land Transportation in the Late War," *Journal of the Royal United Services Institute for Defence Studies* 66 (1921): 700–703.
42. Van Creveld, *Supplying War*, 110–11, 125.
43. Sir Frederick Maurice, *The Last Four Months: The End of the War in the West* (London: Cassell, 1919), 56; Brown, *British Logistics*, 186.
44. Van Creveld, *Supplying War*, 143.
45. Henniker, *Transportation on the Western Front*, 160; Taylor, "Land Transportation," 707.
46. Johnson, *Breakthrough!*, 115.
47. Henniker, *Transportation on the Western Front*, 156–58.
48. Brown, *British Logistics*, 165.
49. *Why Germany Capitulated on November 11, 1918: A Brief Study Based on Documents in the Possession of the French General Staff* (London: Hodder and Stoughton, 1919), 39–40.
50. "Floated to Victory on a Wave of Oil," *New York Times*, November 23, 1918, 3.
51. Yergin, *Prize*, 167.
52. "Floated to Victory," 3.
53. Paul Foley, U.S. Naval Institute Proceedings, November 1924, quoted in Williamson et al., *American Petroleum Industry*, 292.
54. John W. Frey and H. Chandler Ide, eds., *A History of the Petroleum Administration for War, 1941–1945* (Washington, DC: U.S. Government Printing Office, 1946), 8.
55. Paul Foley, U.S. Naval Institute Proceedings, November 1924, quoted in Williamson et al., *American Petroleum Industry*, 292.
56. Venn, *Oil Diplomacy*, 3.
57. Waltz, *Theory*, 123–28; Posen, "Nationalism."
58. Overy, *Why the Allies Won*, 228.

59. Frey and Ide, *History of the Petroleum Administration for War*, 1.
60. Ibid., 271.
61. Cohen, *Japan's Economy*, 142.
62. Ibid., 144.
63. Edwin P. Hoyt, *Japan's War: The Great Pacific Conflict: 1853–1952* (New York: McGraw-Hill, 1986), 398; Lester Brooks, *Behind Japan's Surrender: The Secret Struggle That Ended an Empire* (New York: McGraw-Hill, 1968), 54.
64. Shannon McCune, *Intelligence on the Economic Collapse of Japan in 1945* (Lanham, MD: University Press of America, 1989), 32–33.
65. Cohen, *Japan's Economy*, 146–47.
66. Mark P. Parillo, *The Japanese Merchant Marine in World War II* (Annapolis, MD: Naval Institute Press, 1993), 209.
67. Cohen, *Japan's Economy*, 143.
68. Parillo, *Japanese Merchant Marine*, 210.
69. Ibid., 42–44, 212.
70. Ibid, 42.
71. Overy, *Why the Allies Won*, 229
72. Quoted in Cohen, *Japan's Economy*, 146.
73. Parillo, *Japanese Merchant Marine*, 42–44, 213; Cohen, *Japan's Economy*, 144, 146; Overy, *Why the Allies Won*, 229.
74. Cohen, *Japan's Economy*, 143–44.
75. Parillo, *Japanese Merchant Marine*, 41, 213.
76. Major-General Okada Kikaasaburo, quoted in Parillo, *Japanese Merchant Marine*, 39.
77. Robert A. Pape, "Why Japan Surrendered," *International Security* 18, no. 2 (1993): 154–201; Pape, *Bombing to Win*; Ward Wilson, "The Winning Weapon? Rethinking Nuclear Weapons in Light of Hiroshima," *International Security* 31, no. 4 (2007): 162–79.
78. Pape, "Why Japan Surrendered," 156–57, 178–79.
79. Edward J. Drea, "Missing Intentions: Japanese Intelligence and the Soviet Invasion of Manchuria," *Military Affairs* 48, no. 2 (1984): 67.
80. Brooks, *Japan's Surrender*, 20.
81. John Toland, *The Rising Sun: The Decline and Fall of the Japanese Empire, 1836–1945* (New York: Modern Library, 1970), 756.
82. Ibid., 754–55.
83. Ibid., 754–58, 767, 769, 775, 795–96.
84. McCune, *Economic Collapse*, 54
85. Drea, "Missing Intentions," 68–69.
86. Ibid.
87. Brooks, *Japan's Surrender*, 66–67.
88. Quoted in Toland, *Rising Sun*, 807.

3. QUALITATIVE METHODS FOR TESTING THE THEORY

1. Note that the time-unit approach is a well-established practice in political science research. For example, the voluminous quantitative literature on the democratic peace defines observations as dyad-years, which derives from the independent variable (the regime type of two potential belligerents) rather than the dependent variable (the presence or absence of war). Granted, the democratic peace literature is atypical in that its core prediction is a nonevent, the lack of war between democracies, which is particularly difficult to test. But there is no reason a similar logic cannot be applied to studies of observable events like anticipatory strategies.

2. Alexander L. George and Andrew Bennett, *Case Studies and Theory Development in the Social Sciences* (Cambridge, MA: MIT Press, 2004), 161–62.

3. U.S. Department of Defense fuel procurement numbers are misleading because they omit oil received as in-kind contributions from allies. Full information is not available, but bread crumbs exist. For example, during the six-week operation to topple Saddam Hussein (Operation Iraqi Freedom, March 19 to May 1, 2003), Kuwait provided the U.S. military with $450 million worth of free oil, or roughly 21.4 million barrels (based on the preferential price of $21 per barrel). That suggests an average usage of 3.5 million barrels a week, atop the average weekly usage of 2.7 million barrels of purchased oil per week. In other words, when free Kuwaiti oil is taken into account, the U.S. military consumed at least 37.2 million barrels during the six weeks of war, compared with the 16.2 million barrels that it paid for. The real numbers for military consumption are probably much higher for two reasons. First, military demand during the six-week phase of active combat operations almost certainly exceeded the average consumption of 2.7 million barrels per week calculated above from purchased sources. Second, the United States has no shortage of major oil-exporting allies in the region. Saudi Arabia, the United Arab Emirates, and others may have also contributed free oil that has not yet been disclosed. On top of this, Kuwait donated an additional 23.8 million barrels from the end of the war until the comments of Kuwaiti Member of Parliament (MP) Nasir al-Sana on March 16, 2005. Fuel numbers from the Department of Defense also do not include the oil used by private security contractors working with U.S. troops during the conflict, which again suggests that the "true" demand figure for the complete military effort is substantially higher than commonly assumed. "Kuwait, US in Fuel Payment Row," *al-Jazeera*, March 16, 2005, https://www.aljazeera.com/archive/2005/03/200841014255183636.html; Office of the Secretary of Defense, *Allied Contributions*, appendix C; Anthony Andrews, *Department of Defense Fuel Spending, Supply, Acquisition, and Policy* (Washington, DC: Congressional Research Service, 2009), 2; Moshe Schwartz, Katherine Blakeley, and Ronald O'Rourke, *Department of Defense Energy Initiatives: Background and Issues for Congress* (Washington, DC: Congressional Research Service, 2012), 7.

4. Stephen Van Evera, *Guide to Methods for Students of Political Science* (Ithaca, NY: Cornell University Press, 1997), 38–39, 83; Imre Lakatos, "Falsification and the Methodology of Scientific Research Programmes," in *Criticism and the Growth of Knowledge*, ed. Imre Lakatos and Alan Musgrave (Cambridge: Cambridge University Press, 1970), 115.

5. For example, George and Bennett claim that "the strongest possible supporting evidence for a theory is a case that is least likely for that theory but most likely for all alternative theories." If the predictions of the most-likely alternative theories fail but those of the least-likely theory prove accurate, then the least-likely theory is strongly confirmed because it "[has] already proven [its] robustness in the presence of countervailing mechanisms." George and Bennett, *Case Studies*, 121–22.

6. Van Evera, *Guide to Methods*, 51–52.

7. On "risky predictions," see John Gerring, "Is There a (Viable) Crucial-Case Method?," *Comparative Political Studies* 40, no. 3 (2007): 233–37.

8. The claim that least-likely cases are particularly valuable for causal inference is based on the logic of Bayesian updating. Ibid., 234.

9. Jack S. Levy, "Qualitative Methods in International Relations," in *Evaluating Methodology in International Studies*, ed. Frank P. Harvey and Michael Brecher (Ann Arbor: University of Michigan Press, 2002), 144.

10. Van Evera, *Guide to Methods*, 52–53.

11. The logic here equates to what Mill described as the "method of agreement." John Stuart Mill, *A System of Logic, Ratiocinative and Inductive: Being a Connected View of the Principles of Evidence, and Methods of Scientific Investigation* (London: John W. Parker, 1843), 450–54.

12. More specifically, the analysis is a subtype of congruence testing especially suited to "multiple within-case comparisons," in which "the investigator makes a number of paired observations of values on the IV and DV across a range of circumstances within a case." Stephen Van Evera refers to this as "congruence procedure 2." Van Evera, *Guide to Methods*, 61–62.

13. Under the common assumption that social science is probabilistic, not determinative, a single disconfirming case is not enough to reject a theory. For a theory to stand, however, the bulk of the case studies should confirm it. While in traditional qualitative research there is no widely accepted standard for how many anomalous cases it takes to disconfirm a theory, Charles Ragin has established benchmarks for qualitative comparative analysis for how many cases must support a theory for it to count as statistically significant. Ragin, *Fuzzy-Set Social Science*, 109–15. The book does this analysis in chapter 7 and finds that coercive vulnerability is usually a sufficient cause of anticipatory strategies, and we know this with 90 percent confidence, whereby "usually a sufficient cause" is a standard benchmark that means the theory is right at least 65 percent of the time.

14. George and Bennett, *Case Studies*, 184.

15. Ibid., 189–91.

16. In reality, a petroleum deficit did exist in the British case, but British leaders did not recognize it until after 1918. Therefore, I code the case as no deficit.

17. George and Bennett, *Case Studies*, 182–83.

18. Van Evera, *Guide to Methods*, 64.

19. David Collier, James Mahoney, and Jason Seawright, "Claiming Too Much: Warnings about Selection Bias," in *Rethinking Social Inquiry: Diverse Tools, Shared Standards*, ed. Henry E. Brady and David Collier (Lanham, MD: Rowman & Littlefield, 2004), 96–97.

4. BRITISH VULNERABILITY AND THE CONQUEST OF MESOPOTAMIA

1. V. H. Rothwell, "Mesopotamia in British War Aims, 1914–1918," *Historical Journal* 13, no. 2 (1970): 273–94; Raymond Leslie Buell, "Oil Interests in the Fight for Mosul," *Current History* 17, no. 6 (1923): 931–38.

2. Long forgotten now, the United States was amid an oil scare prompted by geological studies suggesting that wartime demand—including the oil provided to Britain and France—had drained American oil fields dry, leaving the country unable to meet its petroleum demands. Britain's monopolization of Middle Eastern reserves caused significant fear of British intentions in the United States, severely damaging relations between the two countries. John A. DeNovo, "The Movement for an Aggressive American Oil Policy Abroad, 1918–1920," *American Historical Review* 61, no. 4 (1956): 857–61.

3. Marian Jack, "The Purchase of the British Government's Shares in the British Petroleum Company 1912–1914," *Past & Present*, no. 39 (1968): 167.

4. Ibid., 140, 148–49; Sumida, "British Naval Operational Logistics," 461.

5. Sumida, "British Naval Operational Logistics," 460–61; Fletcher, "Coal to Oil," 153–54.

6. Engdahl, *Century of War*, 28.

7. Jack, "Purchase," 141.

8. The remaining 60 percent of the company was controlled by Dutch interests, which APOC claimed were susceptible to German influence.

9. Jack, "Purchase," 139, 141–42, 146, 150, 167.

10. Rothwell, "Mesopotamia," 274.

11. American Petroleum Institute, *Petroleum Facts and Figures, Centennial Edition*, 432–37.

12. Sumida, "British Naval Operational Logistics," 464.

13. Rothwell, "Mesopotamia," 273–88; Elie Kedourie, *England and the Middle East: The Destruction of the Ottoman Empire, 1914–1921* (Boulder, CO: Westview Press, 1987), 29–30.

14. Kedourie, *England and Middle East*, 30–31.

15. Rothwell, "Mesopotamia," 277–79, 286.

16. Helmut Mejcher, "Oil and British Policy towards Mesopotamia, 1914–1918," *Middle Eastern Studies* 8, no. 3 (1972): 377–78.

17. Ibid., 386.

18. Britain depended heavily on American oil throughout the war, receiving 80 percent of its petroleum imports from the United States in 1914 and 1915. Michael B. Stoff, *Oil, War, and American Security: The Search for a National Policy on Foreign Oil, 1941–1947* (New Haven, CT: Yale University Press, 1980), 4.

19. "Minutes of a Meeting of the War Cabinet," July 5, 1917, CAB 23/3, accessed May 28, 2015, http://www.nationalarchives.gov.uk/documentsonline/cabinetpapers.asp.

20. Sumida, "British Naval Operational Logistics," 470.

21. "Oil Fuel Situation," statement by the Fourth Sea Lord to the War Cabinet, June 30, 1917, CAB 24/18, accessed May 28, 2015, http://www.nationalarchives.gov.uk/documentsonline/cabinetpapers.asp.

22. Quoted in Sumida, "British Naval Operational Logistics," 470n85.

23. Quoted in Yergin, *Prize*, 177.

24. Williamson et al., *American Petroleum Industry*, 272.

25. Russia and North America (the United States and Mexico) accounted for 91 percent of global production in 1917. The Middle East produced only 1 percent, virtually all of which came from the British concession in Persia. American Petroleum Institute, *Petroleum Facts and Figures, Centennial Edition*, 432–37.

26. Williamson et al., *American Petroleum Industry*, 267; Sumida, "British Naval Operational Logistics," 470.

27. "Oil Fuel Reserve for Navy in Home Waters," Admiralty Memorandum for the War Cabinet, January 3, 1919, CAB 24/72, accessed May 28, 2011, http://www.nationalarchives.gov.uk/documentsonline/cabinetpapers.asp.

28. Admiral Sir Edmond Slade, "Petroleum Situation in the British Empire," Admiralty Memorandum for the Imperial War Cabinet, July 29, 1918, CAB 14/59, accessed May 28, 2011, http://www.nationalarchives.gov.uk/documentsonline/cabinetpapers.asp.

29. Ibid.

30. Ibid.

31. Ibid.

32. Rothwell, "Mesopotamia," 289; Mejcher, "Oil and British Policy," 385–87.

33. Rothwell, "Mesopotamia," 289–90.

34. Ibid., 290–91.

35. Ibid., 273; Mejcher, "Oil and British Policy," 388.

36. Buell, "Oil Interests," 933.

37. Stoff, *Oil, War*, 3.

5. THE OIL STRATEGIES OF NAZI GERMANY

1. Quoted in Yergin, *Prize*, 326.

2. Williamson Murray and Allan R. Millet, *A War to Be Won: Fighting the Second World War* (Cambridge, MA: Belknap Press of Harvard University Press, 2000), 291.

3. Ibid.

4. Albert Speer, *Inside the Third Reich: Memoirs* (New York: Macmillan, 1970), 406.

5. Walter Warlimont, *Inside Hitler's Headquarters, 1939–45* (New York: F. A. Praeger, 1964), 505.
6. Quoted in Frey and Ide, *History of the Petroleum Administration for War*, 6–7.
7. "Petro Fig-Fax," *American Petroleum Institute Quarterly* 15, no. 2 (1945): 1.
8. Alan S. Milward, *The German Economy at War* (London: University of London, Athlone Press, 1965), 171.
9. United States Strategic Bombing Survey, *Overall Report (European War)* (Washington, DC: U.S. Government Printing Office, 1945), 44.
10. Quoted in United States Strategic Bombing Survey, *Overall Report (European War)*, 44.
11. Joel Hayward, "Hitler's Quest for Oil: The Impact of Economic Considerations on Military Strategy, 1941–1942," *Journal of Strategic Studies* 18, no. 4 (1995): 94.
12. Overy, *Why the Allies Won*, 64–66.
13. Angus Maddison, *The World Economy* (Paris: Development Centre of the Organisation for Economic Co-operation and Development, 2006), 440–41, 463, 476, 560. Germany's GDP per capita surpassed that of the Soviet Union, Italy, and Japan.
14. Richard J. Overy, *War and Economy in the Third Reich* (Oxford: Oxford University Press, 1994), 38–40.
15. U.S. Census Bureau, *Statistical Abstract of the United States* (Washington, DC: U.S. Government Printing Office), multiple volumes; Overy, *War and Economy*, 38.
16. Overy, *War and Economy*, 4.
17. Ibid., 5, 52.
18. Ibid., 53.
19. Ibid., 55–56.
20. Ibid., 56.
21. Joel Darmstadter, *Energy in the World Economy: A Statistical Review of Trends in Output, Trade, and Consumption since 1925* (Baltimore: Johns Hopkins Press, 1972), table X, 622–51. From 1924 to 1933, Germany produced one-fifth of global coal supplies, an output second only to the United States. Thomas Parke Hughes, "Technological Momentum in History: Hydrogenation in Germany 1898–1933," *Past & Present*, no. 44 (1969): 16.
22. B. R. Mitchell, *International Historical Statistics: Europe, 1750–1993*, 4th ed. (London: Macmillan, 1998), 736, 738; Mitchell, *International Historical Statistics: The Americas, 1750–1993*, 4th ed. (London: Macmillan, 1998), 581. Several factors contributed to the lag in motorization, including late industrialization, the severe economic crisis, the excellent German railway system and comparative paucity of roads, and high taxes on automobiles. Overy, *War and Economy*, 69.
23. On prohibited weapons, see Gerhard L. Weinberg, *Hitler's Foreign Policy 1933–1939: The Road to World War II*, Combined ed. (New York: Enigma Books, 2005), 37, 127–28.
24. Ibid., 35–36, 127–28.
25. Paivi Lujala, Jan Ketil Rod, and Nadja Thieme, "Fighting over Oil: Introducing a New Dataset," *Conflict Management and Peace Science* 24, no. 3 (2007): 239–56.
26. Anderson, *Fundamentals*, 25.
27. A. E. Gunther, "The German War for Crude Oil in Europe 1934–1945: Chapter I—The North German Industry: Struggle of Party and Technologist," *Petroleum Times* 29 (November 8, 1947): 1095.
28. Maurice Pearton, *Oil and the Romanian State* (Oxford: Clarendon Press, 1971), 202.
29. Gunther, "North German Industry," 1095–96.
30. Ibid., 1095.
31. Hughes, "Technological Momentum," 122.
32. Ibid., 118–25.

33. Ibid., 127; Overy, *Why the Allies Won*, 230.
34. Hughes, "Technological Momentum," 129–30.
35. Overy, *War and Economy*, 72.
36. Ibid., 82–83.
37. Ibid., 63, 72, 81–82.
38. Weinberg, *Hitler's Foreign Policy*, 271.
39. Arthur Schweitzer, "Foreign Exchange Crisis of 1936," *Journal of Institutional and Theoretical Economics* 118, no. 2 (1962): 243–77.
40. Ibid., 259, 265.
41. Ibid., 256, 267.
42. Ibid., 265–67.
43. Ibid., 272–76.
44. Adolf Hitler, "Untitled Memorandum," in *Documents on German Foreign Policy 1918–1945, Series C (1933–1937), The Third Reich: First Phase*, vol. 5 (March 5–October 31, 1936), Document No. 490 (Washington, DC: U.S. Government Printing Office, 1949), 853–62.
45. On "race" and "space" as Hitler's driving ideology, see Weinberg, *Hitler's Foreign Policy*, 6–13.
46. Contra the conventional view among historians that the USSR was Hitler's primary enemy, Tooze argues that by 1938, the United States had assumed that mantle. J. Adam Tooze, *The Wages of Destruction: The Making and Breaking of the Nazi Economy* (New York: Penguin Books, 2008).
47. Berenice A. Carroll, *Design for Total War: Arms and Economics in the Third Reich* (The Hague: Mouton, 1968), 47–48; Weinberg, *Hitler's Foreign Policy*, 273.
48. Georg Thomas, "Memorandum on the Supply Situation in the Field of Fuels and Its Effect on the Wehrmacht, March 9, 1936," Document 1301-PS, in *Nazi Conspiracy and Aggression* (Washington, DC: U.S. Government Printing Office, 1946), 3:868–908.
49. Weinberg, *Hitler's Foreign Policy*, 273.
50. Hitler, "Untitled Memorandum."
51. Erich von Manstein, *Aus einem Soldatenleben 1887–1939* (Bonn: Athenäum-Verlag, 1958), 241, quoted in R. L. DiNardo, *Mechanized Juggernaut or Military Anachronism? Horses and the German Army of World War II* (New York: Greenwood Press, 1991), 15.
52. Ryan, *Wartime Woodburners*, 13.
53. Milward, *German Economy*, 12; United States Strategic Bombing Survey, *Effects of Strategic Bombing*, 73.
54. DiNardo, *Mechanized Juggernaut?*, 118.
55. Thomas, "Memorandum on the Supply Situation."
56. American Petroleum Institute, *Petroleum Facts and Figures, Centennial Edition*; A. E. Gunther, "The German War for Crude Oil in Europe 1934–1945: Chapter IV—Mobilisation Plans," *Petroleum Times* 29 (December 20, 1947): 1272–74.
57. United States Strategic Bombing Survey Oil Division, *Oil Division Final Report*, 2nd ed. (Washington, DC: U.S. Government Printing Office, 1947), 1.
58. Hitler's reasoning about the weakness of the Anglo-French threat is laid out in the November 10, 1937, memorandum, "Minutes of the Conference in the Reich Chancellery," also known as the "Hossbach Memo," *Documents on German Foreign Policy, 1918–1945*, 29–39.
59. *The German Oil Industry Ministerial Report Team 78*, 2nd ed. (Washington, DC: U.S. Government Printing Office, 1947), 16, table 6.
60. Heinrich Hassmann, *Oil in the Soviet Union: History, Geography, Problems*, trans. Alfred M. Leeston (Princeton, NJ: Princeton University Press, 1953), 55; Pearton, *Oil and the Romanian State*, 202.

61. Hitler, "Untitled Memorandum."
62. Raymond G. Stokes, "The Oil Industry in Nazi Germany, 1936–1945," *Business History Review* 59, no. 2 (1985): 258.
63. Technical Sub-Committee on Axis Oil Chiefs of Staff Committee, *Oil as a Factor in the German War Effort, 1933–1945* (London: Offices of the Cabinet and Minister of Defence, 1946), 4. This target was not met.
64. Gunther, "North German Industry," 1096.
65. Arnold Krammer, "Fueling the Third Reich," *Technology and Culture* 19, no. 3 (1978): 402.
66. Edward E. Ericson, *Feeding the German Eagle: Soviet Economic Aid to Nazi Germany, 1933–1941* (Westport, CT: Praeger, 1999), 202.
67. Postwar estimates indicate that blockade leakages were small. At most, only three hundred thousand tons of oil produced outside of Europe made its way to Germany through neutral countries. Chiefs of Staff Committee, *Oil as a Factor*, 11.
68. Overy, *War and Economy*, 195. This is the standard interpretation. For a dissenting view, see Tooze, *Wages of Destruction*, 662–63.
69. Production includes Austrian output of 144,000 tons but excludes output from Polish territories occupied after the invasion. Gunther, "The German War for Crude Oil in Europe 1934–1945: Chapter IV—Mobilisation Plans," 1273; Dietrich Eichholtz, *War for Oil: The Nazi Quest for an Oil Empire*, trans. John Broadwin (Washington, DC: Potomac Books, 2012), 9, 13, 15; United States Strategic Bombing Survey Oil Division, *Oil Division Final Report*, 18. Demand figures represent actual civilian and military demand in 1939. Civilian fuels were not yet being rationed. Chiefs of Staff Committee, *Oil as a Factor*, 165.
70. Rebecca Haynes, *Romanian Policy towards Germany, 1936–40* (New York: St. Martin's Press, 2000), 26.
71. Dennis Deletant, *Hitler's Forgotten Ally: Ion Antonescu and His Regime, Romania 1940–44* (New York: Palgrave Macmillan, 2006), 26.
72. Haynes, *Romanian Policy*, 108–9.
73. Pearton, *Oil and the Romanian State*, 251.
74. Misha Glenny, *The Balkans: Nationalism, War, and the Great Powers, 1804–2011* (New York: Penguin Books, 1999), 459.
75. Haynes, *Romanian Policy*, 129.
76. Gerhard L. Weinberg, *Germany and the Soviet Union 1939–1941* (Leiden, Netherlands: E. J. Brill, 1954), 128–31.
77. Andreas Hillgruber, *Hitler, König Carol Und Marschall Antonescu: Die Deutsch-Rumänischen Beziehungen, 1938–1944* (Wiesbaden: F. Steiner, 1954), 249.
78. Quoted in Ericson, *Feeding*, 68.
79. Ibid., 71, 77; Weinberg, "Germany and the Soviet Union," 56.
80. Ericson, *Feeding*, 53–54, 77.
81. Quoted in Ericson, *Feeding*, 103.
82. Ibid., 3, 105, 109, 111, 114; James E. McSherry, *Stalin, Hitler, and Europe* (Cleveland, OH: World, 1968), 76.
83. Ericson, *Feeding*, 112–13.
84. Robert Goralski and Russell W. Freeburg, *Oil & War: How the Deadly Struggle for Fuel in WWII Meant Victory or Defeat* (New York: Morrow, 1987), 59.
85. Quoted in Ericson, *Feeding*, 112–13.
86. McSherry, *Stalin, Hitler, and Europe*, 193.
87. Ericson, *Feeding*, 179.
88. Ibid., 3, 105–14, 198; McSherry, *Stalin, Hitler, and Europe*, 76.
89. Ericson, *Feeding*, 173–74.

90. German forces in the Soviet Union consumed 330,000 tons monthly, compared with an estimated demand of 250,000 tons per month. Van Creveld, *Supplying War*, 157.
91. Murray and Millet, *War to Be Won*, 127.
92. Van Creveld, *Supplying War*, 171, 173, 176–77.
93. Ibid., 150.
94. Quoted in Warlimont, *Inside Hitler's Headquarters*, 226.
95. Overy, *Why the Allies Won*, 232.
96. Murray and Millet, *War to Be Won*, 275; Overy, *Why the Allies Won*, 231; Anand Toprani, "The First War for Oil: The Caucasus, German Strategy, and the Turning Point of the War on the Eastern Front, 1942," *Journal of Military History* 80, no. 3 (2016): 815–54.
97. United States Strategic Bombing Survey, *Effects of Strategic Bombing*, 67.
98. Quote is from the United States Strategic Bombing Survey, *Overall Report (European War)*, 40; see also United States Strategic Bombing Survey, *Effects of Strategic Bombing*, 77.
99. United States Strategic Bombing Survey, *Effects of Strategic Bombing*, 78.
100. National Research Council, *Producer Gas*, v, 3, 12, 17, 20.
101. Ryan, *Wartime Woodburners*, 20.
102. R. J. Overy, "Transportation and Rearmament in the Third Reich," *Historical Journal* 16, no. 2 (1973): 395–96.
103. Overy, *Why the Allies Won*, 231.
104. United States Strategic Bombing Survey, *Effects of Strategic Bombing*, 73; National Research Council, *Producer Gas*, 18.
105. National Research Council, *Producer Gas*, 18.
106. United States Strategic Bombing Survey, *Effects of Strategic Bombing*, 78.
107. Speer, *Inside the Third Reich*, 346.
108. Quoted in the United States Strategic Bombing Survey, *Overall Report (European War)*, 41.
109. Speer, *Inside the Third Reich*, 346.
110. United States Strategic Bombing Survey, *Overall Report (European War)*, 41.
111. Milward, *German Economy*, 167.
112. Speer, *Inside the Third Reich*, 350.
113. Ibid., 347–48.
114. Quoted in Milward, *German Economy*, 167.
115. Speer, *Inside the Third Reich*, 350–51.
116. United States Strategic Bombing Survey, *Effects of Strategic Bombing*, 80.
117. Ericson, *Feeding*, 174; Speer, *Inside the Third Reich*, 406.
118. Overy, *Why the Allies Won*, 233.
119. Milward, *German Economy*, 171.
120. "Petro Fig-Fax," 1.

6. AMERICAN EFFORTS TO AVOID VULNERABILITY

1. American Petroleum Institute, *Petroleum Facts and Figures, 40th ed.* (Dallas: DeGolyer and MacNaughton, 1984), 4–11; "Oil Production—Barrels, BP Statistical Review of World Energy—All Data, 1965–2018."
2. American Petroleum Institute, *Petroleum Facts and Figures, Centennial Edition*, 432–37; American Petroleum Institute, *Petroleum Facts and Figures, 40th ed.*, 4–11; "Oil Production—Barrels."
3. Richard Corliss, "The 'Dallas' Shot That Was Heard Round the World," *Los Angeles Times*, November 23, 1990.
4. Karen R. Merrill, "Texas Metropole: Oil, the American West, and U.S. Power in the Postwar Years," *Journal of American History* 99, no. 1 (2012): 197.

5. Darren Dochuk, "Blessed by Oil, Cursed with Crude: God and Black Gold in the American Southwest," *Journal of American History* 99, no. 1 (2012): 56, 59.
6. Gerring, "Crucial-Case Method," 233–37.
7. Beaver, "'Deuce and a Half,'" 253, 259.
8. American Petroleum Institute, *Petroleum Facts and Figures, Centennial Edition*, 432–37.
9. Anderson, *Fundamentals*, 10–11.
10. Gerald D. Nash, *United States Oil Policy, 1890–1964: Business and Government in Twentieth Century America* (Pittsburgh: University of Pittsburgh Press, 1968), 5.
11. John A. DeNovo, "Petroleum and the United States Navy before World War I," *Mississippi Valley Historical Review* 41, no. 4 (1955): 642–43, 645, 656; Anderson, *Fundamentals*, 327; Sumida, "British Naval Administration," 11.
12. DeNovo, "Petroleum and the United States Navy," 646–48.
13. Nash, *United States Oil Policy*, 21.
14. John Ise, *The United States Oil Policy* (New Haven, CT: Yale University Press, 1926), 356.
15. Nash, *United States Oil Policy*, 18.
16. DeNovo, "Petroleum and the United States Navy," 648.
17. Ibid., 647, 649–51.
18. E. David Cronon, ed., *The Cabinet Diaries of Josephus Daniels, 1913–1921* (Lincoln: University of Nebraska Press, 1963), 29–30.
19. Ibid., 43.
20. Frey and Ide, *History of the Petroleum Administration for War*, 8, 171–72; Williamson et al., *American Petroleum Industry*, 267; Stoff, *Oil, War*, 4; Nash, *United States Oil Policy*, 24.
21. Williamson et al., *American Petroleum Industry*, 285.
22. Yergin, *Prize*, 163.
23. Clark, *Oil Century*, 136–37; Nash, *United States Oil Policy*, 43–44.
24. Quoted in "Future Oil Supply Needed by Country; Geological Survey Director Says We Must Conserve Resources or Enter Foreign Fields," *New York Times*, January 5, 1920.
25. Nash, *United States Oil Policy*, 45.
26. DeNovo, "Movement," 861.
27. Stephen J. Randall, *United States Foreign Oil Policy since World War I: For Profits and Security* (Montreal: McGill-Queen's University Press, 2005), 16–17; DeNovo, "Movement," 860; Nash, *United States Oil Policy*, 52.
28. Ise, *United States Oil Policy*, 461.
29. Quoted in DeNovo, "Movement," 859–60.
30. Ise, *United States Oil Policy*, 337–38, 356, 370–71.
31. Venn, *Oil Diplomacy*, 98; Nash, *United States Oil Policy*, 44–46; DeNovo, "Movement," 869; Randall, *United States Foreign Oil Policy*, 2, 29.
32. For an excellent survey of these efforts, see Stephen D. Krasner, *Defending the National Interest: Raw Materials Investments and U.S. Foreign Policy* (Princeton, NJ: Princeton University Press, 1978).
33. Nash, *United States Oil Policy*, 59–60.
34. Randall, *United States Foreign Oil Policy*, 22.
35. Frey and Ide, *History of the Petroleum Administration for War*, 15, 172–73.
36. Ibid., 174–78.
37. Ibid., 1, 5, 6, 8, 15, 75–76, 82–83, 88, 110, 125, 128, 174.
38. Ibid., 174, 178; Edward W. Chester, *United States Oil Policy and Diplomacy: A Twentieth Century Overview* (Westport, CT: Greenwood Press, 1983), 19.

39. Harold Ickes, "We're Running Out of Oil," *American Magazine*, January 1944, 85. At this time, large quantities of Alaskan oil had yet to be discovered.
40. Nash, *United States Oil Policy*, 172.
41. Frey and Ide, *History of the Petroleum Administration for War*, 293.
42. Ickes, "Running Out," 26, 27.
43. American Petroleum Institute, *Petroleum Facts and Figures, Centennial Edition*, 432.
44. Frey and Ide, *History of the Petroleum Administration for War*, 75–76, 82–83, 125.
45. Harold L. Ickes, "Oil from Coal: A 'Must' for America," *Collier's*, December 4, 1943.
46. Krammer, "Technology Transfer," 77, 79–82, 85–88, 97.
47. Global production in 1939 amounted to about 5.7 million barrels per day; the Middle East contributed just 300,000 barrels daily to that figure. Only three Middle Eastern countries were producing oil in commercial quantities when the war broke out in 1939: Iran, contributing about 200,000 barrels per day; Iraq, producing about 80,000 barrels per day; and Saudi Arabia, producing a meager 10,000 barrels daily. By contrast, the United States produced about 3.5 million barrels each day. Iran had been producing since 1913, whereas Iraqi production came online in 1927, and Saudi Arabia in 1936. American Petroleum Institute, *Petroleum Facts and Figures, Centennial Edition*, 432–37.
48. Quoted in Frey and Ide, *History of the Petroleum Administration for War*, 277–78.
49. Ibid., 277; Chester, *United States Oil Policy*, 236.
50. Ickes, "Running Out."
51. Chester, *United States Oil Policy*, 238.
52. Venn, *Oil Diplomacy*, 100; David E. Long, *The United States and Saudi Arabia: Ambivalent Allies* (Boulder, CO: Westview Press, 1985), 15.
53. Nash, *United States Oil Policy*, 172–73, 175; Chester, *United States Oil Policy*, 236, 241.
54. Joseph E. Pogue, "Must an Oil War Follow This War?," *Atlantic Monthly*, March 1944, 43, 45.
55. Chester, *United States Oil Policy*, 235, 239–40.
56. In fact, Eddy appears in the famous photograph of Ibn Saud and FDR on the deck of the *Quincy*, crouched next to the king and listening to a point made by a gesticulating Roosevelt, as if he were about to translate for Ibn Saud.
57. William A. Eddy, *FDR Meets Ibn Saud* (Washington, DC: America-Mideast Educational and Training Services, 1954), 32–34.
58. Thomas W. Lippman, *Saudi Arabia on the Edge: The Uncertain Future of an American Ally* (Dulles, VA: Potomac Books, 2012), 252.
59. Tidelands oil referred to petroleum found within three miles of the U.S. coast that was recoverable with the emerging technology of offshore drilling. States such as Louisiana, Texas, and California wanted these resources to be under state control. Federal ownership was already presumed over resources more than three miles from the coast.
60. Stoff, *Oil, War*, 192–94.
61. "X" [George F. Kennan], "The Sources of Soviet Conduct," *Foreign Affairs* 25, no. 4 (1947), 566–82.
62. For an excellent telling of the domestic politics behind the new U.S. defense stance, see Benjamin O. Fordham, *Building the Cold War Consensus: The Political Economy of U.S. National Security Policy, 1949–1951* (Ann Arbor: University of Michigan Press, 1998).
63. For examples of American planners incorporating Allied requirements into overall "free world" consumption, see "National Security Problems Concerning Free World Petroleum Demands and Potential Supplies, Report by the Secretary of the Interior and Petroleum Administrator for Defense to the National Security Council, December 8, 1952," Confidential, Declassified August 31, 1977, Truman Library, Papers of Harry S. Truman, President's Secretary's File, National Security File, Gale Document No. Gale|CK2349383053, accessed September 11, 2019, http://tinyurl.gale.com.proxy.library.nd.edu/tinyurl/Bofpc1; James S.

Lay, *A Report to the National Security Council by the Executive Secretary on a National Petroleum Program: Interim Report by the National Security Council on a National Petroleum Program (NSC 97/2)* (Washington, DC, 1951); Committee on Interstate and Foreign Commerce, United States House of Representatives, *Fuel Investigation: Petroleum and the European Recovery Program* (Washington, DC: United States GPO, 1948).

64. Committee on Interstate and Foreign Commerce, Special Subcommittee on Petroleum Investigation, United States House of Representatives, *Petroleum Investigation–Petroleum Supplies for Military and Civilian Needs, Final Report* (Washington, DC, 1947), 2.

65. David Alan Rosenberg, "The U.S. Navy and the Problem of Oil in a Future War: The Outline of a Strategic Dilemma, 1945–1950," *Naval War College Review* 29, no. 1 (1976): 55.

66. Bernard Brodie, *Foreign Oil and American Security*, ed. Frederick Sherwood Dunn (New Haven, CT: Yale Institute of International Studies, 1947), 2.

67. Committee on Interstate and Foreign Commerce, United States House of Representatives, *Fuel Investigation*, 1–2.

68. David S. Painter, *Oil and the American Century: The Political Economy of U.S. Foreign Oil Policy, 1941–1954*, The Johns Hopkins University Studies in Historical and Political Science (Baltimore: Johns Hopkins University Press, 1986), 216–17.

69. Chapman, *National Security Problems*, 6.

70. Committee on Interstate and Foreign Commerce, United States House of Representatives, *Fuel Investigation*, 6–7.

71. Painter, *Oil and the American Century*, 216–17.

72. Stoff, *Oil, War*, 146.

73. For obvious reasons, American officials assumed that Soviet oil, the world's other great supply, would be unavailable. Committee on Interstate and Foreign Commerce, United States House of Representatives, *Fuel Investigation*, 6; *Twentieth Century Petroleum Statistics*.

74. Darmstadter, *Energy*, 381, 395; *Twentieth Century Petroleum Statistics*.

75. Russia produced about 410,000 barrels daily in 1945 and 730,000 barrels daily in 1950. Darmstadter, *Energy*, 396; American Petroleum Institute, *Petroleum Facts and Figures, Centennial Edition*, 437.

76. Frey and Ide, *History of the Petroleum Administration for War*, 87, 255.

77. Clark, *Oil Century*, 241.

78. Michael J. Cohen, *Fighting World War Three from the Middle East: Allied Contingency Plans, 1945–1954* (London: Frank Cass, 1997), 32.

79. [USSR: Comprehensive Report to President Truman], *American Relations with the Soviet Union, A Report to the President by the Special Counsel to the President*, September 24, 1946, 12, Top Secret, Declassified March 5, 1973, Truman Library, Clark M. Clifford Papers, Gale Document No. Gale|Ck2349349366, accessed September 11, 2019, http://tinyurl.gale.com.proxy.library.nd.edu/tinyurl/BofsY.

80. Randall, *United States Foreign Oil Policy*, 257–60.

81. James S. Lay, *A Report to the National Security Council by the Executive Secretary on a National Petroleum Program (NSC 97)* (Washington, DC, 1950), 4.

82. Lay, *Interim Report*, 2–9.

83. *A Report to the National Security Council by the NSC Planning Board on a National Petroleum Program (NSC 97/3)* (Washington, DC, 1953), 19, 25, 28, 30, 32.

84. The Soviets could project power much more capably in the Middle East than in the Far East. However, imports would be vulnerable to Soviet naval forces across vast spans of ocean.

85. Military agreements were not as important in the Western Hemisphere, which was beyond the reach of Soviet power in any case.

86. Chester, *United States Oil Policy*, 235, 239–40.
87. Randall, *United States Foreign Oil Policy*, 257.
88. Bruce Riedel, *Kings and Presidents: Saudi Arabia and the United States since FDR* (Washington, DC: Brookings Institution Press, 2018), 43.
89. Chapman, *National Security Problems*, 18.
90. Ibid., 36, 41–42.
91. Chester, *United States Oil Policy*, 105.
92. Crude oil cost $17.30 per barrel in 1953 compared with $11.78 per barrel in 1969, in 2016 dollars. "BP Statistical Review of World Energy—Underpinning Data, 1965–2016."
93. In 1967, worldwide oil production was about 37 million barrels per day, while consumption was about 35.5 million barrels per day. Joseph Mann, "A Reassessment of the 1967 Arab Oil Embargo," *Israel Affairs* 19, no. 4 (2013): 699.
94. Christopher R. W. Dietrich, "'More a Gun at Our Heads Than Theirs': The 1967 Arab Oil Embargo, Third World Raw Material Sovereignty, and American Diplomacy," in *Beyond the Cold War: Lyndon Johnson and the New Global Challenges of the 1960s*, ed. Francis J. Gavin and Mark Atwood Lawrence (Oxford: Oxford University Press, 2014), 222.
95. Mann, "Reassessment," 696–97.
96. "Texas Oil Output Quotas Increased to High in August," *Wall Street Journal*, July 21, 1967.
97. Mann, "Reassessment," 697–98.
98. *Report Entitled: "The Middle East 1967–75 - an Appraisal of U.S. Interests and Policies." Topics Include: General Background Information; Requirements for a U.S. Policy from 1967–1975; Policy Planning; U.S. Interests in the Middle East; U.S.-Soviet Confrontation in the Middle East from 1967–1975; Soviet Threat to the Middle East* (Washington, DC: Central Intelligence Agency, 1967), 3–6.
99. Excess capacity existed historically because the Texas Railroad Commission set output limits for individual producers in the Texas-Louisiana-Oklahoma region so as to avoid the ruinous boom-bust cycle of overproduction followed by price crashes that obtained in the early twentieth century.
100. Yergin, *Prize*, 553–54; George J. Busenberg, *Oil and Wilderness in Alaska: Natural Resources, Environmental Protection, and National Policy Dynamics* (Washington, DC: Georgetown University Press, 2013), 11.
101. *Statement by Secretary of Defense Robert S. McNamara before the Senate Armed Services Committee on the Fiscal Year 1969–73 Defense Program and 1969 Defense Budget* (Washington, DC, 1968), 22.
102. *Middle East 1967–75*, 10–11.
103. Francis Fukuyama, *The Soviet Union and Iraq since 1968* (Santa Monica, CA: RAND Corporation, 1980), 26.
104. *Twentieth Century Petroleum Statistics*, multiple volumes; American Petroleum Institute, *Petroleum Facts and Figures*, 40th ed., 4–11; *BP Statistical Review of World Energy* (London: British Petroleum Company, 1985).
105. "Curbs Found Costly: Oil Import Quota Spurs Inquiry," *New York Times*, March 12, 1969.
106. United States Cabinet Task Force on Oil Import Control, *The Oil Import Question: A Report on the Relationship of Oil Imports to the National Security* (Washington, DC: U.S. Government Printing Office, 1970), 20.
107. Ibid., 124–25, 128.
108. Ibid., 129 (emphasis in the original).
109. Ibid., 135.

110. Ibid., 132–33.

111. Richard Nixon, "Statement about the Report of the Cabinet Task Force on Oil Import Control," in Peters and Woolley, *The American Presidency Project* (1970).

112. Joshua Rovner and Caitlin Talmadge, "Hegemony, Force Posture, and the Provision of Public Goods: The Once and Future Role of Outside Powers in Securing Persian Gulf Oil," *Security Studies* 23, no. 3 (2014): 548–81.

113. W. Taylor Fain, *American Ascendance and British Retreat in the Persian Gulf Region* (New York: Palgrave Macmillan, 2008), 2, 5.

114. "An Assessment of Future U.S. Policy toward the Persian Gulf Region as a Result of British Intentions to Withdraw Militarily from That Area by the End of 1971," memorandum from the National Security Council Interdepartmental Group for Near East and South Asia, 4, July 30, 1970, Department of State, N.D., US Declassified Documents Online, accessed April 17, 2018, http://tinyurl.galegroup.com/tinyurl/6m6vz0. Other documents refer to this as "Future US Policy in the Persian Gulf."

115. James R. Jones, "Behind LBJ's Decision Not to Run in '68," *New York Times*, April 16, 1988.

116. "National Security Study Memorandum 66: Policy toward the Persian Gulf, from Henry A. Kissinger," July 12, 1969, Box H-207, National Security Council Institutional Files, Richard Nixon Presidential Library and Museum, Yorba Linda, California, accessed April 5, 2018, https://www.nixonlibrary.gov/sites/default/files/virtuallibrary/documents/nssm/nssm_066.pdf.

117. "Future U.S. Policy."

118. "Memorandum from the President's Assistant for National Security Affairs (Kissinger) to President Nixon," October 22, 1970, *Foreign Relations of the United States, 1969–1976*, vol. E-4, *Documents on Iran and Iraq, 1969–1972*, ed. Monica Belmonte and Edward C. Keefer (Washington, DC: U.S. Government Printing Office, 2006), Document 91, accessed May 11, 2018, https://history.state.gov/historicaldocuments/frus1969-76ve04/d91.

119. "Future U.S. Policy," 8–9.

120. "Memorandum from the President's Assistant for National Security Affairs (Kissinger) to President Nixon," 3 (emphasis in the original).

121. "Future U.S. Policy," 9, 12.

122. "Memorandum from the President's Assistant for National Security Affairs (Kissinger) to President Nixon," 2.

123. Drezner, "Allies, Adversaries."

124. "Future U.S. Policy," 18–20.

125. "Comments on Fact Paper B-2," October 10, 1969, Folder "Agency Comments to Staff, April-October 1969: OEP—Comments on Fact Papers," Record Group 220, Records of the Cabinet Task Force on Oil Import Control, 1969–1970, box 21, Richard Nixon Presidential Library and Museum, Yorba Linda, CA; "Comments on Fact Paper A-8," undated, Folder "Agency Comments to Staff, April-October 1969: OEP—Comments on Fact Papers," Record Group 220, Records of the Cabinet Task Force on Oil Import Control, 1969–1970, box 21, Richard Nixon Presidential Library and Museum, Yorba Linda, CA.

126. For a skeptical view of the net benefits of conquering oil, see Meierding, "Oil Wars Myth." Notably, however, research suggests that two of the client states, Iraq and Libya, were predisposed toward aggression because they were revolutionary petro-states. Colgan, *Petro-Aggression*.

127. "Memorandum from the President's Assistant for National Security Affairs (Kissinger) to President Nixon," 1.

128. Notably, the proxy threat also exacerbated the traditional invasion threat; close ties to local regimes already armed with Soviet weapons would make it easier for the Soviets to operate military forces in the region. *Middle East 1967–75*, 16.

129. Long, *Ambivalent Allies*, 54.

130. Granted, it could be argued that the War of Attrition was not purely revisionist in nature because Nasser hoped to reclaim Egyptian territory lost to Israel in the 1967 war. In a sense, then, he was trying to return to the status quo—just a few years too late. Nevertheless, his resort to force signaled, at the very least, a comfortability with military adventures. It is also important to remember that the 1967 war instigated by Nasser was itself a failed attempt to upend the status quo.

131. Salim Yaqub, *Imperfect Strangers: Americans, Arabs, and US–Middle East Relations in the 1970s* (Ithaca, NY: Cornell University Press, 2016), 32.

132. Ibid., 39–41.

133. Gregory Winger, "Twilight on the British Gulf: The 1961 Kuwait Crisis and the Evolution of American Strategic Thinking in the Persian Gulf," *Diplomacy & Statecraft* 23, no. 4 (2012): 664.

134. Ibid. The extent to which British intervention was decisive in preventing an attack is difficult to discern. Skeptics argue that Iraqi officials may have just been bluffing with no serious plans to invade. Historical evidence remains ambiguous. Dust storms made it impossible for British reconnaissance to visually confirm reported troop movements. However, the British picked up multiple signals of impending invasion from several independent human intelligence sources, and Prime Minister Harold Macmillan stuck to his claim that "they were out there." Richard A. Mobley, "Gauging the Iraqi Threat to Kuwait in the 1960s," *Studies in Intelligence* 45, no. 11 (2001): 22–23.

135. Mobley, "Iraqi Threat."

136. "Future U.S. Policy," 12–13.

137. Long, *Ambivalent Allies*, 54.

138. Britain hoped to unify nine small sheikhdoms—Bahrain, Qatar, and the seven Trucial States (Abu Dhabi, Ajman, Dubai, Sharjah, Fujairah, Ras al-Khaimah, and Umm al-Quwain)—but Bahrain and Qatar opted for independence instead. In December 1971, the United Arab Emirates (UAE) was formed, composed solely of the Trucial States. Quote from "Future U.S. Policy," 12.

139. Riedel, *Kings and Presidents*, 50.

140. Roham Alvandi, *Nixon, Kissinger and the Shah: The United States and Iran in the Cold War* (Oxford: Oxford University Press, 2014), 52–53.

141. "Future U.S. Policy," 21–24.

142. "National Security Decision Memorandum 92: US Policy toward the Persian Gulf," November 7, 1970, *Foreign Relations of the United States, 1969–1976*, vol. E-4, *Documents on Iran and Iraq, 1969–1972*, ed. Monica Belmonte and Edward C. Keefer (Washington, DC: U.S. Government Printing Office, 2006), Document 97, accessed February 26, 2018, https://history.state.gov/historicaldocuments/frus1969-76ve04/d97.

143. Alvandi, *Nixon, Kissinger and the Shah*, 51.

144. "Future U.S. Policy," 25.

145. Long, *Ambivalent Allies*, 40–41.

146. This made Iran the largest regional purchaser of American arms, just eking past Israel, which received $7 billion in weapons over the same period.

147. Andrew Scott Cooper, *The Oil Kings: How the U.S., Iran and Saudi Arabia Changed the Balance of Power in the Middle East* (New York: Simon and Schuster, 2011), 66.

148. [Middle East Tensions; Attached to Cover Memorandum Dated July 26, 1973], "United States. National Security Council. Staff. Top Secret, Memorandum of Conversation, July 24, 1973," Digital National Security Archive (DNSA) collection, Kissinger Con-

versations, Supplement I, 1969–1977, accessed May 15, 2018, http://proxy.library.nd.edu/login?url=https://search-proquest-com.proxy.library.nd.edu/docview/1679086586?accountid=12874.

149. [Iran–U.S. Relations], "United States. National Security Council. Staff. Top Secret, Memorandum of Conversation. July 27, 1973," DNSA Collection, Kissinger Conversations, Supplement I, 1969–1977, accessed February 27, 2018, http://proxy.library.nd.edu/login?url=https://search-proquest-com.proxy.library.nd.edu/docview/1679087652?accountid=12874.

150. Alvandi, *Nixon, Kissinger and the Shah*, 51.

151. Quoted in Cooper, *Oil Kings*, 42.

152. Yergin, *Prize*, 562–65.

153. "Transcript of a Telephone Conversation between the President's Assistant for National Security Affairs (Kissinger) and John B. Connally," *Foreign Relations of the United States, 1969–1976*, vol. 36, *Energy Crisis, 1969–1974*, ed. Linda Qaimmaqami (Washington, DC: U.S. Government Printing Office, 2011), document 137, accessed May 21, 2018, https://history.state.gov/historicaldocuments/frus1969-76v36/d137.

154. Military sales were just a small part of the broader phenomenon of petrodollar recycling, which included all variety of commerce. For instance, Gulf countries also repatriated dollars by investing billions in American financial assets.

155. "Memorandum from the President's Assistant for National Security Affairs (Kissinger) to President Nixon."

156. The companies present at the Vienna negotiations were Royal Dutch-Shell, British Petroleum, Exxon, Atlantic Richfield, and Standard Oil of California. Six countries sent delegates to negotiate: Abu Dhabi, Iran, Iraq, Kuwait, Saudi Arabia, and Qatar. Algeria and Libya sent observers but were not direct parties to the negotiations, having already negotiated side deals with the international oil companies on prices. Clyde H. Farnsworth, "Higher Oil Prices under Discussion," *New York Times*, October 9, 1973.

157. Michael Getler, "Combat Costing Israel Heavily," *Washington Post*, October 9, 1973.

158. Yergin, *Prize*, 587.

159. OAPEC communique, quoted in "Arab Countries Reduce Their Petroleum Production 5% as Latest Protest against Western Support for Israel," *Wall Street Journal*, October 18, 1973.

160. Clayton, *Market Madness*, 111.

161. Roy Licklider, "The Power of Oil: The Arab Oil Weapon and the Netherlands, the United Kingdom, Canada, Japan, and the United States," *International Studies Quarterly* 32, no. 2 (1988): 218 (emphasis in the original).

162. Clayton, *Market Madness*, 110–12.

7. EMPIRICAL TESTS WITH FUZZY-SET QCA

1. Fuzzy-set QCA also allows for other forms of causal complexity, such as equifinality and asymmetric causation, that are consistent with, though not as fundamental to, this particular theory.

2. Carsten Q. Schneider and Claudius Wagemann, *Set-Theoretic Methods for the Social Sciences: A Guide to Qualitative Comparative Analysis* (Cambridge: Cambridge University Press, 2012), 78.

3. Charles C. Ragin, *Redesigning Social Inquiry: Fuzzy Sets and Beyond* (Chicago: University of Chicago Press, 2008), 177.

4. Ragin has since adapted QCA for large-N research designs as well. Ibid., 7.

5. The logic of regression is to identify an "average case" based on the distribution mean and then define the boundaries of what counts as significant variation based on how far a case falls from the average case (typically by calculating the standard deviation of the

sample). As a result, the cut points for what counts as "significant variation" may be statistically meaningful but are not necessarily *substantively* meaningful.

6. Of course, there is much debate about whether the United States remains the world's lone superpower or has been surpassed by China. The weight of the evidence today suggests the United States remains unparalleled in its ability to project power and to defend its sea lines of communication. See Stephen G. Brooks and William C. Wohlforth, *America Abroad: The United States' Global Role in the 21st Century* (New York: Oxford University Press, 2016). China and Russia, the closest rivals to the United States, thus far have little chance of posing a serious disruption threat to U.S. imports. Over time, however, this is likely to change. Currently, the United States has the power to deny large amounts of oil to China. See Mirski, "Stranglehold."

7. Domestic production can also be vulnerable to military power, but I assume that imports are always more vulnerable than home output. There are always more and easier pathways to sever imports than to destroy production.

8. A telling example is the experience of Spain during World War II. Officially neutral, Spain was free to buy Western Hemisphere oil, some of which it illicitly sold to Hitler through Nazi-occupied France. However, the country took great pains to disguise its efforts to avoid trouble from the Allied countries. Chiefs of Staff Committee, *Oil as a Factor*, 11.

9. The outcome must be present for assessing the consistency of necessity. In fuzzy sets, present means all cases where the outcome is greater than zero, indicating that the case is at least a partial member in the set.

10. Schneider and Wagemann, *Set-Theoretic Methods*, 143.

11. Ragin, *Fuzzy-Set Social Science*, 110–15. Following Mahoney, I calculate one binomial across all paths, not one binomial per path. This would also be equivalent to looking at the variable of coercive vulnerability (D·T) as a macrocondition. James Mahoney, "Strategies of Causal Assessment in Comparative Historical Analysis," in *Comparative Historical Analysis in the Social Sciences*, ed. James Mahoney and Dietrich Rueschemeyer (New York: Cambridge University Press, 2003), 345–46, 346n7.

12. Ragin, *Fuzzy-Set Social Science*, 110–15. Ragin's other benchmarks are 0.50, which means that the causal factor is a necessary condition to produce the outcome "more often than not," and 0.80, which indicates that the cause is "almost always" necessary for the outcome.

13. The sample N is too small to meet the "almost always" benchmark proportion (0.80) with 90 percent confidence, even if every case passed the consistency test.

14. Schneider and Wagemann, *Set-Theoretic Methods*, 160.

15. Ibid., 157–60.

16. Because of limited diversity, the truth table algorithm will provide more than one potential solution: a complex solution, an intermediate solution, and a parsimonious solution. Each solution simply reflects a different level of logical simplification on what is the same underlying answer. The solution reported here is the Intermediate Solution, for which Ragin and others strongly advocate.

CONCLUSION

1. Stephen Wilmot, "Prepare for the Electric Car Revolution," *Wall Street Journal*, December 14, 2016; "The Electric Car Revolution," *New York Times*, July 18, 2017.

2. International Energy Agency, *World Energy Outlook 2018* (Paris: Organization for Economic Cooperation and Development, 2018), 29.

3. International Energy Agency, *World Energy Outlook 2018*, 29, 36, 43, 138–39, 153, 521.

4. Charles F. Wald and Tom Captain, *Energy Security: America's Best Defense* (New York: Deloitte LLC, 2009).

5. *Defense Energy: Observations on DOD's Investments in Alternative Fuels* (Washington, DC: United States Government Accountability Office, 2015), 11; Timothy Gardner, "US Military Marches Forward on Green Energy, Despite Trump," Reuters, March 1, 2017.

6. International Energy Agency, *World Energy Outlook 2018*, 138, 144.

7. "Country Analysis Brief: China," U.S. Energy Information Administration, updated May 14, 2015, https://www.eia.gov/beta/international/analysis.php?iso=CHN.

8. Liang Fang, a professor at China's National Defense University, February 11, 2015, quoted by Nadège Rolland, *China's Eurasian Century? Political and Strategic Implications of the Belt and Road Initiative* (Seattle, WA: National Bureau of Asian Research, 2017), 112n83.

9. China's lack of a blue water navy stands in strong contrast to the thorough anti-access/aerial denial (A2/AD) capabilities it has amassed to make U.S. naval intervention in the South China Sea and Chinese territorial waters highly costly.

10. Steven Lee Myers, "With Ships and Missiles, China Is Ready to Challenge US Navy in Pacific," *New York Times*, August 29, 2018.

11. *BP Statistical Review of World Energy*, 68th ed. (London: BP Amoco, 2019), 12, 14, 15.

12. International Energy Agency, *World Energy Outlook 2018*, 138, 144.

13. According to Google Earth, the shortest distance between the Chinese border and the Iranian border is about 750 miles as the crow flies. Actual driving routes across the mountainous expanse between the two countries are significantly longer.

14. International Energy Agency, *World Energy Outlook 2018*, 138, 144, 145.

15. Michael Clarke, "The Belt and Road Initiative: China's New Grand Strategy?," *Asia Policy*, no. 24 (2017): 71–79.

16. "Brief: Belt and Road Initiative," The World Bank, March 29, 2018, https://www.worldbank.org/en/topic/regional-integration/brief/belt-and-road-initiative#02.

17. Rolland, *China's Eurasian Century?*, 127–28.

18. Xi quoted in Rolland, *China's Eurasian Century?*, 122. See also ibid., 48–52, 116–18, 127–28, 135–37.

19. Ibid., 111–13.

20. Christopher Len, "China's Maritime Silk Road and Energy Geopolitics in the Indian Ocean: Motivations and Implications for the Region," in *Asia's Energy Security and China's Belt and Road Initiative*, ed. Erica Downs, Mikkal E. Herberg, Michael Kugelman, Christopher Len, and Kaho Yu (Seattle, WA: National Bureau of Asian Research, 2017), 50.

21. John Frittelli, Anthony Andrews, Paul W. Parfomak, Robert Pirog, Jonathan L. Ramseur, and Michael Ratner, *US Rail Transportation of Crude Oil: Background and Issues for Congress* (Washington, DC: Congressional Research Service, 2014).

22. Beining Zhuang, "Spotlight: China-Myanmar Oil, Gas Project Benefits Both," *Xinhua*, May 10, 2017; Gregory B. Poling, "Kyaukpyu: Connecting China to the Indian Ocean," in *China's Maritime Silk Road: Strategic and Economic Implications for the Indo-Pacific Region*, ed. Nicholas Szechenyi (Washington, DC: CSIS, 2018), 5–6.

23. Mirski, "Stranglehold."

24. Rolland, *China's Eurasian Century?*, 82–85.

25. Benoit Faucon, "World News: China Offers Iran $3 Billion Oil Deal," *Wall Street Journal*, January 18, 2019.

26. Jonathan Hillman, "Game of Loans: How China Bought Hambantota," in Szechenyi, *China's Maritime Silk Road*, 8; Maria Abi-Habib, "How China Got Sri Lanka to Cough Up a Port," *New York Times*, June 25, 2018.

27. Jayanna Krupakar, "China's Naval Base(s) in the Indian Ocean: Signs of a Maritime Grand Strategy?," *Strategic Analysis* 41, no. 3 (2017): 207, 209.

28. "Yanbu's Joint Venture Refinery Shines as Example for Beneficial China-Saudi Energy Cooperation," *Xinhua*, July 9, 2018.

29. Krupakar, "China's Naval Base(s)," 220n23, 220n25, 221n51; Minnie Chan, "First Djibouti . . . Now Pakistan Port Earmarked for a Chinese Overseas Military Base," *South China Morning Post*, July 20, 2018.

30. Len, "Maritime Silk Road," 48; Hillman, "Game of Loans," 8.

31. Maria Abi-Habib, "China's 'Belt and Road' Plan in Pakistan Takes a Military Turn," *New York Times*, December 19, 2018.

32. Krupakar, "China's Naval Base(s)," 215–16.

33. Jesse Barker Gale and Andrew Shearer, "The Quadrilateral Security Dialogue and the Maritime Silk Road Initiative," in Szechenyi, *China's Maritime Silk Road*, 31.

34. Gurmeet Kanwal, "Pakistan's Gwadar Port: A New Naval Base in China's String of Pearls in the Indo-Pacific," in Szechenyi, *China's Maritime Silk Road*, 14.

35. Krupakar, "China's Naval Base(s)," 216.

Index

Page numbers in italics refer to figures and tables.

Abadan refinery, 84
Abu Dhabi, 155–56
Aden, 142
Alaskan oil fields, 122, 127, 142, 158, 202n39
Algeria, 142, 156
alliances, 37–38. *See also* indirect control; security partnerships
Alsace, 93
alternative fuels, 29–31, 110–13, 132, 175. *See also* coal; coal-to-oil hydrogenation; synthetic fuel
American Civil War, 50–51
Anglo-French blockades: on Germany in World War I, 95, 101; on Nazi Germany, 22, 94, 102, 104, 105, 107–8, 114
Anglo-Persian Oil Company (APOC), 55, 82–83, 85, 195n8
Angola, 23
anticipatory strategies, 1–5; as additive, 42; defined, 3–4; extreme, 6, 13, 32, 40–41, 69–70, 76, 151, 167–68; fuzzy-set scoring and, 159, 167–72; spectrum of, *33*; summary of, *39*. *See also* direct control; indirect control; self-sufficiency; strategic anticipation theory
Arab-Israeli conflict, 140–42, 144, 155–56. *See also* Six-Day War (1967); Suez Crisis; Yom Kippur War (1973)
Arab nationalism, 142, 148–52
ARAMCO (Arabian American Oil Company), 127, 153–54, 181, 187n5
Asquith, Herbert Henry, 84–85
Associated Oil Company, 121
atomic bombs, 63, 65–66, 131
attrition warfare: Nazi Germany and, 94, 102–3, 109, 114; in World War I, 192n40 (*see also* World War I)
Austria, 93, 101, 199n69
Austro-Prussian War (1866), 50–51
automobiles: alternative fuels for, 110–11; invention of, 46, 190n67; mass production of, 56, 98. *See also* motorization; motor transit; transportation
Azerbaijan, 179

Baghdad, 85
Baghdad Pact, 142
Bahrain, 137–38, 148–50, 154, 156, 206n138
Baku oil fields, 110
balance of power: location of oil and, 44–47. *See also* great powers
Balfour, Arthur, 85, 87, 90
Bangladesh-China-India-Myanmar Economic Corridor (BCIMEC), 179–80
Barbarossa, Operation, 13, 93
Basra, 149
Belt and Road Initiative (BRI), 5, 178–82
Bennett, Andrew, 194n5
Benz, Karl Friedrich, 190n67
Bérenger, Henry, 58
Bergius, Friedrich, 98
Bessarabia dispute, 106–7
Blau, Operation, 93, 110
blitzkrieg strategy, 19, 53, 94, 102–3, 105, 109, 114
blockades, 5, 9, 21–22, 27; on Britain, 49, 58, 80–81, 85–88, 189n52; on Germany, 94, 95, 101, 102, 104, 105, 107–8, 114, 199n67; on Japan, 59–62
boycotts, 12, 186n36, 187n14. *See also* embargos
Bradley, Omar, 93
Britain: American oil and, 196n18; case study approach and, 68, 72, 74, 76; coal reserves, 46; coercive vulnerability, 80–91; direct control strategies, 2, 34, 76, 80, 87; grand strategy, 81, 88; great power status, 10, 71; India and, 83–84, 147; invasion of Mesopotamia, 13, 39, 80, 90–91, 121, 173; Middle East policy, 84–86, 89–91, 120–22, 138, 146–51, 195n2; military power, 103; petroleum deficit, 17, 20, 80–81, 85–88, 195n16; petroleum reserves, 46; pre-war oil policy, 13, 81–86, 89; threat to imports, 82–84, 88–91. *See also* Anglo-French blockades
British Expeditionary Force, 56
British Fourth Army, 57–58
British Royal Air Force, 111

INDEX

British Royal Navy: blockade on, 80–81, 85–88; coal-fueled ships, 81–82; oil and, 45, 52, 55–56, 119; Persian oil concession and, 82–84
Brodie, Bernard, 131
Bruning, Heinrich, 98

California, 202n59
Calinescu, Armand, 106
Canada: import restrictions on oil from, 139–40, 145; oil production, 134, *135*
Caribbean Sea, 135
Carter, Jimmy, 2, 115
Carter Doctrine, 2
case studies. *See* qualitative case study research design
causal processes, 4, 13–14, 68. *See also* process tracing
CENTCOM, 2
Central Geological Survey (Germany), 97
Central Intelligence Agency, 129, 144
Central Treaty Organization (CENTO), 142–43
Chapman, Oscar, 139
charcoal, 29–31, 36
China: anticipatory strategies, 14, 176–82; Belt and Road Initiative (BRI), 5, 178–82; coercive vulnerability, 178; grand strategy, 178; great power status, 11, 47, 175, 208n6; imported oil, 5, 183n9; indirect control strategies, 5–6, 178, 181–82; Iran and, 209n13; military power, 177, 181–82, 209n9; petroleum deficit, 176–77; potential blockade of, 5, 9; threat to imports, 176–77
China-Central Asia-West Asia Economic Corridor (CCWAEC), 179–80
China-Pakistan Economic Corridor (CPEC), 179–80, 182
Churchill, Winston, 81, 82, 119
civilian oil consumption, 20, 35, 61; in Nazi Germany, 110–11; in U.S., 120–21, 124–26, 131, 137
Clarke, J. C., 86
Clausewitz, Carl von, 20, 53
Clayton, Blake, 156
Clifford, Clark, 136
climate change, 174–75
coal: abundance of, 44, 46, 81–82; compared to oil, 42; global supply of, 197n21; great power status and, 47; military effectiveness and, 49–54; transportation and, 28–29, 48; World War I and, 56
coal-to-oil hydrogenation, 93, 97–98, 103, 106; Allied bombing of German facilities, 111–13; in U.S., 126. *See also* synthetic fuel

coercion: defined, 24–26, 188n20. *See also* oil coercion
coercive vulnerability, 12–14; determinants of, 15–23 (*see also* import threat; petroleum deficit); level of, 40–42, 68, 173, 189n36; responses to (*see* anticipatory strategies). *See also* Britain; Nazi Germany; United States
Cohen, Jerome, 60–61
Cold War, 28, 75, 116, 129–41, 174
Colgan, Jeff D., 7, 186n41
Colombia, 123, *135*
Colorado, 122
command of the commons, 7, 185n27
compellence, 9, 188n20. *See also* coercion
conflict: oil and, 6–8; trade and, 5. *See also* war; *specific wars and conflicts*
congruence testing, 4, 76–77, 195n12
conjunctural causation, 160
Constantinople, 84
cost of oil. *See* oil prices
costs: assessment of, 33; of direct control, 60, 80; of indirect control, 38; overview of, 25–26; predicted outcomes and, 40–42; of self-sufficiency, 35–37
crisp-set scoring systems, 161
cross-case analysis, 67, 69, 74
Curzon, George Nathaniel, 58, 85
Czechoslovakia, 101

Daimler, Gottlieb, 190n67
Daniels, Josephus, 118–19, 121
D'Arcy, William Knox, 82
Day, David T., 118, 120, 121
De Bunsen, Maurice, 84
De Bunsen Committee, 85, 90
democratic peace, 193n1
denial strategies, 25–26
DeNovo, John, 121
dependence, 47. *See also* coercive vulnerability
Desert Shield, Operation, 2
Desert Storm, Operation, 2
deterrence, 9
direct control, 12, 24, 173; costs and risks of, 39, 60, 80; defined, 3; fuzzy-set scoring, 167–68; overview of, 32–34, 38–39; predicted outcomes, 41–42. *See also* Britain; Germany; Japan; Nazi Germany
disruptibility. *See* import threat
Djibouti, 181, 182
Drake, Edwin L., 44
Dubai, 156

Dutch East Indies: Japanese attack on, 39, 60, 62; oil production, 89
Dutch oil policy, 122, 195n8

economic value of oil, 3, 12, 24; anticipatory strategies and, 27–32, 48–49
Eddy, William, 128, 202n56
Eden, Anthony, 2
Edgar, E. Mackay, 121
Edison, Thomas, 45
Egypt: 1967 oil embargo, 141; Arab nationalism in, 142; Israel and, 8, 155, 206n130; Soviet Union and, 149; Suez Crisis and, 2, 34; Yemen and, 139
Eisenhower, Dwight D., 34, 131, 137–41, 143, 158
electric cars, 174–75
electricity, 31, 45
Elk Hills Naval Petroleum Reserve, 137
embargos, 21–23, 187n14; by Arab states (1967), 140–41; by OAPEC (1973), 8–9, 21, 37, 154–57, 187n15. *See also* boycotts
endogeneity, of natural resources and relative power, 44, 46
endogeneity problems, potential for, 73–74, 187n10, 189n50
environment, fossil fuels and, 174–75
Europe, Western: alternative transportation fuels, 29–31; Mideast oil and, 148, 151, 156, 174 (*see also* Middle East); motorization in, 132; U.S. defense of, 117, 130–31, 136–38, 156, 158. *See also* Britain; France; Germany; NATO
external balancing, 37, 189n43
extraction, 18–19, 125, 133, 187n6; early drilling methods, 44–45. *See also* oil production

Faisal, King, 21, 150–51, 153, 157
Farben, IG, 96, 98, 101, 103, 126
Feder-Bosch contract, 98
Fisher, John, 81
Forrestal, James, 129
fossil fuel emissions, 174–75
fracking, 6–7, 187n7
France: anticipatory strategies, 2; case study approach and, 72; great power status, 10, 71; Middle East policy, 138; military power, 103; Mosul and, 85, 90–91; naval power, 55; oil embargos and, 22; petroleum deficit, 20; petroleum reserves, 46. *See also* Anglo-French blockades
Franco-Prussian War (1870–1871), 50–52

fuels. *See* alternative fuels; coal; oil; synthetic fuel
fuzzy-set qualitative comparative analysis (fsQCA), 4, 14, 159–61, 207n1; analysis of necessary conditions, 168–70; analysis of sufficient conditions, 170–72; summary interpretation of results, 172
fuzzy-set scoring systems, 161–68, 208n9

Gadhafi, Muʿammar, 153
Galicia, 45, 93
Gallipoli Campaign (1915), 84
Geddes, Eric, 90
geography: balance of power and location of oil, 44–47; threat to imports and, 21
geological surveys: Germany, 97; Middle East, 127; United States, 118, 120, 121, 125, 195n2
George, Alexander L., 194n5
Germany: case study approach and, 68, 72, 74–75; civilian oil consumption, 20; coal reserves, 46, 197n21; direct control strategies, 75; great power status, 10, 71; Japan and, 61–62; military mobility, 26, 191n9; military resources, 57; motorization, 197n22; naval power, 55; petroleum needs, 19; petroleum reserves, 46; self-sufficiency, 70–71; submarine warfare, 49, 58, 80–81, 86–88, 120, 135; threat to imports, 93, 119. *See also* Nazi Germany
glut, 123, 129, 140
Göring, Hermann, 100–101, 107–8
Graham, Billy, 116
grand strategy, 9; Britain, 81, 88; China, 178; Nazi Germany, 94; United States, 130
great powers: balance of power, 44–47; oil and, 1–2, 4–5; qualifying countries, 10–11, 71. *See also specific countries*
Greece, 129
Guam, 127
gusher wells, 187n8; Spindletop, 47, 117

Halder, Franz, 108
Hankey, Maurice, 85, 90
Hardinge, Lord, 84
Hard Surface, Operation, 139
Harmsworth, Alfred, 87
Hawaii, 127
Hiroshima, 63
Hitler, Adolf, 13, 22, 75, 92–114, 198n58. *See also* Nazi Germany
Hossbach Memo, 198n58
Hughes, Llewelyn, 185n27
Hu Jintao, 179

INDEX

Hull, Cordell, 127
Hussein, King, 149
Hussein, Saddam, 2, 38
hydrogenation. *See* coal-to-oil hydrogenation

Ickes, Harold, 125–27, 129
import threat: defined, 3, 15; determination of coercive vulnerability and, 12, 15–17, 20–23; domestic production and, 208n7; estimates of, 186n1; fuzzy-set scoring, 163–67; predicted outcomes, 40–42. *See also* Britain; China; Germany; Nazi Germany; United States
India: Britain and, 83–84, 147; China and, 176–77; oil demand, 174
Indian Ocean, 176–77, 181–82
indirect control, 12, 24, 173; defined, 3; fuzzy-set scoring, 167–68; overview of, 32–35, 37–38; predicted outcomes, 41–42. *See also* China; Nazi Germany; United States
Indonesia, 137
industrial production, 28, 31
internal combustion engines, 29–31, 53, 59, 132
International Energy Agency, 174
international relations scholarship, 4–5
international security. *See* security needs
Iran: China and, 179–82; nuclear program, 12; oil embargos and, 23; oil production, 127; shah of, 82, 150–54, 157; Soviet Union and, 136, 138, 143, 148–50; Strait of Hormuz and, 2, 7–9, 11, 21; "Twin Pillars" policy and, 152–54; United States and, 206n146. *See also* Persia
Iran-Iraq War, 186n36
Iraq, 175, 205n126, 206n134; 1967 oil embargo, 140; Soviet Union and, 142–43, 149; United States and, 2
Iraqi Freedom, Operation, 194n3
iron, 12, 42, 46, 47
Israel, 206n130; Egypt and, 8, 155, 206n130; Iran and, 152; Sinai Peninsula and, 8, 156. *See also* Arab-Israeli conflict
Italy: naval power, 45, 55; petroleum reserves, 46. *See also* Mussolini, Benito

Jack, Marian, 81, 83
Japan: anticipatory strategies, 2; case study approach and, 68, 72, 76; civilian oil consumption, 20; coercive vulnerability, 13, 59–66; direct control strategies, 76; great power status, 10, 71; invasion of Dutch East Indies, 39, 60, 62; Mideast oil and, 148, 156; naval power, 45, 55; oil substitutes, 29–31, 111; petroleum deficit, 20, 59–66; petroleum needs, 144, 158; petroleum reserves, 46; U.S. oil and, 143, 144; World War I and, 58; World War II surrender, 49, 59–66
Johnson, Lyndon B., 139, 141, 146
Joint Chiefs of Staff, 129, 136, 158
Jordan, 141, 153
Jutland, Battle of (1916), 55

Kazakhstan, 177, 179–81
Kennan, George F., 129
Kennedy, John F., 139
kerosene, 44, 45
Ketsu-Go, Operation, 64
Kissinger, Henry, 147, 149, 153–54, 156
Knox, William F., 127
Korean War, 129
Krauch, Carl, 101
Kurdish uprisings, 142, 149
Kuwait: 1967 oil embargo, 140; 1973 oil embargo, 156; indirect control strategies and, 37; Iraq and, 152; Operation Desert Storm and, 2; Operation Iraqi Freedom and, 194n3; Soviet Union and, 143, 148–49; U.S. and, 154
Kwantung Army, 63–64

Latin America, 123, 130, 133. *See also* Venezuela
Lay, James, 136
League of Nations, 104
Lend-Lease aid, 128
Levy, Jack, 75
Leyte Gulf, Battle of, 62
Libya, 205n126; 1967 oil embargo, 140–41; 1973 oil embargo, 155–56; Soviet Union and, 142–43
Licklider, Roy, 156
Lincoln, George A., 145
Lippman, Thomas, 128
Lloyd George, David, 85, 90
logistics, 26. *See also* supply lines
Long, Austin, 185n27
Long, Walter Hume, 121–22
longitudinal analysis, 67–69, 73
Louisiana, 146, 202n59
Ludendorff, Erich, 90
Ludendorff offensives (1918), 26
Luftwaffe, 36, 100, 109, 111–12, 126. *See also* Nazi Germany
Lynn, John, 50

MacArthur, Douglas, 31
Macmillan, Harold, 206n134
Maduro, Nicolás, 12
magnitude of damage from oil cutoffs, 3, 17, 40, 160

Mahoney, James, 208n11
Marshall Plan, 129, 132
Marxism, 148–49
Marxist National Liberation Front, 150
Mauritius, 182
means-ends calculations, 187n10
mechanized warfare, 26–27, 43, 48–49, 54, 87, 173
Mercedes-Benz, 111
Mesopotamia: British interest in, 85; British invasion of, 13, 39, 80, 90–91, 121, 173; petroleum resources, 89–91
Mesopotamian Expeditionary Force, 84
Messines, 58
Mexico: import restrictions on oil from, 145; oil exports to Britain, 89, 119–20; oil exports to U.S., 119–20, 145; oil production, 119–20, 123, 134, *135*
Middle East: Anglo-American rivalry in, 120–22, 195n2; Anglo-German rivalry in, 83–84, 89; Britain and, 84–86, 89–91, 120–22, 138, 146–51, 195n2; China and, 177–78; Europe and, 116; geological surveys, 127; indirect control strategies and, 37–38; Japan and, 116; oil prices, 133, 153–54; oil production, 138, 196n25; oil reserves, 134; Soviet Union and, 130, 136, 142, 146–51, 158, 203n84, 206n128; U.S. strategic relationships in, 2, 126–28, 141, 146–54, 174. *See also* Mesopotamia; Organization of Arab Petroleum Exporting Countries (OAPEC); Organization of Petroleum Exporting Countries (OPEC); *specific countries*
MIDEASTFOR, 154
military aviation: Allied bombing of Nazi Germany, 111–13; German Luftwaffe, 36, 100, 109, 111–12, 126; Japanese kamikaze attacks, 63; oil and, 46, 54, 131. *See also* British Royal Air Force
military force, 9, 24–25
military mobility: oil and, 26–27, 31–32, 50–59; railroads and, 50–52
military rationing, 162–63
military value of oil: coal and, 49–54; effectiveness and, 19, 48–66; for flexibility and speed, 53–54, 59; future wars and, 124–25; for logistics, 26, 51, 54, 60; in mechanized warfare, 26–27, 43, 48–49, 54, 87, 173; oil reserves and, 157; rarity of oil and, 43–44; research on, 24; strategic anticipation and, 3–4, 12–13, 27–28, 48–49; for training activities, 27, 111, 113. *See also* attrition warfare; blitzkrieg strategy; naval forces
Mill, John Stuart, 194n11

minor powers, 10–11, 71
Molotov, Vyacheslav, 65
Molotov-Ribbentrop Pact, 107
Monroe Doctrine, 134
Mossadegh, Mohammad, 34, 38, 138
Mosul, 85, 90–91
motorization, 96–99, 103, 110, 117, 132, 197n22. *See also* automobiles; mechanized warfare; motor transit
motor transit: oil and, 28–31, 53–54; World War I and, 56–59
Mussolini, Benito, 104, 108
Mutual Defense Assistance Agreement, 138
Myanmar, 180–81

Nagasaki, 63
Nasser, Gamal Abdel, 2, 34, 149, 206n130
Nasserism, 142
national power, raw materials and, 46
National Security Council (NSC), 129, 136, 144, 146–47
National Security Decision Memorandum (NSDM 92), 152–54
NATO (North Atlantic Treaty Organization), 129; Mideast oil and, 148, 151, 174; U.S. oil and, 130–31, 143, 144. *See also* Europe, Western
natural gas, 28–29
naval forces: coal-powered vessels, 52; oil and, 45–46, 54–56. *See also* blockades; British Royal Navy; U.S. Navy
Nazi Germany, 92–114; Anglo-French blockade on, 94, 102, 104, 105, 107–8, 114; anticipatory strategies, 93–94, 97–101, 104–14, 174; attrition warfare, 94, 102–3, 109, 114; blitzkrieg strategy, 94, 102–3, 105, 109, 114; Caucasus campaign, 110, 114; civilian oil consumption, 110–11; coercive vulnerability, 13, 93–94, 96–97, 104, 105–6, 109–10, 114; direct control, 110–14; economic stimulus programs, 95–96, 99; foreign exchange crisis, 100–101; Four-Year Plan, 94, 100–101, 104–5; grand strategy, 94; indirect control, 106–9; invasion of Poland, 105, 114; invasion of Soviet Union, 52, 93–94, 109, 200n90; military power, 92–93, 96–97, 102–5, 108–14; motorization, 96–99, 103, 110; oil production, 96–98, 102–3; petroleum deficit, 92–93, 96–97, 100–114; self-sufficiency, 97–101, 104–6; synthetic fuel production, 36, 93, 97–98, 103, 106, 174; territorial expansion, 101–3; threat to imports, 93–94, 97, 104–9; within-case analysis, 73. *See also* Germany
necessary conditions, analysis of, 168–70

INDEX

Nevada (battleship), 118–19
New Policies Scenario (NPS), 174–77
Nicholas II, 84
Nigeria, 23
Nixon, Richard M., 131, 143, 146–47, 149–50, 152–58
Nixon Doctrine, 152
NSC. *See* National Security Council
nuclear power, 28
nuclear weapons. *See* atomic bombs
null cases, 68

OAPEC. *See* Organization of Arab Petroleum Exporting Countries
Obama, Barack, 12
Office for Petroleum Coordinator for National Defense, 124
Office of Emergency Preparedness (OEP), 145, 158
offshore drilling, 202n59
oil: conflict and, 6–8; energy units, 188n30; great power politics and, 1–2, 4–5; rarity of, 43–44; value of (*see* economic value of oil; military value of oil)
oil age, 11
oil coercion: defined, 8–9; effectiveness of, 12; genesis of, 49–54; military and, 3–4, 173 (*see also* military value of oil); myths about, 9; potential targets of, 12; reverse, 12. *See also* coercive vulnerability; import threat; petroleum deficit
oil companies: Mexican oil and, 119–20; Mideast oil and, 139, 153–54; military supplies and, 121; prices and, 143
oil demand: global, 174–75; U.S., 19, 131–32, 141. *See also* petroleum deficit
oil glut, 123, 129, 140
oil prices, 143, 156; 1973 embargo and, 157; Middle East and, 133, 153–54; oil supply and, 187n4
oil production: by country (*see specific countries*); global, 196n25, 202n47, 204n93; self-sufficiency and, 35; technology of, 18–19, 44–45; threat to imports and, 208n7. *See also* extraction
oil reserves: estimates of, 17, 187n9 (*see also* geological surveys); expansion of, 186n3; indigenous, 18–19; scarcity of, 43–44; self-sufficiency and, 35
oil scarcity ideology, 6–7
oil substitutes: in Japan, 61–62; military and, 48, 59; transportation and, 28–29, 36, 110–13. *See also* alternative fuels

oil supply, inelastic, 187n4
"oil weapon" concept, 12, 17, 157. *See also* oil coercion
Olson, Mancur, 189n52
Oman, 149, 181, 182
Organization of Arab Petroleum Exporting Countries (OAPEC), 186n34; 1973 oil embargo, 8–9, 21, 37, 154–57, 187n15; South African oil embargo, 23
Organization of Petroleum Exporting Countries (OPEC), 153, 186n34
Ottoman Empire, 46; German influence in, 83–84; partition of, 80, 85

Pakistan, 138, 179–82
Palestine Liberation Organization (PLO), 149. *See also* Arab-Israeli conflict
Panama Canal Zone, 127
Pape, Robert A., 63–64, 188n20
Paris Climate Accords, 174–75
Patton, George S., 124
Pearl Harbor, Japanese attack on, 2, 60
peat, 29, 36, 113, 132
People's Liberation Army Navy (PLAN), 177, 181
Persia, 46; British oil concession, 82–84; petroleum resources, 89–91. *See also* Iran
Persian Gulf oil. *See* Middle East
Persian Gulf War, 37–38
Peru, 123, *135*
petro-dollar recycling, 154, 207n154
petroleum. *See* oil
Petroleum Administration for War (PAW), 124–25
petroleum deficit: defined, 3, 15; determination of coercive vulnerability, 12, 15–20; estimates of, 186n1; fuzzy-set scoring, 162–63; indigenous oil resources and, 18–19; predicted outcomes and, 40–42. *See also* Britain; China; Japan; Nazi Germany; United States
Petroleum Industry War Council, 125
petroleum reserves. *See* oil reserves
Petroleum Reserves Corporation (PRC), 127
Philippine Sea, Battle of, 62
pine root oil, 61, 111
Poland, 101, 103, 105, 108, 199n69
Posen, Barry, 7
predicted outcomes, 39–42
probability of oil cutoffs, 3, 40, 160, 162, 183n6
process tracing, 4, 14, 67–68, 77–79
producer gas, 110–11
prosperity concerns, 27–32, 48–49

INDEX 217

Prussia, 50–52, 190n4
punishment strategies, 25

Qasim, Abd al-Karim, 149
Qatar, 137–38, 206n138; 1973 oil embargo, 156; Soviet Union and, 148–49
qualitative case study research design, 13, 67–79
qualitative comparative analysis (QCA), 160–68, 195n13. *See also* fuzzy-set qualitative comparative analysis (fsQCA)

radicalism, 148, 150–52
Ragin, Charles, 4, 14, 160, 169–70, 195n13, 207n4, 208n12, 208n16
railroads: military use of, 50–52, 190n4, 191n9, 191n25, 192nn40–41; in World War I, 57–58
Rapid Deployment Joint Task Force, 2
refineries, 186n3
regression analysis, 159, 160, 171, 207n5
Reilly, Sidney, 82
renewable energy, 28
resource curse, 6–7
resource wars, 6–7
reverse coercion, 12
Rhineland, militarization of, 97, 100, 104
Ribbentrop, Joachim von, 107–8
risks: of direct control, 39, 60, 80; of indirect control, 38; predicted outcomes and, 40–42
Rockefeller, John D., 45, 115
Rolland, Nadège, 178
Romania: kerosene and, 44; oil exports to Britain, 89; oil exports to Nazi Germany, 93, 100, 103–7, 114, 174; oil production, 44–45; petroleum deficit, 17; threat of Soviet invasion, 106–7
Rommel, Erwin, 92
Roosevelt, Franklin D., 60, 124, 127–28, 202n56
Ross, Michael, 6, 186n41
Rothschild family, 82
Royal Dutch-Shell, 82
rubber, 42
Russia: case study approach and, 72; European oil market and, 8; naval power, 55; oil exports to Britain, 89; oil exports to Nazi Germany, 93, 100, 103–5, 107–9, 114, 174; oil production, 45, 46–47, 87, 97, 135, 147, 177, 179, 196n25, 203n75. *See also* Cold War; Union of Soviet Socialist Republics (USSR)

San Remo agreement (1920), 91, 121
Sato, Naotake, 64–65
Saud, Ibn, 128, 202n56

Saudi Arabia: 1967 oil embargo, 140–41; 1973 oil embargo, 155–56; China and, 181; indirect control strategies and, 37; oil production, 8, 96; Operation Desert Shield and, 2; Soviet Union and, 143, 148–49; subsidy policies, 188n29; "Twin Pillars" policy and, 152–54; United States and, 127–28, 137–38, 152–54, 157, 194n3
Schelling, Thomas C., 9, 188n20
scope conditions, 10
sea lines of communication (SLOCs), 177, 179, 181–82, 208n6
sea transportation of oil, 135, 177, 179, 181–82, 208n6; Strait of Hormuz, 2, 7–9, 11, 21; Strait of Malacca, 5, 176, 179, 180; Suez Canal, 2, 34. *See also* blockades; transportation
security competition, 47
security needs, 6–8, 12; anticipatory strategies and, 12, 40; expansionism and, 189n49; petroleum deficit and, 19–20. *See also* military value of oil
security partnerships, 37–38, 138–40, 180–81. *See also* alliances; indirect control
self-sufficiency, 2, 12, 23–24, 173; defined, 3; fuzzy-set scoring, 167–68; in international relations scholarship, 8; overview of, 32–33, 35–37; predicted outcomes, 41–42. *See also* Germany; Nazi Germany; United States
set theory, 159. *See also* fuzzy-set qualitative comparative analysis (fsQCA)
Seychelles, 181, 182
shah of Iran, 82, 150–54, 157
Sherman, William Tecumseh, 50–51
Sinai Peninsula, 8; Yom Kippur War (1973) and, 149, 155–56
Sinopec, 180, 181
Six-Day War (1967), 140–42
Slade, Edmond, 88–90
Smith, George Otis, 121
smuggling, 22
Somme, Battle of the (1916), 57
South Africa, 23
Southern Watch, Operation, 38
South Yemen, 142, 143; Soviet Union and, 149–50. *See also* Yemen
Soviet Union. *See* Union of Soviet Socialist Republics (USSR)
Spain, 22, 208n8
Speer, Albert, 92, 104, 111–12
Spindletop gusher well, 47, 117
Sri Lanka, 180–81
Stalin, Joseph, 64–65, 106–9, 136
Stalingrad, 110

Standard Oil Company, 45, 121
steamships, 52
Stern, Roger, 6–7
Stewart, Lyman, 116
Stimson, Henry L., 127
stockpiling, 36–37
Strait of Hormuz, 2, 7–9, 11, 21
Strait of Malacca, 5, 176, 179, 180
strategic anticipation theory, 15–47; causal logic, 24 (*see also* military value of oil); dependent variables, 12, 23–24, 32–39 (*see also* anticipatory strategies); independent variables, 3, 12, 15–23, 39–42 (*see also* coercive vulnerability); predicted outcomes, 39–42, 167–68; qualitative case study research design, 13, 67–79 (*see also* fuzzy-set qualitative comparative analysis); scope conditions, 10, 71
strategic resources, 6–7, 12, 42–47. *See also* coal; oil
Suez Crisis, 2, 34
sufficient conditions, analysis of, 170–72
supply lines, 51, 54, 60
Sweden, 30
Sykes-Picot Agreement, 85, 90
synthetic fuel, 61, 110–13; costs of, 36. *See also* coal-to-oil hydrogenation
Syria, 91; 1967 oil embargo, 140; Arab nationalism in, 142; attack on Israel, 155; Soviet Union and, 149–50

Taiwan, 5, 9
Teapot Dome, Wyoming, 122
Technical Oil Mission, 126
territorial expansion, 38–39, 189n49
Texas, 47, 117, 146, 202n59
Texas Railroad Commission, 140, 204n99
Thomas, Georg, 102–4
threat to imports. *See* import threat
Thuringia oil field, 97
tidelands oil, 137, 202n59
Toland, John, 65
Tooze, Adam, 198n46
total war, 102
Toyoda, Soemu, 62, 66
trade: conflict and, 5. *See also* economic value of oil
trade embargos. *See* embargos
transportation: clean energy and, 174–75; coal and, 28–29, 48; disruption of imports and, 21 (*see also* blockades; import threat); oil and, 28–32, 189n39; oil substitutes and, 28–31, 36, 110–13. *See also* automobiles; Belt and Road Initiative (BRI); military mobility; motorization; motor transit; naval forces; railroads
Tripartite Treaty, 136
Trucial Oman Scouts (TOS), 150
Trucial States, 143, 206n138; Soviet Union and, 148–49; U.S. and, 154
trucks, 53–54, 57–58
Truman, Harry S., 64, 129, 131, 136–39
Truman Doctrine, 129
Trump, Donald, 12, 175, 182
Turkey, 129, 138, 143
"Twin Pillars" policy, 152–54

Union of Soviet Socialist Republics (USSR): great power status, 10, 71; invasion of Afghanistan, 2; invasion of Manchuria, 63–66; Middle East and, 130, 136, 142, 146–51, 158, 203n84, 206n128; military power, 103; naval forces, 203n84; Suez Crisis and, 34; territorial expansion, 129–31, 136; threat to Allied oil imports, 133–36; World War II and, 52, 59, 93–94, 109, 200n90. *See also* Cold War; Russia
Union Oil Company, 121
United Arab Emirates, 194n3, 206n138
United States, 115–58; anticipatory strategies, 2, 37–38, 71, 116, 120–22, 125–26, 131, 138–40, 148–51, 157–58; case study approach and, 67–68, 72, 74–75; case I (1918–1920), 120–23; case II (1921–1941), 123; case III (1941–1945), 123–28; case IV (early Cold War), 130–41; case V (1969–1975), 141–57; coal reserves, 46, 197n21; coercive vulnerability, 13–14, 116, 120, 130, 138, 141–42, 154–55, 157; Cold War and, 28, 75, 116, 129–41; geological surveys, 118, 120, 121, 125, 195n2; grand strategy, 130; great power status, 10–11, 71, 208n6; import dependence, 7; import restrictions, 139, 143–46; indirect control, 37–38, 116, 138–40, 148–51, 157–58; Iran and, 182; isolationism, 130; Mideast oil and, 2, 91, 120–22, 126–28, 141, 146–54, 174, 194n3, 195n2; military power, 7, 9, 103, 127, 130, 177 (*see also* U.S. Army; U.S. Navy); military sales, 206n146, 207n154; OAPEC oil crisis (1973) and, 8–9, 21, 37, 154–57; oil glut, 123; oil production, 46–47, 96–97, 117, 123–25, 132–33, 139, 141, 143–44, 157–58, 196n25, 204n99; Ottoman Empire and, 80; petroleum deficit, 116, 120, 130–33, 136–46, 154–56; petroleum needs, 19, 131–32, 141; petroleum reserves, 36–37, 120–25, 130, 137,

141, 157–58, 189n41, 195n2; pre-war oil policy, 117–20; rationing of civilian oil consumption, 120–21, 124–26, 131, 137; role of oil in culture of, 115–16; Saudi Arabia and, 127–28, 137–38, 152–54, 157, 194n3; security partnerships, 138–40; self-sufficiency, 71, 116, 120–22, 125–26, 131, 157–58; synthetic fuel production, 126; threat to imports, 116, 130, 133–36, 138, 141–42, 145–51, 154–56, 208n6; World War I and, 58, 86–89, 120–23; World War II and, 59, 123–28
United States Geological Survey, 118, 121
United States Strategic Bombing Survey, 111, 113
United States Strategic Petroleum Reserve (SPR), 36–37, 189n41
U.S. Army, 117
U.S. Department of Commerce, 144, 158
U.S. Department of Defense, 129, 136–37, 144–45, 158, 175, 194n3
U.S. Department of State, 144, 158
U.S. Department of the Interior, 133, 136, 139, 144
U.S. Department of the Treasury, 144
U.S. Military Training Mission, 138
U.S. Navy, 45, 55, 117–19, 177
USSR. *See* Union of Soviet Socialist Republics
Utah, 122
utilities, 28, 31

Van Creveld, Martin, 190n4
Van Evera, Stephen, 195n12
Vantage, Operation, 149
Venezuela, 12; oil exports to U.S., 124, 139, 145; oil production, 123, 134–35, *135*, 138
Venn, Fiona, 46, 58
Versailles, Peace of, 97, 104
Vienna negotiations, 155, 207n156
Vietnam, 37, 141, 146, 152; oil demand in, 175
Volkswagen, 111

Waltz, Kenneth N., 35, 189n38, 189n43
Wang Jisi, 179

war: fear of oil coercion and, 2; prosperity concerns and, 27–28; uncertainty of, 53–54. *See also* conflict; direct control; *specific wars and conflicts*
War of 1859, 50
War of Attrition, 206n130
weak states, 10
Wehrmacht, 92, 102–3, 108. *See also* Nazi Germany
Western Hemisphere: oil production, 117, 134–35, *135*, 138–40; Soviet power and, 203n85; Spain and, 208n8
whale oil, 44
Wilson, Woodrow, 118–22
within-case analysis, 73–74
wood, 29–30, 36
World Bank, 178
World War I: ammunition requirements, 57; Anglo-French blockade on Germany, 95, 101; armies in, 56–59; attrition warfare, 192n40; German submarine warfare, 49, 58, 80–81, 86–88, 173; military mobility, 26; military value of oil during, 48–49, 52–59; oil coercion and, 16, 49, 54–66, 87; railroads and, 52; United States and, 120–23
World War II: Allied bombing of German oil facilities, 111–13; Allied control over oil, 59; American oil and, 196n18; balance of power and, 47; blockade on Nazi Germany, 22, 94, 102, 104, 105, 107–8, 114; German submarine warfare, 135; Japanese surrender in, 49, 59–66; oil demand, 175; United States and, 123–28. *See also* Nazi Germany

Xi Jinping, 5, 178

Yemen, 152. *See also* South Yemen
Yemen crisis (1963), 139
Yom Kippur War (1973), 155–56
Yonai, Mitsumasa, 65–66

Zahedi, Ardeshir, 153
Zionism, 150–51

CPSIA information can be obtained
at www.ICGtesting.com
Printed in the USA
LVHW091923290120
645204LV00010B/20/J